EQUALITY IN KENYA'S 2010 CONSTITUTION

This book makes a significant contribution to ongoing global conversations on the various understandings of equality. It illuminates the many ways in which diverse equality guarantees clash, or are interrelated. It also sets out principled approaches on how they can be coherently interpreted to address the myriad inequalities in Kenya.

Taking a comparative approach, the book considers how other jurisdictions including the United States, United Kingdom, Canada, South Africa, India and Botswana have approached the conceptualisation, interpretation and application of various equality concepts.

Equality in Kenya's 2010 Constitution

Understanding the Competing and Interrelated Conceptions

Victoria Miyandazi

•HART•
OXFORD • LONDON • NEW YORK • NEW DELHI • SYDNEY

HART PUBLISHING

Bloomsbury Publishing Plc

Kemp House, Chawley Park, Cumnor Hill, Oxford, OX2 9PH, UK

1385 Broadway, New York, NY 10018, USA

29 Earlsfort Terrace, Dublin 2, Ireland

First published in Great Britain 2021

A catalogue record for this book is available from the British Library.

Library of Congress Cataloging-in-Publication data

Names: Miyandazi, Victoria, 1989- author.

Title: Equality in Kenya's 2010 constitution : understanding the competing and interrelated conceptions / Victoria Miyandazi.

Description: Oxford, UK ; New York, NY : Hart Publishing, an imprint of Bloomsbury Publishing, 2021. | Includes bibliographical references and index.

Identifiers: LCCN 2020052047 (print) | LCCN 2020052048 (ebook) | ISBN 9781509941193 (hardback) | ISBN 9781509945290 (paperback) | ISBN 9781509941216 (pdf) | ISBN 9781509941209 (Epub)

Subjects: LCSH: Equality before the law—Kenya. | Discrimination—Law and legislation—Kenya. | Constitutional law—Kenya.

Classification: LCC KSK2100 .M59 2021 (print) | LCC KSK2100 (ebook) | DDC 342.676208/5—dc23

LC record available at https://lccn.loc.gov/2020052047

LC ebook record available at https://lccn.loc.gov/2020052048

ISBN: HB: 978-1-50994-119-3
ePDF: 978-1-50994-121-6
ePub: 978-1-50994-120-9

Typeset by Compuscript Ltd, Shannon

This book is dedicated to my mother, Martha Betty Echayo, whose fight for equality, justice and women's rights inspires me

ACKNOWLEDGEMENTS

Writing this monograph has been a great journey for me. To put words to an idea is not always an easy task and there are several people I would like to thank for making this possible. First and foremost, I would like to express my heartfelt gratitude to my DPhil supervisor, Professor Sandra Fredman, for her guidance, invaluable comments and unrelenting dedication. Thank you to my DPhil examiners, Professor Mark Freedland and Professor Christina Murray, for their helpful feedback, guidance and constructive criticism on the various chapters of this monograph.

A debt of gratitude is owed to my family, my dear mother, Martha Betty Echayo, who has been my constant source of positivity, motivation and encouragement, and my sisters Luckystar, Ruth, Faith and Mercy, who have been my little angels in terms of urging me on and reading through my drafts.

CONTENTS

TABLE OF CASES

Kenya

Botswana

Canada

India

South Africa

United Kingdom

United States

African Commission on Human and Peoples' Rights

European Court of Justice

Inter-American Court of Human Rights

UN Human Rights Committee

TABLE OF STATUTES

TABLE OF REGIONAL AND INTERNATIONAL INSTRUMENTS

1

Introduction

Kenyans' overwhelming support for the adoption of a new Constitution on 27 August 2010 demonstrated their common desire for an entirely new legal framework with a commitment to equality at its core.[1] The strong emphasis on equality is in reaction to the previous constitutional dispensation's exclusion of a large portion of Kenyans from governance and the socio-economic system.[2] Those who were most affected included women, persons with disabilities, minority groups and marginalised communities. Such exclusion led to these groups experiencing inequalities in access to socio-economic resources and services, land, jobs and political participation. A major factor that aggravated such inequalities was the divisive ethnicised politics in the country whereby regions consisting of ethnic communities that were not in power and did not have close proximity to those in power were sidelined in terms of socio-economic development. Such inequalities, particularly the allocation of public resources along ethnic lines, were largely responsible for the tensions that resulted in the 2007–08 post-election violence, which left over 1,333 people dead and thousands more displaced.[3] The clamour for a new Constitution was thus driven by the yearning of Kenyans for a resolution of the long-standing marginalisation and inequality in the country.

The entrenchment of major equality provisions in the 2010 Constitution, most of which were previously absent,[4] establishes a crucial constitutional framework for addressing the above-mentioned past injustices. However, the conception of equality is expressed in multiple ways in the 2010 Constitution, opening up the question of whether a coherent conception of equality can be discerned or developed.

The Constitution contains different articulations of equality, both in the equality clause (Article 27) and elsewhere in the Constitution. For example, it includes a status-based conception of equality through the requirement of non-discrimination

[1] 67% of Kenyans voted for the 2010 Constitution, and 31% voted against it.

[2] Constitution of Kenya Review Commission (CKRC), *The Final Report of the Constitution of Kenya Review Commission. Approved for issue at the 95th Plenary Meeting held on 10 February 2005* (2005) 103.

[3] Truth Justice and Reconciliation Commission (TJRC), *Report of the Truth, Justice and Reconciliation Commission* Volume IIB (Kenya TJRC 2013) 312.

[4] eg the Constitution of Kenya 2010 Art 27(3) on equal rights of men and women; and Art 27(6) on affirmative action.

on grounds such as sex and disability (Article 27(4)); a redistributive conception of equality through the inclusion of socio-economic rights (Article 43) and affirmative action (Article 27(6)); and recognition of cultural and religious diversity (Article 56 and the Preamble). These provisions reflect different – sometimes complementary and other times potentially conflicting – conceptions of equality. In relation to interrelated conceptions of equality, it is hard to apply socio-economic rights to further redistributive equality without considering status-based inequality, as those discriminated against because of their status (eg women and persons with disabilities) are disproportionately poor. The Constitution also requires the State to give priority to delivering the socio-economic rights of vulnerable individuals and groups (Article 20(5)(b)), confirming the link between socio-economic rights and status-based inequality. In terms of competing equalities, the notion of affirmative action clashes with equal treatment at a prima facie level, while recognition of cultural and religious diversity may at times interfere with gender equality.

In developing a coherent and mutually supportive way of understanding the broader conception of equality in the Constitution, all the equality principles in the Constitution will be examined with a specific emphasis on potentially conflicting and interrelated conceptions of equality. Current equality jurisprudence says little, if anything, on how the multiple competing and interrelated conceptions of equality in the 2010 Kenyan Constitution should be harmoniously conceptualised, interpreted and applied. Various courts have taken contradictory positions on the matter.[5] Therefore, because of the lack of clarity in this area, the concept remains open textured, offering limited guidance to governmental actors, legal practitioners and other pertinent players on what is required of them by law in addressing inequalities. The lack of clarity also has great implications for the Constitution's transformative vision and the aspirations of Kenyans for a more just society.

At this fairly nascent stage in the implementation of the Constitution, this book aims to shed more light on the various ways in which different equality guarantees clash or are interrelated, and proposes principled approaches as to how they can be coherently interpreted to address the myriad inequalities in Kenya. This is done in eight chapters. This chapter provides the necessary background of the issues analysed in the book. Chapter 2 considers how provisions in the Kenyan Constitution should be interpreted, with a special emphasis on equality. It argues that the 2010 Constitution is transformative, and hence, to achieve the aims therein, a purposive and contextual approach to interpretation should be adopted. The discussion sets the stage for the analysis made in subsequent chapters on how to interpret competing and interrelated conceptions of equality.

Chapter 3 gives an overview of inequalities in the country to fully understand what informed the 2010 Constitution's strong emphasis on equality and examines the multiple and competing understandings of equality in the Constitution. It then considers whether a coherent conception of equality can be discerned from

[5] See Ch 3, text to nn 101–07.

these competing conceptions and the extent to which the equality guarantees in the Constitution can be said to advance the promise of transformative constitutionalism. The chapter develops an analytical framework within which rival and interrelated concepts of equality can be understood and harmoniously applied. This provides the necessary background and explanation of competing and interrelated conceptions of equality to be analysed in subsequent chapters.

Taking the discussion in Chapter 3 on multiple and competing conceptions of equality further, Chapter 4 examines whether there is a coherent conception of equality underlying the list of grounds for non-discrimination in Article 27(4) of the Constitution, which can be drawn on in expanding the list of enumerated grounds and adding analogous (similar) grounds. Chapter 5 expounds on the discussion of competing equalities in Chapter 3 by examining the various notions of affirmative action in the Constitution, their aims, the conceptual and interpretive challenges to their implementation and how they can be effectively applied. Finalising the discussion of competing conceptions of equality, Chapter 6 explores the tense relationship that exists between gender equality and recognition of cultural and religious diversity. It examines how the conflict between the two arises and how it can be overcome.

On interrelated conceptions of equality, Chapter 7 provides the conceptual framework for understanding the complex but mutually reinforcing and important relationship between socio-economic rights and status-based equality. It particularly argues that efforts to realise socio-economic rights should consider its interrelationship with status-based equality as status-based discrimination is a major cause and consequence of socio-economic deprivation. Accordingly, it observes that those discriminated against because of their status (eg women and persons with disabilities) are disproportionately poor. This suggests that identity characteristics and discrimination play a key role in perpetuating socio-economic disadvantage. The chapter thus recommends that the State, judiciary and other stakeholders, in seeking to implement and enforce socio-economic rights, should consider the interrelationship between the two to avoid reinforcing disadvantage. Chapter 8 then applies the conceptual framework developed in Chapter 7 on the need to apply an equality-sensitive approach to the enforcement and adjudication of socio-economic rights. This is by considering the extent to which Kenyan courts have and can take into account the interrelationship between socio-economic rights and status-based equality when adjudicating claims that touch on both issues. It also shows how a failure to apply an equality-sensitive approach in some of the current socio-economic rights cases that have a bearing on equality runs the risk of reinforcing disadvantage and makes recommendations on how this can be avoided.

The book then ends with a general conclusion providing a summary of the two core principled approaches proposed in the various chapters for the harmonious interpretation of the Constitution's equality concepts; the *equal concern and respect approach* and the *multi-dimensional equality approach*.

Various interpretive and analytical methodologies are used in addressing the book's central inquiry of whether a coherent conception of the competing and interrelated equality notions in the Constitution can be discerned or developed. This includes an analysis of the actual constitutional text, drafting documents, case law and academic literature expounding on equality concepts. Alongside these, comparative law is considered as a helpful tool in making sense of the equality clause and related provisions in the 2010 Constitution, especially when considering constitutional silences (both in relation to the text and drafting history) in contentious equality questions.

A reference to comparative jurisprudence is important for four main reasons. First, Kenya adheres to the common law tradition and thus courts consider and use foreign judgments, particularly those from other common law jurisdictions, as persuasive precedents.[6] Second, since constitutional norms such as equality are regarded as being transcendent universal legal principles applicable to all human beings regardless of national boundaries, courts and academics globally can be considered as engaging in the interpretation of the same norms.[7]

Third, in terms of the genealogy of Kenya's 2010 Constitution, there are traces of constitutional borrowing of equality provisions in the 2010 Constitution, particularly from South Africa. Furthermore, the South African Constitution, on which the drafters of the Kenyan Constitution drew heavily,[8] was itself subject to influences from other jurisdictions. It is particularly noted that 'the South African constitutional text was modelled largely on the Canadian Charter of Rights and Freedoms, with liberal borrowings from Germany and the United States of America'.[9] Therefore, to the extent that the South African Constitution influenced the Kenyan Constitution, jurisprudence from these countries is informative in filling the vacuum left by the 'temporary absence of (preferred) indigenous jurisprudence' once it is determined that such jurisprudence is applicable to the Kenyan context.[10] The use of comparative law in instances of constitutional borrowing is, however, mitigated by the application of the country's own context.[11] This is important because, as Christina Murray, one of the members of the 2010 Constitution's drafting Committee rightly observes, 'the Bill of Rights is comprehensive and richly informed by international and comparative experience. But, in its emphases and through language and clauses that speak to the country's history, it is completely Kenyan'.[12]

[6] Judicature Act Cap 8, Laws of Kenya, s 3(1)(c).

[7] S Choudhry, 'Globalization in Search of Justification: Toward a Theory of Comparative Constitutional Interpretation' (1999) 74 *Indiana Law Journal* 819, 825.

[8] G Musila (ed), *Handbook on Election Disputes in Kenya: Context, Legal Framework, Institutions and Jurisprudence* (Nairobi, Law Society of Kenya, GIZ and the Kenyan Judiciary, 2013) 3.

[9] D Davis, 'Constitutional Borrowing: The Influence of Legal Culture and Local History in the Reconstitution of Comparative Influence: The South African Experience' (2003) 1 *International Journal of Constitutional Law* 181, 191.

[10] C McCrudden, 'Common Law of Human Rights? Transnational Judicial Conversations on Constitutional Rights' (2000) 20 *OJLS* 499, 523.

[11] Davis (n 9) 195.

[12] C Murray, 'Kenya's 2010 Constitution' (2013) 61 *Neue Folge Band Jahrbuch des öffentlichen Rechts* 747, 764–66.

Fourth, the use of comparative jurisprudence is justified by the dialogic argument whereby courts and academics from different jurisdictions 'identify the normative and factual assumptions underlying their own constitutional jurisprudence by engaging with comparable jurisprudence of other jurisdictions'.[13] This justification is quite similar to the more expansive 'deliberative approach' whereby 'Judicial accountability depends on the quality of the reasons adduced', which is where the deliberation comes in.[14] Application of a deliberative approach by considering alternative positions in comparative jurisdictions, and whether they are applicable, helps dispel suspicion that judges impose their own subjective predilections. The deliberative approach, through use of comparative material, therefore, assists judges in providing reasons for their decisions that 'are thorough and persuasive'.[15] It helps improve the quality of arguments made by either distinguishing a foreign jurisprudence from the Kenyan position or insisting on its desirability when it is found that the purpose or context in which the foreign position has been developed is similar to the Kenyan one.[16]

Reference to comparative law is, however, done cautiously, noting the dangers of its use.[17] For instance, it is said to be 'at odds with one of the dominant understandings of constitutionalism: that the constitution of a nation emerges from, embodies, and aspires to sustain or respond to that nation's particular history and political traditions'.[18] Another concern voiced is that of 'cherry picking' jurisdictions that might lead to inaccurate conclusions.[19] Nevertheless, the reference to comparative law does not suggest that equality and non-discrimination jurisprudence from other jurisdictions should simply be blindly imported. Such an attempt would be futile. It is carefully applied in line with the four justifications laid out above, while making sure to address the similarities or differences of the comparative experience with the Kenyan context and historical background.

In relation to context, given that the law does not operate in a vacuum but is undeniably a product of its social context, Kenya's political, legal and social context is also looked at in the various chapters to understand the context-specific problems equality provisions are addressing to make their conceptualisation effective and responsive.[20]

[13] ibid.

[14] S Fredman, 'Foreign Fads or Fashions: The Role of Comparativism in Human Rights Law' (2015) 64(3) *ICLQ* 631, 634.

[15] ibid.

[16] Choudhry (n 7) 825.

[17] See A Scalia, 'Keynote Address: Foreign Legal Authority in the Federal Courts' (2004) 98 *Proceedings of the ASIL Annual Meeting* 305; R Hirschl, 'The Rise of Comparative Constitutional Law: Thoughts on Substance and Method' (2008) 2 *Indiana Journal of Constitutional Law* 11; McCrudden (n 10); Choudhry (n 7).

[18] Choudhry (n 7) 822.

[19] McCrudden (n 10) 507.

[20] See C McCrudden, 'Legal Research and the Social Sciences' (2006) *LQR* 632, 633–34; P Selznick, '"Law in Context" Revisited' (2003) 30(2) *Journal of Law and Society* 177, 181.

This book largely focuses on the role of Kenyan courts in the development of indigenous equality jurisprudence, as the achievement of greater equality is partly dependent on courts tasked with constitutional interpretation, a core element in the effective implementation of rights.[21] Nevertheless, it is acknowledged that constitutional competence for the realisation of rights is a *shared* competence. Hence, the book is alive to constraints that impinge on the judiciary's functions, noting that the judiciary has an important yet limited role to play when considering its job in relation to other constitutional actors such as Parliament and the executive, tasked with implementation of judicial decisions. Moreover, since equality is dependent in part on the adoption of political, economic and social policies that are sensitive to the rights of the marginalised and disadvantaged, its application implicates more actors than the judiciary.

No such comprehensive study on equality has so far been undertaken in relation to the Kenyan Constitution. This book's area of focus is therefore of value as it seeks to provide clarity in this area of law in Kenya, particularly because the courts are still struggling with the best ways to conceptualise, interpret and apply the concept. The study is also a significant contribution to the ongoing global conversations on the various understandings of equality.

[21] B Sihanya, 'Constitutional Implementation in Kenya, 2010–2015: Challenges and Prospects' (2011) *FES Kenya Occasional Paper* 5, 23.

2

Interpretation of Kenya's 2010 Constitution

This chapter examines how Kenya's 2010 Constitution should be interpreted with a special emphasis on equality. It sets the stage for discussions in subsequent chapters on the conceptualisation, interpretation and application of competing and interrelated conceptions of equality in the Constitution. The chapter is divided into three main sections. Section I argues that the 2010 Constitution is transformative and hence requires new judicial approaches to interpretation in order to fulfil the Constitution's transformative vision. Several questions are interrogated including: What is a transformative Constitution? Why can the Kenyan Constitution be said to be transformative? What is it transforming from? And, what does this mean for constitutional interpretation?

On the other hand, Section II looks at the past approaches to constitutional interpretation in Kenya, to better understand the position taken in the 2010 Constitution. Lastly, Section III embarks on an analysis of Article 259 of the Constitution, which provides guidelines on how constitutional provisions should be interpreted. It argues that the guidelines provide a set of factors to be taken into consideration in interpretation that support a purposive and contextual approach.

I. The Transformative Nature of Kenya's 2010 Constitution and its Effect on Constitutional Interpretation

The design and nature of the Constitution is important in deciding what the proper interpretation of constitutional provisions, including equality, should be. This chapter argues that the 2010 Kenyan Constitution is a *transformative charter*, which serves as a blueprint for social change. This argument is supported by the Kenyan Supreme Court and High Court, although these courts do not develop the idea fully.[1] Several Kenyan scholars have also described the 2010 Constitution as

[1] See *In the Matter of the Principle of Gender Representation in the National Assembly and the Senate Advisory Opinion No 2 of 2012* (SC) Majority Advisory Opinion [41]; *John Kabui Mwai & 3 Others v Kenya National Examination Council & 2 Others* [2011] eKLR (HC) [6] (*Kabui Mwai).*

being a transformative one.[2] Hence, it is essential to determine what is meant by transformative constitutionalism. Moreover, since the term was developed based on the South African history of apartheid, it is important to deduce the main principles of transformative constitutionalism and apply them to the Kenyan context.

A. What is Transformative Constitutionalism?

Klare, writing in relation to the 1996 South African Constitution, coined the term transformative constitutionalism. He interprets it as

> a long-term project of constitutional enactment, interpretation, and enforcement committed (not in isolation, of course, but in a historical context of conducive political developments) to transforming a country's political and social institutions and power relationships in a democratic, participatory, and egalitarian direction. Transformative constitutionalism connotes an enterprise of inducing large-scale social change through nonviolent political processes grounded in law.[3]

Albertyn and Goldblatt add that, for a Constitution to be transformative, 'a complete reconstruction of the State and society, including a redistribution of power and resources along egalitarian lines is needed'.[4] The transformative project thus involves 'the eradication of systemic forms of domination and material disadvantage based on race, gender, class and other grounds of inequality'.[5] Therefore, a Constitution's transformative nature gives rise to broader constitutional objectives that are not only significant in developing a more equal society, but are also important in informing constitutional interpretation. These include what Klare refers to as constitutional post-liberal readings comprising of notions such as social rights, a substantive conception of equality, affirmative State duties, horizontality which extends democratic norms and values into the private sphere, participatory governance, multiculturalism, and historical self-consciousness.[6] He defines a post-liberal Constitution as 'one that may plausibly be read not only as open to but committed to large-scale, egalitarian social transformation'.[7]

[2] See G Musila, 'The Transformative Promise of the 2010 Constitution and New Electoral Laws' in G Musila (ed), *Handbook on Election Disputes in Kenya: Context, Legal Framework, Institutions and Jurisprudence* (Nairobi, Law Society of Kenya, GIZ and the Kenyan Judiciary, 2013); NW Orago, 'Limitation of Socio-Economic Rights in the 2010 Kenyan Constitution: A Proposal for the Adoption of a Proportionality Approach in the Judicial Adjudication of Socio-Economic Rights Disputes' (2014) 16 *Potchefstroom Electronic Law Journal* 169, 172.

[3] KE Klare, 'Legal Culture and Transformative Constitutionalism' (1998) 14 *South African Journal of Human Rights* 146, 150.

[4] C Albertyn and B Goldblatt, 'Facing the Challenge of Transformation: Difficulties in the Development of an Indigenous Jurisprudence of Equality' (1998) 14 *South African Journal of Human Rights* 248, 249.

[5] ibid 249.

[6] Klare (n 3) 153–55.

[7] ibid.

In terms of interpreting the Constitution in a manner that considers transformative constitutionalism, Langa views this exercise as being three pronged.[8] The first approach relates to the fact that transformative constitutionalism requires a backward-looking and forward-thinking approach to constitutional interpretation. Langa states that this is what the Epilogue of the Interim South African Constitution described as 'a historic bridge between the past of a deeply divided society characterised by strife, conflict, untold suffering and injustice, and a future founded on the recognition of human rights …'.[9] In support of this position, Baxi opines that 'For the constitutional transformative to remain, as it were, "true" to itself, it needs to re-organise both collective memory and forgetfulness'.[10]

The second approach to transformation, according to Langa, relates to a change in legal culture.[11] Klare defines legal culture as 'professional sensibilities, habits of mind, and intellectual reflexes … [the] inarticulate premises culturally and historically ingrained in the professional discourse and outlook'.[12] He argues that in relation to the legal culture in South Africa pre 1998, courts took a more formalistic approach to law and were 'highly structured, technicist, literal and rule-bound'.[13] Langa therefore posits that transformation in this sense would mean a change in the legal culture to a culture of justification, which Mureinik refers to as

> a culture in which every exercise of power is expected to be justified; in which the leadership given by government rests on the cogency of the case offered in defence of its decisions, not the fear inspired by the force of its command. The new order must be a community built on persuasion, not coercion.[14]

In relation to this approach, Langa calls for a paradigm shift from past ideas of formal constitutional interpretation that presented the law as being neutral and objective to a commitment to 'substantive reasoning', which examines 'the underlying principles that inform laws themselves and judicial reaction to those laws'.[15]

The third approach touches on the idea that change is constant. Langa states that the transformation agenda does not end once we reach the other side of the bridge, which is our desired destination. Put differently, constitutional transformation should be viewed as a continuum. It is not only peculiar to changing a history of injustice, but is also the idea that change is constant and that society should always be open to change and contestation.[16] Transformative constitutionalism

[8] P Langa, 'Transformative Constitutionalism' (2006) 17 *Stellenbosch Law Review* 351.

[9] Constitution of the Republic of South Africa, Act 200 of 1993; Langa (n 8) 352.

[10] U Baxi, 'Preliminary Notes on Transformative Constitutionalism' in O Vilhena, U Baxi and F Viljoen (eds), *Transformative constitutionalism: Comparing the Apex Courts of Brazil, India and South Africa* (Johannesburg, Pretoria University Law Press, 2013) 28.

[11] Langa (n 8) 356–58.

[12] Klare (n 3) 166–67.

[13] ibid 168.

[14] E Mureinik, 'A Bridge to Where? Introducing the Interim Bill of Rights' (1994) 10 *South African Journal of Human Rights* 31, 32.

[15] Langa (n 8) 357.

[16] ibid 354.

thus echoes the need to eradicate past disadvantage, as well as inequalities that may arise in future in the creation of a more egalitarian society. The achievement of these goals is partly dependent on courts tasked with constitutional interpretation, which is a core element in the effective implementation of the Constitution.[17]

B. Why Can the Kenyan Constitution be Said to be Transformative? What is it Transforming from? And What Does this Mean for Interpretation?

i. A Backward-looking and Forward-thinking Approach

In relation to this first approach to transformation, the 2010 Constitution is meant to be a bridge from a past fraught with inequalities and injustices, to a future where there is respect for human rights coupled with a redistributive agenda and recognition of minorities. As illustrated in Chapter 1, Kenyan society pre 2010 was plagued with many injustices and gross violations of human rights. The 2010 Constitution, by recognising historical injustices, seeks to redress the plight of those who have been marginalised and disadvantaged in the past and aims to create a more just society in future. This is through the inclusion of far-reaching affirmative action provisions.[18] It seeks to narrow down the large economic disparities between regions through the creation of the Equalisation Fund[19] and to improve the general welfare of individuals by inclusion of justiciable socio-economic rights.[20] The Constitution also gives women a political voice by introducing principles such as the requirement that 'not more than two-thirds of the members of elective or appointive bodies shall be of the same gender'.[21] Thus, the 2010 Constitution is transformative as it adopts the post-liberal notions of social rights and affirmative action that Klare espouses above.[22] In this regard, the Constitution can be seen as restructuring the State to ensure the equitable redistribution of power and resources.[23] Indeed, in terms of the Constitution being a bridge from a past characterised by gross injustices, Willy Mutunga CJ stated in his concurring opinion in *Jasbir Singh Rai & 3 Others v Tarlochan Singh Rai Estate of & 4 Others* that

> [t]here is no doubt that the Constitution is a radical document, that looks to a future that is very different from our past, in its values and practices. It seeks to make a

[17] B Sihanya, 'Constitutional Implementation in Kenya, 2010–2015: Challenges and Prospects' (2011) *FES Kenya Occasional Paper* 5, 23.

[18] Art 27(6) of the 2010 Constitution provides for application of affirmative action programmes and policies to 'redress any disadvantage suffered by individuals or groups because of past discrimination'.

[19] Constitution of Kenya 2010, Art 204.

[20] ibid Art 43.

[21] ibid Art 27(8).

[22] Text to n 6.

[23] Orago (n 2) 172–73.

> fundamental change from the 68 years of colonialism, and 50 years of independence. In their wisdom, the Kenyan people decreed that past to reflect a *status quo* that was unacceptable and unsustainable, through … a modern Bill of Rights that provides for economic, social and cultural rights to reinforce the political and civil rights, giving the whole gamut of human rights the power to radically mitigate the *status quo* and signal the creation of a human-rights State in Kenya; mitigating the *status quo* in land … These instances, among others, reflect the will and deep commitment of Kenyans, reflected in fundamental and radical changes, through the implementation of the Constitution.[24]

Having settled the application of the first principle of transformative constitutionalism to the Kenyan context, the question that follows is, therefore, what this means for constitutional interpretation. This chapter postulates that it should mean, as Baxi puts it above, that courts should, in interpreting the Constitution, have both 'collective memory and forgetfulness'. Thus, on the one hand, constitutional interpretation should be alive to the history of inequalities and the deeply rooted ethno-regional marginalisation in the country. On the other hand, it should also seek nation-building goals such as guaranteeing the protection of human rights in general and improving *everyone's* socio-economic conditions. In interpreting the Constitution in light of this principle, Kenyan courts should also take a contextual approach in order to breathe life into transformative notions of equality as discussed in Chapter 3, bearing in mind historical and ongoing inequalities.[25]

ii. Change in Legal Culture

The 2010 Constitution aims to cure the problems of the Kenyan judiciary's past legal culture, whereby, as a number of commentators have argued, the judiciary lacked independence and basically acted as the 'poster child' for the executive.[26] Mutua describes the past judiciary as one that showed no ability or inclination to uphold the rule of law against the control of the executive and individual senior government officials and, hence, ruled consistently in favour of the ruling elite in cases involving corrupt practices and political interests.[27] It turned into 'an ineffective guard of the fundamental liberties of the people … guided more by the concern over maintenance of order than the administration of justice'.[28] Kenya's first Chief Justice under the 2010 Constitution, Willy Mutunga, acknowledged

[24] *Jasbir Singh Rai & 3 Others v Tarlochan Singh Rai Estate of & 4 Others* [2013] eKLR (SC) [89] (*Rai v Rai*).

[25] Ch 3, text to nn 75–98.

[26] F Jjuuko (ed), *The Independence of the Judiciary and the Rule of Law: Strengthening Constitutional Activism in East Africa*, vol 2 (Kampala, Kituo cha Katiba, 2005) 129; M Mutua, 'Justice Under Siege: The Rule of Law and Judicial Subservience in Kenya' (2001) 23 *Human Rights Quarterly* 96; and GK Kuria and AM Vazquez, 'Judges and Human Rights: The Kenyan Experience' (1991) 35 *Journal of African Law* 142.

[27] Mutua (n 26) 99.

[28] P Mwangi, *The Black Bar: Corruption and Political Intrigue within Kenya's Legal Fraternity* (Nairobi, Oakland Media Services, 2001) 104.

that the institution under the previous Constitution was 'so frail in its structures; so thin on resources; so low on its confidence; so deficient in integrity; so weak in its public support that to have expected it to deliver justice was to be wildly optimistic'.[29] It was a legal culture where judicial decisions were made as a result of fear inspired by the force of executive commands, entirely at odds with the more desirable culture of justification as earlier advocated for.[30]

The previous Constitution provided that the President had an independent right to appoint the Chief Justice while Court of Appeal and High Court judges were to be 'appointed by the President acting in accordance with the advice of the Judicial Service Commission' (JSC).[31] However, every member of the JSC was effectively a presidential appointee. Accordingly, under section 68 of the 1963 Constitution, the JSC consisted of the Chief Justice (a presidential appointee under section 61(1)), the Attorney General (a presidential appointee under section 109), two persons designated by the President among the High Court and Court of Appeal judges, and the chairperson of the Public Service Commission (a presidential appointee under section 106(2)).

The President's broad powers to appoint members of the JSC greatly jeopardised the independence of this institution in offering advice on appointment of judges. This, in turn, posed a threat to judicial independence, accountability and performance, compounded by the fact that the criteria for selecting and vetting candidates for the JSC was neither transparent nor publicly known.[32] These challenges led to serious repercussions for the workings of the judiciary. In 1998 a report based on the judiciary's own investigation led by appellate Justice Kwach highlighted that mediocrity in judicial performance was a serious problem.[33] Jjuuko additionally points out that the 2003 Ringera Committee, when recommending the removal of various judges and magistrates, called for meritorious appointments,[34] strongly suggesting that judicial appointments had been driven by considerations other than merit.[35] The evident lack of judicial independence elicited more allegiance to the Presidency and ruling political regime than to the rule of law and delivery of justice.

Judicial reforms have been undertaken post 2010 in an effort to re-legitimise the judiciary and restore public confidence in the institution. There is increased independence of the judiciary as the JSC has been reshaped so that, rather than merely advising the President as under the previous Constitution, it is now tasked

[29] W Mutunga, *Progress Report on the Transformation of the Judiciary: The First Hundred and Twenty Days, 19 October 2011* (2011).

[30] Text to nn 14 and 15.

[31] Previous Constitution of Kenya 1963, s 61(1) and (2).

[32] Republic of Kenya, *Final Report of the Task Force on Judicial Reforms* (Nairobi, Government Printer, 2010) 24.

[33] Republic of Kenya, *Report of the Committee on the Administration of Justice: Summary of Recommendations 24* (1998). See also Jjuuko (n 26) 129.

[34] Jjuuko (n 26).

[35] ibid.

with the recruitment of judges and magistrates.[36] The candidates selected are then recommended to the President for appointment.[37] Such recommendation holds much weight as the candidates are always approved and appointed by the President. Moreover, most of the members of the new JSC are not presidential appointees and even the two members appointed by the President to represent the public are to be approved by the National Assembly.[38] Judicial independence has also been improved by creation of the Judicial Fund under Article 173 of the Constitution, which is administered by the Chief Registrar of the judiciary. Financial autonomy helps to eliminate control of the judiciary by the executive.

Additionally, the Constitution provides for the vetting of judges and magistrates to reform the judiciary and weed out corrupt and incompetent judges.[39] The Judges and Magistrates Vetting Board (the Board) was established by the Vetting of Judges and Magistrates Act 2011. The Board consists of nine members, six of whom are Kenyans (three lawyers and three non-lawyers) and the other three are non-citizens and eminent judges from the Commonwealth.[40] The diversity of the Board's members, who are drawn from different professional and jurisdictional backgrounds, is meant to instil public confidence in the vetting process and to ensure independence and fairness.[41] The Board was tasked with the vetting of judges and magistrates who were in office as of 27 August 2010 when the new Constitution was passed.[42] A number of judges were dismissed. Some of the reasons given for their removal included: lack of impartiality, manipulating the law to achieve a result that favoured impunity, being aware of human rights violations such as the torture of suspects and doing nothing about it, incompetence and negligence, dishonesty, questionable integrity, and conduct unbecoming of a professional judge.[43]

Mureinik's description of a constitutional culture of justification built on persuasion and not coercion also refers to the need for development of rich progressive jurisprudence. Mutunga CJ states that such rich jurisprudence should avoid mechanist approaches which characterised many of the judicial decisions under the previous Constitution.[44] According to him, a mechanical jurisprudence is one like that made under the previous Constitution where the High Court in

[36] Constitution of Kenya 2010, Art 172.

[37] ibid Art 172(1)(a).

[38] ibid Art 171(2).

[39] ibid s 23 of the Sixth Schedule.

[40] Vetting of Judges and Magistrates Act No. 2 of 2011, ss 7 and 9.

[41] Judges and Magistrates Vetting Board, *Restoring Confidence in the Judiciary* (Interim Report, 2013) XIV and XVI.

[42] R Jillo, 'Court Orders Vetting of Judges to Start Thursday', *Capital News* (Nairobi, 21 February 2012).

[43] *First Announcement: Judges and Magistrates Vetting Board Determinations Concerning the Judges of the Court of Appeal* [2012] eKLR; I Lucheli, 'Vetting Board Finds Five High Court Judges Unfit to Serve', *The Standard* (Nairobi, 22 December 2012).

[44] W Mutunga, 'The 2010 Constitution of Kenya and Its Interpretation: Reflections from the Supreme Court Decisions' (University of Fort Hare Inaugural Distinguished Lecture Series, 16 October 2014) 3.

the *Kibaki v Moi & 2 Others* case reached 'an apparently technically sound decision that the election of a sitting President could not be challenged because the losing opponent had not achieved the pragmatically impossible task of serving the relevant legal documents directly upon the sitting President'.[45] Another example is the decision in *Gibson Kamau Kuria v Attorney General*, where section 84 of the previous Constitution, which granted the High Court original jurisdiction to hear cases under the Bill of Rights, was declared inoperable in 1988.[46] This was because the rules regarding procedures for enforcement of fundamental rights had not been made by the then Chief Justice, Cecil Miller, as was required of him by the Constitution.[47] Claims of violation of fundamental rights, like the applicant's claim in the *Gibson Kamau Kuria* case that impounding his passport violated his right to travel to and from Kenya as protected by the Constitution, could therefore not be litigated during this time. The rules were later made in 2001.[48]

Muigai argues that a reading of cases like that of *Gibson Kamau Kuria* shows that the courts were affected by the previous conservative judicial culture of seeing their role as maintaining the status quo by 'upholding the powers of government in the face of any challenge'.[49] Consequently, in adjudicating cases that had a political angle, 'courts started from the position that they did not wish to hear the substance of the complaint; they then proceeded to look for a technical reason to dismiss the cases without hearing them'.[50] Muigai observes that, even when courts decided to hear the merits of a case, the conclusion was more or less the same, a decision in favour of the government.[51] The two case examples show that the development of rich jurisprudence requires courts, as guardians of the Constitution's supremacy, to give compelling reasons for their decisions that go to the root of disputed issues in a case and meet the ends stipulated in the Constitution.[52] It also requires courts to avoid having undue regard to technicalities.

What does a change in legal culture mean for interpretation? In order to embrace the new legal culture, constitutional interpretation is no longer to be based on the influence of the executive and the ruling regime. Constitutions are open textured and give judges room for interpretation, and their discretion is to be guided by the values and principles provided for in the Constitution, as discussed below. Unlike the previous Constitution, the 2010 Constitution

[45] *Kibaki v Moi & 2 Others (No 2)* (2008) 2 KLR (EP) 308 (HC); ibid.

[46] *Gibson Kamau Kuria v Attorney General*, High Court Miscellaneous Civil Case No. 550 of 1988 (unreported).

[47] See ibid; Mutunga (n 44).

[48] Jjuuko (n 26) 133.

[49] G Muigai, 'Political Jurisprudence or Neutral Principles: Another Look at the Problem of Constitutional Interpretation' (2004) *East African Law Journal* 1, 8–9.

[50] ibid 10.

[51] ibid 10–11.

[52] Mutunga (n 44) 3–4; R Pound, 'Mechanical Jurisprudence' (1908) 8(8) *Columbia Law Review* 605, 605.

recognises justiciable socio-economic rights, affirmative action and more extensive equality guarantees. The implementation of such rights requires a bench that is independent, competent, bold enough to give authoritative decisions, and not afraid to hold the executive accountable and check the powers of the legislature. Nonetheless, courts should be careful not to overstep their mandate and interfere with the powers of the legislature and the executive. A change in legal culture also means that courts, when interpreting the Constitution, improve on the quality and depth of reasons given in their decisions to ensure 'coherence, certainty, harmony, predictability, uniformity and stability in the various interpretive frameworks that the Constitution … provide[s]'.[53] This is doubly important because 'constitution making does not end with its promulgation; it continues with its interpretation'.[54]

iii. Embracing the Idea that Change is Constant

In relation to the third approach to transformation, Kenyan courts should, in interpreting the Constitution, permit the development of the law. As espoused by Langa, constitutional interpretation should be cognisant of the fact that society keeps evolving and thus interpretation should allow the natural development of the law to meet these changes.[55] This idea resonates with the provision in Article 259(1)(c) of the Constitution, which requires the Constitution to be interpreted in a manner that 'permits the development of the law'.[56]

This means that Kenyan judges will in time be required to interpret the Constitution in a way that considers changes in social mores. Therefore, courts may have to depart from the originally intended meaning as evident in the constitutional drafting history documents referred to below[57] or from their own earlier judicial interpretations. Indeed, the Supreme Court has acknowledged that 'As times, values, perceptions, and yardsticks of legitimacy and right, keep evolving, … the Supreme Court retains a competence and discretion, when properly moved, and on weighty grounds, to reconsider its precedents, and to vary them as may be appropriate'.[58]

The interpretive role of Kenyan courts should be seen in the context of the possibility of constitutional amendment, which might be a more appropriate forum than leaving it to courts, through novel constitutional interpretation, to incorporate far-reaching changes in social mores. On the other hand, the amendment process for fundamental rights and freedoms is complex and slow.

[53] Mutunga (n 44) 14.

[54] *Re the Speaker of the Senate & Another v Attorney General & 4 Others*, Supreme Court Advisory Opinion No. 2 of 2013 [2013] eKLR [156].

[55] Text to n 16.

[56] See text to nn 102–04.

[57] Text to nn 77–88.

[58] *Rai v Rai* (n 24) [61].

Article 255(1) of the Constitution states that a proposed constitutional amendment touching on the Bill of Rights, national values and principles, and other fundamental articles of the Constitution can only be approved by a national referendum. This shows the difficulty in amending such constitutional provisions.[59] Hence, to some extent, courts may have to apply novel understandings to certain constitutional principles in accommodating developments in society. Nevertheless, in such an event, we cannot wish away the essential question that emerges of whether judges can justifiably make authoritative interpretive decisions that consider changes in social mores, which will in effect amend the Constitution; or if judges should defer such decisions to the legislature or the people through a referendum in respecting the doctrine of separation of powers. The issue of how courts can properly enforce developments in human rights through judicial interpretation while also respecting the doctrine of separation of powers is a difficult one.

There are various schools of thought on the approach that should be taken in such a case. Commentators from the originalist school of thought such as Justice Antonin Scalia would argue that if the Constitution needs to be amended to reflect new societal values, it should be done through proper procedures like the legislative process.[60] Other scholars in support of the deliberative approach would argue that instead of taking either side (judicial interpretation validating developments in society or the legislative process), a better approach would be one that views the decision-making process on such issues as collaborative.[61] This approach views both courts and the legislature as 'contributing to a democratic resolution of human rights disputes' to accommodate changes in social mores through deliberation, such that, 'Rather than courts having a final say, judicial decisions provoke a response from the legislature'.[62] However, in the response by the legislature, Fredman argues for a 'bounded deliberative' approach, which requires deliberation within the confines of achieving the goal of human rights, and does not permit their negation.[63]

The 'bounded deliberative' approach is the most ideal for the Kenyan context to protect fundamental rights and freedoms in the Constitution from being compromised. The process may be more cumbersome in practice but the vital point here is that the deliberative process, however imperfect, may be helpful in arriving at an agreeable position on the effect of a change in social mores.

[59] Noteworthy, as per Art 256(1)(d) of the Constitution, the amendment of other constitutional provisions not listed in Art 255(1) may be effected through a bill passed by not less than two-thirds of the Members of Parliament. Therefore, for such constitutional guarantees, social, political or economic changes can be flexibly incorporated through an Act of Parliament.

[60] A Scalia, 'Originalism: The Lesser Evil' (1988) 57 *University of Cincinnati Law Review* 849, 854.

[61] See T Hickman, 'Constitutional Dialogue, Constitutional Theories and the Human Rights Act 1998' (2005) *PL* 306; M Tushnet, 'Dialogic Judicial Review' (2009) 61 *Arkansas Law Review* 205. See also S Fredman, 'From Dialogue to Deliberation: Human Rights Adjudication and Prisoners' Rights to Vote' (2013) *PL* 292 for an overview of the dialogic model.

[62] Fredman (n 61) 292.

[63] ibid 296–98.

II. Constitutional Interpretation under the Previous Kenyan Constitution

It is important to briefly highlight here the past approaches to constitutional interpretation in Kenya to better understand the position taken in the 2010 Constitution. Since the previous 1963 Constitution did not provide guidelines on how the Constitution should be interpreted, the courts were tasked with the development of a proper approach. Muigai observes that this exercise was 'largely un-principled, *ad hoc*, eclectic, vague, pedantic, inconsistent, contradictory and confusing'.[64] The lack of a principled and coherent approach led to diverse and conflicting approaches to constitutional interpretation which undermined the legal authority of constitutional dictates and their political significance.[65]

Despite the lack of a principled and consistent approach to constitutional interpretation in the grand scheme of things, Ongoya states that two phases of constitutional interpretation in Kenya pre 2010 can be discerned.[66] The first phase was just after independence, where the courts adopted a restrictive approach to constitutional interpretation, equating it with statutory interpretation. The legal precedent at the time was set in the 1969 case of *R v El Mann*, where the then Chief Justice Mwendwa held that 'in one cardinal respect, we are satisfied that a Constitution is to be construed in the same way as any other legislative enactment'.[67] Hence, during this phase, the courts insisted on the application of the literal rule, which requires that the constitutional text must be given its ordinary and plain meaning.

A different stance was taken in the second phase (post 1992), which is represented by the decision in the seminal case of *Timothy Njoya and 6 Others v Attorney General and 4 Others*.[68] In the case, Ringera J held that the Constitution is a living tree which should not be interpreted like any other Act of Parliament because 'it embodies certain fundamental values and principles and must be construed broadly, liberally and purposely or teleologically to give effect to those values and principles'.[69] Hence, the second phase saw a shift from restrictive methods of constitutional interpretation to a more purposive approach.

Nevertheless, a number of other cases expounding on the purposive approach insisted that it must be grounded on the natural and ordinary meaning of the words in the Constitution. For example in *RM (Suing Thro' Next Friend) & 3 Others v Attorney General*,[70] the High Court held that even though the principle set

[64] Muigai (n 49) 2.

[65] ibid.

[66] EZ Ongoya, 'The Law, the Procedures and the Trends in Jurisprudence on Constitutional and Fundamental Rights Litigation in Kenya' (2010) II *Kenya Law Review* 1.

[67] *R v El Mann* [1969] EA 357.

[68] *Timothy Njoya and 6 Others v Attorney General and 4 Others* [2004] 1EA 194 (HC).

[69] ibid.

[70] *RM (Suing Thro' Next Friend) & 3 Others v Attorney General* [2006] 2 KLR 697.

in *R v El Mann* had rightly been replaced by the purposive and living tree approaches, the nourishment given to the living tree, that was the Constitution, must originate from its roots.[71] It can thus be deduced that the reasoning was essentially that the purposive and living tree methods of interpretation were to be anchored on the ordinary meaning of the constitutional text. This is based on the understanding that the latter is the soul of the Constitution, a position with which I agree.

Ongoya concludes that from the jurisprudence on interpretation of the Constitution pre 2010, 'the more the cases one looks at from the Kenyan judiciary, the gloomier the situation looks' in terms of settling on a proper approach to constitutional interpretation.[72] Even in the second interpretive phase, the restrictive principle in *R v El Mann* was still applied in some cases.[73] It was thus evident that clarity on the issue was needed in order to resolve the divergent opinions on constitutional interpretation.

III. Interpretation of Kenya's 2010 Constitution

In the new interpretational phase brought about by the 2010 Constitution, one does not need to derive from case law what the proper approach to constitutional interpretation should be. The Constitution already tells us what this is. Article 259 provides extensive guidelines on how the Constitution should be interpreted. It was included to deal with the lack of clarity on the proper interpretation of the Constitution described in the previous section. It states:

> 259. (1) This Constitution shall be interpreted in a manner that—
>
> (a) promotes its purposes, values and principles;
> (b) advances the rule of law, and the human rights and fundamental freedoms in the Bill of Rights;
> (c) permits the development of the law; and
> (d) contributes to good governance.
>
> …
>
> (3) Every provision of this Constitution shall be construed according to the doctrine of interpretation that the law is always speaking …[74]

Additionally, Article 10 sets out the national values and principles of governance that should guide courts when interpreting the Constitution. These include the principles of 'human dignity, equity, social justice, inclusiveness, equality, human rights, non-discrimination and protection of the marginalised'.[75] Moreover,

[71] ibid.
[72] Ongoya (n 66) 12–13.
[73] eg in *Ngare v Attorney General* [2004] 2 EA 217.
[74] Constitution of Kenya 2010, Art 259.
[75] ibid Art 10(2)(b).

Article 20(4) of the Constitution buttresses the centrality of the guiding principles of interpretation stipulated in Article 10(2) by providing that courts should, in interpreting the Bill of Rights, promote 'the values that underlie an open and democratic society based on human dignity, equality, equity and freedom' as well as 'the spirit, purport and objects of the Bill of Rights'.[76] However, these principles are drafted in broad terms and their content and how they play out is not self-evident from the text. Therefore, alongside a textual inquiry, reference to the original intention and historical and social context is also essential in giving content to such principles.

Consequently, it is clear that the 2010 Constitution envisages that in choosing which interpretive method to apply, judges should not limit themselves to one mode of analysis, but should select tools of interpretation based on the nature of the issue at hand. Article 259 embraces a variety of interpretive methods, including original intent, textualism and a purposive/living tree approach to interpretation, which are briefly explained below.

A. Original Intent

This interpretive principle is sometimes referred to as originalism or historical interpretation. It envisions that all laws should be applied based on 'a serious examination of the intention of the drafters and of the people who adopted the Constitution in the first place'.[77] In Kenya, these intentions can be discovered from the constitutional drafting history documents and writings of the drafters. Accordingly, Kenyans' desire to have a new Constitution and the constitutional review process began with the first Constitutional Review Act passed in 1997. The first attempt at developing a new Constitution in 2005 failed to pass as 57 per cent of the electorate voted against the proposed Constitution. Following the highly disputed 27 December 2007 general election, which resulted in widespread post-election violence across the country, there was renewed agitation by Kenyans for constitutional reform. The violence came to an end through the signing of the Kenya National Dialogue and Reconciliation Agreements (KNDR) in 2008.[78] The fourth agenda item for reform identified by the KNDR team included a need for constitutional and other legal reform to tackle long-term issues such as poverty and inequality.[79]

This agenda steered the second attempt at constitutional review that led to the 2010 Constitution. The process began in 2009 and was headed by the Committee

[76] ibid Art 20(4)(a) and (b).

[77] See Muigai (n 49) 4; K Thomas, 'Selected Theories of Constitutional Interpretation' (2011) *Congressional Research Service* 1, 6.

[78] Committee of Experts on Constitutional Review, *Final Report of the Committee of Experts on Constitutional Review* (2011) 21.

[79] ibid.

of Experts on Constitutional Review (CoE) established under the Constitution of Kenya Review Act of 2008 (the Review Act). In drafting the Constitution, the CoE drew on a variety of resources to assist them in proposing ways of resolving contentious issues. These included public views, thematic and sectoral consultations,[80] the CoE's own internal discussions, and consultations with a Reference Group chosen by the interested groups as required under the Review Act.[81] This means that the 2010 Constitution can be regarded as articulating the views and aspirations of what Kenyan society in general wanted to be entrenched in the constitutional text. Section 4 of the 2008 Constitution of Kenya Review Act also provided 'instructions to drafters' by setting out principles that the new Constitution was to include such as a free and democratic system of government, human rights, gender equality, affirmative action and socio-economic rights.

The CoE also identified contentious issues that had not been agreed upon in the two previous draft Constitutions (the 2004 *Bomas Draft* and 2005 *Wako Draft*, the latter having been rejected in the 2005 referendum) as well as those that were agreed upon.[82] It similarly included as a reference point archived records of the public participation process and views that were received from Kenyans in the making of the two previous constitutional drafts. These included submissions from various regions across the country, vulnerable groups and reports from the past Constitution of Kenya Review Commission (CKRC).[83]

These constitutional drafting history documents are a source of original intent that can be thrown into the crucible to help ascertain the meaning of various concepts in the Constitution and how they should be conceptualised and interpreted. Writings by some of the members of the drafting Committees including Yash Ghai and Christina Murray (chair of the CKRC and member of the CoE respectively) on the intentions behind the inclusion of various constitutional provisions are also valuable sources.

Major proponents of original intent argue that this theory provides a coherent approach to interpretation by stressing the attitudes and assumptions in relation to a constitutional provision at the time it was adopted, and is therefore the best in ensuring consistency and predictability of the law.[84] Mostly, as Fredman's rendition of the originalist argument highlights, this principle is seen as providing legitimacy on the assumption that the role of judges 'is not to answer fundamental moral questions, but to apply the law'.[85] Hence, a reference to original intention,

[80] These were consultations with political parties, religious organisations, the private sector and civil society on their views and proposals.

[81] Committee of Experts on Constitutional Review (n 78) 44.

[82] ibid 20–21.

[83] See ibid 29–30; 'The Review of the Constitution of Kenya under Constitution of Kenya (Amendment) Act, 2008 and the Constitution of Kenya Review Act, 2008', *The Daily Nation* (Nairobi, 16 June 2009).

[84] See Scalia (n 60) 855; Muigai (n 49) 4.

[85] S Fredman, 'Living Trees or Deadwood: The Interpretive Challenge of the European Convention on Human Rights' in N Barber, R Ekins and P Yowell (eds), *Lord Sumption and the Limits of the Law* (Oxford, Hart Publishing, 2016) 47.

which represents 'choices that have been given authority by the [people]' ostensibly prevents judges who are unelected and thus arguably undemocratic from relying on their own 'values and predilections'.[86] However, Fredman challenges this argument by stating that judges cannot neutrally apply the law because all judicial decisions include some value judgements, and that the democratic argument is flawed as drafters, and original intentions generally, at best represent the views of a previous generation.[87]

Indeed, it is rightly observed that original intent 'attempts to freeze meaning within a historical context', which is dangerous as it is almost 'impossible to give words the same meaning across different generations and circumstances'.[88] Therefore, original intent is not sufficient in interpreting the Constitution, more so because to a large extent, framers of a Constitution usually use general terms that could have broad application. They cannot anticipate 'all possible fact situations in which a particular constitutional provision could be applied'.[89] Moreover, courts are called upon to interpret diverse matters, including those relating to competing rights. This would necessitate the application of interpretive methods other than original intent.[90] Therefore, as much as it is an important tool of constitutional interpretation, there are instances where it is essential to consider it alongside other interpretive methods such as the interpretive doctrine that the law is always speaking in Article 259(3) of the Constitution.

B. Textualism

Textualism is referred to as the objective intent conveyed in the language of the text contemporaneous to the drafting and ratification of the Constitution.[91] This suggests that words in the Constitution should be given their 'acontextual meaning', referring to 'the meaning that we would assign them if we had no special information about the context of their use or the intentions of their author'.[92] This interpretive approach is seen as most desirable as it corresponds with the main role of judges, which is to make sense of the written law. It is also helpful in resolving the difficulty in ascertaining original intentions of the people and drafters as the text is seen as 'the surest guide to the adopters' intentions'.[93]

[86] See ibid; R Dworkin, *A Matter of Principle* (Oxford, Oxford University Press, 1985) 34.
[87] Fredman (n 85) 52, 53, 57 and 58.
[88] Muigai (n 49) 4.
[89] See RH Bork, *The Tempting of America: The Political Seduction of the Law* (London, Sinclair-Stevenson, 1990) 162; Thomas (n 77) 6.
[90] Muigai (n 49) 4.
[91] Thomas (n 77) 5.
[92] R Dworkin, *Law's Empire* (Cambridge, MA, Harvard University Press, 1986) 17.
[93] P Brest, 'The Misconceived Quest for the Original Understanding' (1980) 60 *Boston University Law Review* 204, 205.

Nevertheless, despite the desirability of textualism, the application of words in the constitutional text cannot be frozen in time because the applied meanings change as society evolves. Balkin refers to this as the 'text and principle' method of interpretation, which suggests that interpreters must be faithful to the original meaning of the constitutional text and to the principles that underlie the text. However, loyalty to original meaning does not require 'fidelity to *original expected application*', which should be left open for each generation to flesh out in their own time while sticking to the text and principle.[94] Hence, such situations warrant the application of a purposive/living tree approach. It is to this that I now turn.

C. Purposive/Living Tree Approach to Constitutional Interpretation

The purposive approach can be best explained by the definition given by Dickson J in the Canadian case of *R v Big M Drug Mart* relating to the Canadian Charter of Rights and Freedoms.[95] In the case, Dickson J stated that a purposive approach requires the consideration of several factors, including

> the character and larger objects of the *Charter* itself, to the language chosen to articulate the specific right or freedom, to the historical origins of the concepts enshrined, and where applicable, to the meaning and purpose of other specific rights and freedoms with which it is associated in the text of the *Charter*.[96]

Barak expounds on this approach by stating that the purposive approach is 'the context according to which the text is interpreted'.[97] Additionally, he states that a consideration of 'the goals, interests, and values … that the author of the text sought to actualize' as well as those that 'a text of the type being interpreted is designed to actualize' are important components of the purposive approach.[98] This therefore means that, among other factors, the purposive approach considers original intent and textualism.

Barak also includes in his definition the holistic nature of purposive interpretation in the sense that interpreting one text means interpreting all texts related to it.[99] A holistic approach to constitutional interpretation has also been proffered by Kenyan courts.[100] In this approach, the interpretation of one provision should be done in a way that ensures harmony with other related provisions in

[94] JM Balkin, 'Framework Originalism and the Living Constitution' (2009) 103 *Northwestern University Law Review* 549, 551–52.
[95] *R v Big M Drug Mart* [1985] 1 SCR 295.
[96] ibid [344].
[97] A Barak, *Purposive Interpretation in Law* (Princeton, NJ, Princeton University Press, 2007) xiii.
[98] ibid xiii.
[99] ibid xii.
[100] eg *Centre for Rights Education and Awareness (CREAW) & 7 Others v Attorney General* [2011] eKLR (HC) (*CREAW*).

the Constitution. He also points out that judicial discretion is a critical component of purposive interpretation where 'the text does not point to a single, unique legal meaning'.[101] Hence, a purposive approach is a comprehensive interpretive tool that is grounded on the language of the Constitution itself. However, the fleshing out of the relevant applied meaning as required by the context is left to judges, who are to make their own value judgements on the matter.

The use of judicial discretion in deciding the applied meaning of a constitutional text gives rise to the question of where judges get their values. To temper the claims of lack of legitimacy when judges apply their own value judgements, it is important that such decisions are anchored on values and principles explicitly stated in the Constitution.

From this background, I now look at how the 2010 Constitution is to be interpreted under Article 259, which incorporates aspects of the interpretive methods discussed here.

D. How Should Kenya's 2010 Constitution be Interpreted as Required by Article 259?

From the discussions in the three preceding sub-sections, Article 259 of the Kenyan Constitution seems to incorporate all the above-mentioned interpretive methods, with the purposive approach being the overarching method to be applied, while incorporating textualism and, to the extent that context permits, original intent. Indeed, Article 259(1)(a) states that the Constitution should be interpreted in a manner that 'promotes its purposes, values and principles'. This position corresponds with Jackson's argument that the constitutional text and original intent act as the roots upon which subsequent generations can flesh out the different understandings of the text to fit their context as the living tree grows.[102]

However, as mentioned above, textualism should be applied with the understanding that it should not be limited to the original expected application. The text and principle behind it should remain authoritative, but the application of the text should be done in a way that 'permits the development of the law' as stipulated in Article 259(1)(c) of the Constitution.

As for original intent, it is noteworthy that some of the original intentions (such as the need for affirmative action to redress the disadvantage experienced by various groups) are right now converging with the social context but may at some point in time diverge as society is constantly evolving. This resonates with the third principle of transformative constitutionalism, which acknowledges that transformation is permanent and that the idea of change is constant. This is also reflected

[101] Barak (n 97) 207.

[102] VC Jackson, 'Constitutions as "Living Trees"? Comparative Constitutional Law and Interpretive Metaphors' (2006) 75 *Fordham Law Review* 921, 943 and 953.

in the Constitution's support for development of the law in Article 259(1)(c). Therefore, as discussed above, the danger of applying original intent is that it attempts to freeze meaning in a historical context. Hence, courts need to be cognisant of this and move away from original intent when the context changes, or if it is determined that such original intent clashes with a core constitutional value or principle that supersedes it.

The need for development of the law to embrace the idea that change is constant is particularly important when we consider issues that are highly contentious in the country, such as sexual orientation. In relation to constitutional interpretation in such cases, it can be argued for instance that, because there was no consensus on issues such as inclusion of non-discrimination based on sexual orientation during the constitutional drafting process, the silence in the Constitution on the matter means that the question was left for later generations and requires the exercise of judicial discretion. Such discretion is nevertheless limited by the fact that it should always be exercised in light of the values and principles central to the Constitution. Indeed, when interpreting the Constitution, Articles 10(2), 20(4) and 259(1)(a), as highlighted above, provide for values and principles that should be taken into consideration to mitigate judicial discretion.[103] Such an approach resonates with Balkin's presupposition, with which I agree, that the choice of rules, standards and principles, or silence, in a Constitution is not accidental. Drafters use such rules to limit discretion, standards and principles to channel politics but delegate the details for future generations.[104]

Moreover, because of the transformative nature of the Constitution, judges need to consider history and social context in taking a backward-looking and forward-thinking approach to interpretation. Nevertheless, as argued in the section on legal culture, judges should be careful not to interfere with the powers of the legislature and executive when interpreting the Constitution. As much as judges need discretion to interpret broad and open-ended concepts like equality, the exercise of such discretion requires restraint. How this is achieved has been challenging in all constitutional interpretation. The Kenyan Constitution is useful in giving express guidance as to interpretation. At the same time, it leaves a good deal of discretion to judges. This means that much depends on legal culture to ensure that judges do not overstep their mandate.

Various recent judgments of the Kenyan Supreme Court attest to the fact that Article 259 of the Constitution requires a purposive approach to constitutional interpretation which incorporates textualism, context and original intent (to the extent that it is applicable).[105] Mutunga CJ in his dissent in the Supreme Court's *Gender Representation Advisory Opinion*, quoting Article 259, stated that 'In interpreting the Constitution and developing jurisprudence, the Court will always

[103] Text to nn 74–76.
[104] Balkin (n 94) 553.
[105] See n 24; Mutunga (n 44).

take a purposive interpretation of the Constitution as guided by the Constitution itself'.[106] He further quoted Dickson J's statement in *R v Big M Drug Mart* cited earlier that a purposive approach includes an analysis of the purpose of the constitutional guarantee in question in light of the interests it is meant to protect and 'in its proper linguistic, philosophic and historical contexts'.[107] Dissenting opinions, like that of Mutunga CJ, are considered authoritative to the extent that they comprehensively deal with a certain argument that dissenting judges feel must not be disregarded, ensuring clarity.[108]

The Supreme Court has also stated that an analysis of historical, economic, social, cultural and political context is also fundamentally critical in interpreting the Constitution as 'The Constitutional text and letter may not properly express the minds of the framers, and the minds and hands of the framers may also fail to properly mine the aspirations of the people'.[109]

Therefore, a purposive and contextual approach applied in the ways described above is the best method of interpreting the Constitution as envisioned in Article 259.

IV. Conclusion

In conclusion, as has been discussed, the Kenyan Constitution stands out because it provides guidelines on constitutional interpretation. It mandates a purposive and contextual interpretive approach through its transformative nature, which considers both the historical context of inequalities and changes in society. Moreover, the values and principles in the Constitution are open textured and inevitably will require judicial interpretation, which is authorised by the Constitution. At the same time, while taking a purposive approach, judges need to remain accountable for their value judgements by being true to the Constitution as a whole, its values and principles.

[106] *Gender Representation Advisory Opinion*, Dissenting Advisory Opinion (n 1) [8.8].
[107] ibid and text to nn 95–96.
[108] R Raffaelli, *Dissenting Opinions in the Supreme Courts of the Member States, European Parliament Study, Directorate General for Internal Policies Policy Department C: Citizens' Rights and Constitutional Affairs* (2012) 13.
[109] *Re the Speaker of the Senate* (n 54) [156]–[157]; Mutunga (n 44) 10–14; *CREAW* (n 100).

3

Multiple and Competing Conceptions of Equality

According to Loenen, 'Equality is one of the most elusive legal concepts', which has in all major jurisdictions 'generated extensive debates on its proper meaning and interpretation'.[1] Fredman attributes this elusive nature to the fragmentation of the concept of equality into distinct and rival concepts.[2] The term equality carries within it a multiplicity of meanings, especially when looked at from different perspectives. Indeed, some commentators have noted that a further inquiry into *what* must be equalised (eg welfare, rights, political power, incomes or opportunities) and *to whom* (as human beings differ in their personal characteristics) reveals a plethora of competing conceptions.[3]

In relation to equality as equal treatment before the law, could it mean identical treatment such that, for example, everyone should be taxed the same no matter their pay grade? Is this not equality? Fredman rightly argues that 'Experience has shown that equal treatment can in practice perpetuate inequalities' and 'a law which appears equal on its face bears far more heavily on the poor than the rich'.[4] It is for this reason that Sen opines that 'equal consideration for all may demand very unequal treatment in favour of the disadvantaged'.[5] Bearing this in mind and going back to the question of equal taxation for all irrespective of their pay grade, other questions emerge such as the need to protect the poor and marginalised in society, who have been disadvantaged because of past injustices.

The 2010 Kenyan Constitution also faces the conceptual and interpretive challenges that the multiple and competing concepts of equality pose. As this chapter and subsequent ones will illustrate, decisions in current equality cases show that the concept of equality has been variably and inconsistently interpreted. Courts have not yet settled on a reasonable and principled approach to adjudicating equality concepts. The lack of clarity on how to approach the interpretation of the multiple conceptions of equality has led to confusion and conflicting interpretations.

[1] T Loenen, 'The Equality Clause in the South African Constitution: Some Remarks from a Comparative Perspective' (1997) 13 *South African Journal of Human Rights* 401, 402.

[2] S Fredman, *Human Rights Transformed: Positive Rights and Positive Duties* (Oxford, Oxford University Press, 2008) 175.

[3] See A Sen, *Inequality Reexamined* (Oxford, Oxford University Press, 1992) 1–20; LP Pojman and R Westmoreland (eds), *Equality: Selected Readings* (Oxford, Oxford University Press, 1997) 1–2.

[4] S Fredman, *Discrimination Law* (2nd edn, Oxford, Oxford University Press, 2011) 2.

[5] Sen (n 3) 1.

This chapter is centred on Article 27 of the Constitution (the equality clause) and other related equality provisions that contain the various conceptions of equality present in the Constitution. It is divided into four main sections. Section I gives an overview of inequalities in the country to fully understand what informed the 2010 Constitution's strong emphasis on equality. Section II interrogates the understandings of equality that have been encapsulated in the Constitution's equality guarantee and how they can be harmoniously interpreted. An analytical framework is developed on how best to harmoniously interpret the multiple conceptions of equality in the Constitution. Section III explores the extent to which the equality guarantee in the Constitution advances transformative constitutionalism. Finally, to illustrate the need for coherence in interpreting the equality clause and related provisions in the Constitution, Section IV looks at the problem of conflicting decisions in recent case law on similar equality and non-discrimination questions.

I. Historical Overview of Inequalities and Discrimination in Kenya

Generally, equality and non-discrimination issues in Kenya can be looked at in terms of political, social and economic dynamics in the country and how they impact on marginalised groups or lead to certain groups being disadvantaged. This encompasses themes such as inequalities in land ownership, access to resources and services, and ethnicised politics that have led to deep-rooted ethno-regional inequalities through the marginalisation of politically 'dissident regions'. Marginalised and disadvantaged groups in Kenya that bear a disproportionate burden of discrimination are the poor, women, persons with disabilities, ethnic minorities, indigenous communities, and lesbian, gay, bisexual, transgender and intersex persons (LGBTIs).[6] These predominant forms of inequalities and discrimination in Kenya are further explained below.

A. Ethnicised Politics and Ethno-regional Inequalities

Before the passing of the 2010 Constitution, Kenya was a centralised State which gave presidents immense power. This created what Musila describes as a 'winner takes all' system in which the presidency, and by extension the State, became 'the main dispenser of largesse'.[7] The winning party would reward its supporters with more resource allocation and made sure the opposition got the least share of the national cake.

[6] Equal Rights Trust and Kenya Human Rights Commission, *In the Spirit of Harambee: Addressing Discrimination and Inequality in Kenya* (London, Prontaprint Bayswater, 2012) I–VIII.

[7] G Musila, 'A Preliminary Assessment of the Kenyan Truth, Justice and Reconciliation Commission Bill, 2008' (2008) 5 *African Renaissance* 40, 40–41.

The problem with this system of government was that it fuelled ethnic divisions as, since the colonial era, regions in Kenya have been divided and ruled on an ethnic basis. Hence, the struggle to hold on to power also followed ethnic patterns, producing many casualties, with those outside power being 'relegated to the fringes of social, political and economic life'.[8] The actions of successive ruling elites under the previous Constitution, of promoting exclusive economic benefits to sections of the country that promised the most political support, resulted in regional imbalance in the distribution of political appointments.[9] The distribution of public goods such as education facilities, health, and physical infrastructure also followed patterns of access to political power. This inevitably contributed to ethno-regional inequalities because the situation undermined efforts to alleviate poverty and resulted in cross-regional and generational variations in well-being.[10]

As an International Labour Organization report highlights, the Central Province of Kenya was favoured over other provinces in the distribution of resources during the regime of President Jomo Kenyatta (1964–78), who came from the region.[11] In 1970 the province accounted for about 15 per cent of government expenditure on housing. By contrast, Nyanza Province, which was considered a politically 'dissident region', accounted for only 1 per cent, even though the difference in population between Nyanza and Central Province was negligible. Similarly, the report notes that Central Province had 766 people per hospital bed, whereas politically excluded areas like Nyanza, Western and North Eastern Provinces had an average of over 1,000 persons per bed.[12] This was also the case during President Moi's rule (1979–2002), which brought similar advantages for the Rift Valley Province, from which he hailed.[13]

B. Inequality in Relation to Marginalised and Disadvantaged Groups

i. *The Poor*

Over 40 per cent of Kenyans are deemed poor.[14] Poverty and lack of access to basic essentials, including food, water, housing, healthcare and education, of nearly half

[8] ibid.

[9] R Muhula, 'Horizontal Inequalities and Ethno-regional politics in Kenya' (2009) 1 *Kenya Studies Review* 85, 95.

[10] ibid.

[11] International Labour Office, *Employment Incomes and Equality: A Strategy for Increasing Productive Employment in Kenya* (1972) 301.

[12] ibid.

[13] See Society for International Development (SID), *Pulling Apart: Facts and Figures on Inequality in Kenya* (Nairobi, SID, 2004) 21; Truth Justice and Reconciliation Commission (TJRC), *Report of the Truth, Justice and Reconciliation Commission* Volume IIB (Kenya TJRC 2013) 312.

[14] See Kenya National Bureau of Statistics, *Basic Report on Well-Being in Kenya: Based on the 2015/2016 Kenya Integrated Household Budget Survey (KIHBS)* (2018) 44–45; J Cilliers, B Hughes

of the population constitutes an inequality of manifestly unacceptable proportions. It correspondingly signals the official failure of the State under the previous Constitution as well as successive governments to address the plight of the poor. Poverty also exacerbates the effects of the other grounds of discrimination. It is both a reason for discrimination and an effect of discrimination, as those vulnerable to discrimination on the basis of other aspects of their identity, such as gender, disability, sexual orientation or HIV status, tend to have poorer access to education, health and other essential services.[15]

ii. Women

Kenya is ranked 126 out of 155 states globally in gender inequality.[16] This is a result of women's low levels of participation in socio-political fields, economic disempowerment, unfair cultural practices, persistent domestic and gender-based violence, and low enrolment of girls in schools. Many women in Kenya do not hold formal land and property titles, largely because most customary laws exclude women from land inheritance and ownership. It is reported that only 1 per cent of registered land titles in Kenya are held by women and only 5–6 per cent are jointly held.[17] This is despite women making up approximately 80 per cent of the workforce in agriculture and livestock production.[18] This contributes to their socio-economic disadvantage as land is a crucial source of their employment, livelihood and access to credit. Also, only 29 per cent of women in Kenya work in formal wage employment and about 70 per cent of these women feature in the lower income bracket, earning between Ksh 8,000 and Ksh 25,000 (US$103–321) per month.[19] This means that a huge percentage of women work in the informal sector, which has its own challenges in terms of low pay and lack of laws protecting women. Yet nearly 40 per cent of households in the country are run solely by women, contributing to most of these households being affected by poverty.[20]

On top of this, it is women who predominantly provide unpaid domestic and care work to the extended family, restricting them from participating in social, economic and political life. In addition, because part of the unpaid domestic work

and S Turner, *Reducing Poverty in Africa: Realistic Targets for the Post-2015 MDGs and Agenda 2063* (African Futures Paper 10, 2014) 1.

[15] Equal Rights Trust and Kenya Human Rights Commission (n 6) 5.

[16] United Nations Development Programme, *Kenya Human Development Report 2015, Work for Human Development: Briefing Notes for Countries on the 2015 Human Development Report* (2015) 6.

[17] Kenya Land Alliance and FIDA-Kenya, *Women, Land and Property Rights and the Land Reforms in Kenya* (Policy Brief 2006) 1.

[18] ibid.

[19] R Atieno, 'Explaining Female Labour Force Participation: The Case of Kenya's Informal Sector and the Effect of the Economic Crisis' (Annual IAFFE Conference, Buenos Aires, 22–24 July 2010) 3.

[20] UN Committee on the Elimination of Discrimination Against Women (CEDAW), *Consideration of reports submitted by States parties under article 18 of the Convention, Eighth periodic report of States parties due in 2015: Kenya*, 1 June 2016, CEDAW/C/KEN/8 [141].

women perform includes shopping for household goods, women are disproportionately affected by the growing use of Value Added Tax and other consumption taxes. The economic disempowerment of many women makes them susceptible to domestic violence and makes them stay in violent marriages because of their economic dependence.[21] Such dependence likewise prevents them from negotiating safe sex, increasing their risks of contracting HIV/AIDS.[22] Recent statistics show that Kenyan women up to the age of 24 are 5.2 times more likely to contract HIV than men of the same age.[23]

Kenya's 2010 Constitution is a major boost in guaranteeing women's equality rights. Numerous articles incorporate principles of gender equality and require the elimination of cultural norms and practices that are harmful to women. The Kenyan government, while seeking to comply with gender equality provisions in the 2010 Constitution, has put in place laws, policies and programmes to try to address existing gender inequalities. Various initiatives have also been started in a bid to empower women. These include the Uwezo Fund, aimed at enabling women to access finances to promote their businesses and enterprises at the constituency level, and the Women Enterprise Fund, which provides accessible and affordable credit to support women in starting or expanding businesses. However, as has been observed by civil society organisations in Kenya, 'Even where rights are available, enforcement is weak, knowledge of legal rights is poor among both right-holders and duty-bearers and access to justice is problematic'.[24]

iii. Persons with Disabilities

There are approximately 6 million persons with disabilities living in Kenya.[25] These statistics include both moderately and severely disabled persons. Problems facing those with physical and sensory disabilities often arise as a result of lack of access to assistive devices, lack of welfare support and lack of reasonable accommodation; whereas the problems facing those with mental and intellectual disabilities include lack of legal personality and enforced medical treatment.[26] On the whole, persons with disabilities in Kenya are discriminated against in the political, social and economic fields, which leads to them having poor access to education, political

[21] J Smith, C Theano, L Torbett and J Toussaint, 'Women's Land and Property Rights in Kenya – Moving Forward into a New Era of Equality: A Human Rights Report and Proposed Legislation' (2009) 40 *Georgetown Journal of International Law* 1, 3.

[22] ibid 3 and 46–51.

[23] KS Njonjo, *Youth Fact Book: Infinite Possibility of Definite Disaster?* (Nairobi, Institute of Economic Affairs, 2010) 20.

[24] East African Collaboration for Economic, Social & Cultural Rights, *Kenya Civil Society Shadow Report on Economic, Social and Cultural Rights* (2014) 44.

[25] World Health Organization, *The Global Burden of Disease: 2004 Update* (2004) 34. See also, Equal Rights Trust and Kenya Human Rights Commission (n 6) 132.

[26] Equal Rights Trust and Kenya Human Rights Commission (n 6) 131.

representation, health, employment and transportation.[27] The discrimination they face is attributed to, inter alia, lack of awareness and education on disability, which leads to stigma, stereotypes and little attitudinal change towards persons with disabilities.[28]

iv. Minorities and Marginalised Groups

Article 260 of the 2010 Constitution defines a marginalised group as 'a group of people who, because of laws or practices before, on, or after the effective date, were or are disadvantaged by discrimination on one or more of the grounds in Article 27 (4)'. According to the same article, these groups effectively include a community that has a relatively small population; indigenous communities that have retained and maintained their traditional way of life; pastoral and nomadic communities; and 'a settled community that, because of its relative geographic isolation, has experienced only marginal participation in the integral social and economic life of Kenya as a whole'.[29] Groups in Kenya covered by these provisions include: the Ogiek (hunter gatherers); Maasai, Pokot, Samburu, Turkana, Rendille, Orma and Borana (pastoralists or agro-pastoralists); and the Endorois.[30] Other groups that can be included in the list are ethnic minorities such as the Kenyan Nubians and Kenyan Somalis.[31]

Marginalised communities in Kenya have been at the centre of economic marginalisation characterised by a lack of infrastructural development, limited access to social amenities and violation of their land rights. Such economic marginalisation emanated from a legal framework and various policy initiatives that did not take cognisance of minority rights.[32] The failure to enforce judgments upholding minority rights in Kenya has also been a contributing factor.[33] An example of this is the case of *Centre for Minority Rights Development (Kenya) and Another on behalf of Endorois Welfare Council v Kenya*.[34] In the case, the African Commission

[27] PA Nyagudi, 'Overview of the Current Policies, Legislation and Programmes for Persons with Disabilities in Kenya' in *Launch of PWD Web Portal and e-Accessibility Workshop for Persons with Disabilities* (Laico Regency, Nairobi: National Council for Persons with Disabilities, 2012).

[28] Kenya National Bureau of Statistics, *Kenya National Survey for Persons with Disabilities – Main Report* (2008) xvi.

[29] The Constitution of Kenya, 2010, Art 260.

[30] African Commission on Human and Peoples' Rights and International Work Group for Indigenous Affairs, *Report of the African Commission Working Group of Experts on Indigenous Populations/Communities* (2005) 15 and 17.

[31] Equal Rights Trust and Kenya Human Rights Commission (n 6) 78–92.

[32] UN Human Rights Council, *Oral statement on 'Minorities and Effective Participation in Economic Life' by the Centre for Minority Rights Development (CEMIRIDE), UN Human Rights Council Forum on Minority Issues, Third Session, Geneva December 14–15, 2010* (2010) 1.

[33] ibid.

[34] *Centre for Minority Rights Development (Kenya) and Another on behalf of Endorois Welfare Council v Kenya* Communication 276/2003 (ACHPR).

on Human and Peoples' Rights (ACHPR) held that the Kenyan government had, inter alia, violated the Endorois community's right to property, culture and the free disposition of natural resources by evicting the Endorois people from their homes at Lake Baringo. For these violations, the ACHPR recommended that the government should recognise the ownership rights of the Endorois and return to them their ancestral lands. It also recommended that the Endorois should be compensated for their losses and should benefit from the royalties and employment opportunities within the game reserve.[35] However, 10 years on, the recommendations have still not been fully implemented.[36]

v. Lesbian, Gay, Bisexual, Transgender and Intersex Persons

Homosexuality is considered a taboo and repugnant to cultural values and morality in Kenya. The Penal Code, which is a colonial relic in force since 1930, with several subsequent amendments post independence in 1963, criminalises sodomy in sections 162–65.[37] Terms such as 'unnatural offences', 'attempt to commit unnatural offences' and 'indecent practices between males' are used in the Penal Code to describe the kind of punishment that would be meted out to anyone found guilty of being gay under the law. A guilty verdict could mean up to 21 years' imprisonment.[38] The 2010 Constitution has not repealed these provisions.

The Gay and Lesbian Coalition of Kenya and other organisations have been pushing for greater liberties for their members and the deletion of sections 162–65 of the Penal Code.[39] Scholars like Finerty argue that the 2010 Constitution's heightened protection of individual rights, coupled with the increased recognition that discrimination based on sexual orientation or gender identity violates international human rights law, provides a strong framework for arguing that Kenya's anti-sodomy laws are currently unconstitutional.[40] This has not yet been expressly recognised and so the anti-sodomy laws remain on the books. However, there is ongoing litigation challenging the constitutionality of sections 162–65 of the Penal Code, which criminalise private consensual sexual conduct between adults of the same sex.[41]

[35] ibid [80].

[36] R Marlin, '"The Endorois decision" – Four years on, the Endorois still await action by the Government of Kenya' (Minority Rights Group Blogs and Podcasts, 23 September 2014) minorityrights.org/2014/09/23/the-endorois-decision-four-years-on-the-endorois-still-await-action-by-the-government-of-kenya/.

[37] Penal Code Cap. 63, Laws of Kenya.

[38] ibid s 162.

[39] P Orengo, 'Kenya's Gay Movement Seeks Stamp of Approval', *The Standard* (Nairobi, 9 July 2013).

[40] C Finerty, 'Being Gay in Kenya: The Implications of Kenya's New Constitution for Its Anti-Sodomy Laws' (2012) 45 *Cornell International Law Journal* 431, 448–49.

[41] See *EG & 7 Others v Attorney General; DKM & 9 Others (Interested Parties); Katiba Institute & Another (Amicus Curiae)* (Consolidated) [2019] eKLR; *Eric Gitari v Attorney General & Another* [2016] eKLR.

II. What Understandings of Equality are Encapsulated in Article 27 and Related Provisions of the Constitution?

A. Scope of Article 27 – The Equality Clause

Article 27 contains eight sub-sections incorporating multiple concepts of equality. It deals with both equality and non-discrimination in the same provision and its sub-sections refer to both equality and non-discrimination. This implies that the two terms are closely interconnected and difficult to separate. On the relationship between the two, Hepple argues that discrimination law is an essential but not exclusive part of equality law.[42] Principle 4 of the Equal Rights Trust's Declaration of Principles on Equality states that the right to be free from discrimination is subsumed in the right to equality.[43] In addition, the Inter-American Court of Human Rights, referring to the special relationship between the two, has stated that 'The element of equality is difficult to separate from non-discrimination. Indeed, when referring to equality before the law … this principle must be guaranteed with no discrimination'.[44] The consensus therefore seems to be that the right to equality is broader than the right to non-discrimination, which is a free-standing right. However, while conceptually different, the two are interconnected and difficult to separate. The text of the Constitution envisions a close relationship between the two norms, and thus there is no problem with referring to the two of them together in this book as dealt with in the equality clause.

The application of the equality clause extends vertically in relation to protection of people's rights from violation by the State and its organs, and horizontally to rights protection in relationships between private individuals or groups. Article 20(1) of the Constitution states that 'The Bill of Rights applies to all law and binds all State organs and all persons'. By including the word 'all persons' it thus embraces direct horizontality.[45] This was acknowledged by the High Court in *Rose Wangui Mambo & 2 Others v Limuru Country Club & 17 Others*.[46] In the case, the Court held that it had jurisdiction to hear equality claims against private entities and private members' clubs. It stated that the respondents could not be allowed to wave a private entity card to bar the Court from assuming jurisdiction where there are allegations of breach of fundamental rights and freedoms by its members or any other person.[47] The recognition of both vertical and horizontal application of

[42] B Hepple, *Equality: The New Legal Framework* (Oxford, Hart Publishing, 2011) 1.
[43] Equal Rights Trust, *Declaration of Principles on Equality* (London, Equal Rights Trust, 2008) 6.
[44] *Juridical Condition and Rights of the Undocumented Migrants*, Advisory Opinion OC-18/03, Inter-American Court of Human Rights [83].
[45] C Murray, 'Kenya's 2010 Constitution' (2013) 61 *Neue Folge Band Jahrbuch des öffentlichen Rechts* 747, 760–61.
[46] *Rose Wangui Mambo & 2 Others v Limuru Country Club & 17 Others* [2014] eKLR.
[47] ibid [68].

rights and freedoms is particularly fundamental in tackling the deep-rooted social stereotypes and prejudices in society. As will be discussed later on in the chapter, direct horizontality is important in eradicating patterns of systemic disadvantage as most of the discrimination in Kenya occurs in the private sphere.[48]

It is also essential to note that the rights and fundamental freedoms in the Bill of Rights, including the equality clause, are guaranteed not only to citizens, but to 'every person'. The Bill of Rights uses the words 'all persons', 'every person' and 'a person' instead of 'citizen' in providing for rights and obligations. This is with the exception of Article 35, which specifically states that the right of access to information applies only to citizens.[49]

B. Formal and Substantive Conceptions of Equality in the Constitution

Article 27 incorporates both formal and substantive conceptions of equality, which are the two main distinctions commonly used to explain rival concepts of equality. On the one hand, a formal understanding of equality insists on equal treatment, which is the primary goal of anti-discrimination law. It views justice as requiring the symmetrical application of equality in the sense that everyone should be treated the same, regardless of whether sameness in treatment will favour or foreseeably exacerbate the inequality experienced by a disadvantaged group.[50] It is thus an abstract view of justice as it overlooks differences, for example, in social status, access to primary goods, political power, or opportunities, which in many instances result in unequal outcomes.[51] Nevertheless, formal equality is an important first step in breaking down stereotypes and prejudices that are applied to subordinate a certain group of individuals from accessing benefits enjoyed by others, who are similarly situated, because of their personal characteristics.[52]

On the other hand, substantive equality takes into account the differences between individuals and is concerned about the 'situation they end up in'.[53] For this reason, substantive equality acknowledges that justice is not abstract and can only be meaningful when a contextual approach is employed, taking into consideration the social dynamics at play.[54] It recognises that sameness

[48] See text to nn 85–93.

[49] *Famy Care Limited v Public Procurement Administrative Review Board & Another* [2013] eKLR [18].

[50] See Fredman, *Discrimination Law* (n 4) 2–14 and 234; B McLachlin, 'The Evolution of Equality' (1996) 54 *Advocate* 559, 560; Pojman and Westmoreland (n 3) 2; E Holmes, 'Anti-Discrimination Rights Without Equality' (2005) 68 *MLR* 175, 176.

[51] Fredman, *Discrimination Law* (n 4) 2 and 235.

[52] See ibid 14; McLachlin (n 50) 560.

[53] Holmes (n 50) 178.

[54] Fredman, *Discrimination Law* (n 4) 235.

in treatment can in reality exacerbate inequality because of past and ongoing discrimination.[55] Substantive equality is therefore interested in identifying inequality of outcomes and tries to remedy disadvantage by eliminating factors that exacerbate or lead to such inequality in outcome.[56] These are the two core distinctions that are used to explain the multiple notions of equality interrogated in the book.

Article 27(1) of the Constitution contains the main formal understanding of equality. It provides that 'Every person is equal before the law and has the right to equal protection and equal benefit of the law'. This provision can be said to entail aspects of formal equality since the idea of equality before the law has been said to require blindness to a person's individual characteristics by insisting on the consistent application of the law to all.[57] Hence, the State should be neutral in the way it treats its citizens and should not favour some over others.

Nevertheless, it is important to note that 'equal benefit of the law' also includes a substantive conception of equality since it acknowledges that you may be equal before the law and still not get the equal benefit of it. For instance, deaf persons cannot equally benefit from the right to healthcare if healthcare facilities lack sign language interpreters.[58] This shows that 'equal benefit of the law' goes further than requiring symmetrical treatment. It may also require reasonable accommodation in situations where a group of people are discriminatorily excluded from entitlements to benefits meant to be equally enjoyed by all persons. These words, 'equal benefit of the law', are also used in section 15(1) of the Canadian Charter and it was hoped they would be understood in this way, in that it was meant to extend beyond a duty to refrain from discriminating to include a positive duty to redress and even eradicate poverty.[59] Some aspects of formal equality can also be found in Article 27(3), which provides for the equal treatment of men and women in all spheres of life.

The rest of Article 27, including sub-sections (2)–(8), can be said to entail a more substantive conception of equality. The sub-sections incorporate notions such as full and equal enjoyment of rights, equal opportunities for women and men in all spheres of life, an expansive and open list of grounds for non-discrimination, affirmative action, the principle of genuine need, and gender quotas. All these notions, and in particular the inclusion of affirmative action in Article 27(6), are a strong indication of the Constitution's emphasis on substantive equality.

[55] ibid 14.

[56] A Phillips, 'Defending Equality of Outcome' (2004) 12(1) *Journal of Political Philosophy* 1, 1–2.

[57] eg *Regents of the University of California v Bakke* 438 US 265 (1978) [288]–[290], where the US Supreme Court stated that equality before the law requires blindness to people's personal characteristics.

[58] See *Eldridge v British Columbia (Attorney General)* [1997] 3 SCR 624.

[59] B Porter, 'Expectations of Equality' (2006) 33 *Supreme Court Law Review* 23, 27.

C. The Equality Clause as Creating an Analytical Framework Incorporating Both Formal and Substantive Conceptions of Equality

The inclusion of both formal and substantive conceptions of equality in Article 27 is essential in achieving greater equality. It resonates with Dworkin's presupposition that the guarantee of equality should be based on finding an answer to the question: what does treatment as an equal require? Dworkin stresses that it is a primary obligation of government not only to treat people with concern and respect, but also to treat them with *equal* concern and respect.[60] Such treatment implicates two different kinds of rights, 'the right to *equal treatment*' and 'the right to *treatment as an equal*'.[61] According to him, the former relates to the neutral treatment of everyone in terms of 'equal distribution of some opportunity or resource or burden' and the latter involves 'the right, not to receive the same distribution of some burden or benefit, but to be treated with the same respect and concern as anyone else'.[62] On the relationship between the two, Dworkin opines that 'the right to treatment as an equal is fundamental, and the right to equal treatment, derivative' as in some scenarios 'the right to treatment as an equal will entail a right to equal treatment'.[63]

The formal and substantive conceptions of equality in Article 27 have a similar relationship; substantive equality seeks to answer the 'meta question' of what treatment as an equal entails, which in some cases would mean guaranteeing formal equality in terms of equal treatment. The two concepts are essential in achieving full equality since 'Injustice arises when equals are treated unequally and also when unequals are treated equally'.[64]

However, the two concepts often conflict. For example, affirmative action applies unequal treatment when remedying past and ongoing disadvantage experienced by a particular group in order to achieve substantive equality. This may be regarded as breaching formal equality, which is difference-blind. Collins explains that the tension between the two is created because formal equality determines a procedure rather than an outcome, whereas substantive equality regards as questionable any rule or practice including equal treatment that does not lead to an equal outcome.[65]

Hence, in providing a pragmatic and comprehensive approach (that considers the tension between the two norms), what is envisioned is an analytical framework similar to the contextual approach developed by Goldstone J in the

[60] R Dworkin, *Taking Rights Seriously* (Cambridge, MA, Harvard University Press, 1977) 272–74 and 326–28.

[61] ibid 273.

[62] ibid.

[63] ibid.

[64] Pojman and Westmoreland (n 3) 2.

[65] H Collins, 'Discrimination, Equality and Social Inclusion' (2003) 66(1) *MLR* 16, 17–18.

South African Constitutional Court decision in *President of the Republic of South Africa and Another v Hugo*.[66] He opined that equal treatment on the basis of equal worth and freedom cannot be achieved by insisting on identical treatment in all cases. All equality cases before the Court therefore require 'a careful and thorough understanding of the impact of the discriminatory action upon the particular group concerned to determine whether its overall impact is one which furthers the constitutional goal of equality or not'.[67] This enquiry has been described as contextual because it 'considers, inter alia, the position of the complainant in the society and whether she has suffered from past patterns of disadvantage'.[68] By insisting on an analysis of the impact, Goldstone J thus, arguably, prefers the substantive over the formal approach to equality. Nevertheless, a consideration of the impact might warrant equal treatment. A similar position is taken in this book.

Therefore, a conceptualisation of Article 27 that considers all its sub-sections as creating an analytical framework to determine what treatment as an equal requires for different people is argued for. This analytical framework will be helpful in guiding courts, lawyers and other relevant actors towards a desirable conceptualisation of equality concepts in the Constitution.

Moreover, in terms of the constitutional text, the sub-sections of the equality clause – in their inclusion of different equality concepts fundamental to achieving greater equality – reflect Fredman's four-dimensional view of the goals of equality. In this view, substantive equality should simultaneously: redress disadvantage through, for instance, the egalitarian redistribution of resources (the redistributive dimension); address stigma, stereotyping, prejudice and violence directed against certain individuals or groups (the recognition dimension); facilitate participation and political voice, particularly for marginalised groups, to advance social inclusion (the participative dimension); and accommodate difference and bring about structural change by confronting the root causes of inequality that lead to patterns of disadvantage (the transformative dimension).[69] These facets of equality are interdependent and work together in addressing the harms of inequality and discrimination in a polity as opposed to each dimension on its own.[70] Therefore, all these dimensions should be considered when addressing equality-related cases.

An approach that views these four-dimensional goals as mutually exclusive may fail to correctly situate the multiple root causes of injustice in determining what treatment as an equal requires and devising proper remedies.[71] There are occasions where it is hard not to combine these dimensions. For instance, the *recognition* of

[66] *President of the Republic of South Africa & Another v Hugo* 1997 (4) SA 1 (CC) (*Hugo*).

[67] ibid [41].

[68] C Albertyn, 'Substantive Equality and Transformation in South Africa' (2007) 23 *South African Journal of Human Rights* 253, 259.

[69] Fredman, *Discrimination Law* (n 4) 25–33; and S Fredman, 'Substantive Equality Revisited' (2016) 14(3) *International Journal of Constitutional Law* 712.

[70] ibid.

[71] N Fraser and A Honneth, *Redistribution or Recognition? A Political-Philosophical Exchange* (London, Verso, 2003) 11.

different cultures and religions is important in the creation of a difference-friendly society 'where assimilation to majority or dominant cultural norms is no longer the price of equal respect'.[72] However, there are cultural and religious beliefs that entrench gender inequality by allowing the application of harmful cultural practices such as the exclusion of women from owning land. Thus, to tell the difference between the two, a consideration of the first dimension (*redressing disadvantage*) working together with the second dimension (*recognition* – respect for human dignity and worth) and the fourth dimension (*transformative* – accommodation of difference and structural change) is necessary. Such a multidimensional approach would require that cultural and religious diversity be accommodated only to the extent that it does not breach women's human dignity both in redressing social exclusion and defeating gender prejudices.

In looking at the Constitution's drafting history, the drafters seem to have supported such a conceptualisation of the multiple notions of equality in the Constitution. This conclusion can be extrapolated from a reading of the *Beginner's Guide to the Proposed Constitution*, which was a useful compilation of background information for the public on the 2010 Constitution before its adoption, provided by the Committee of Experts on Constitutional Review.[73] The first dimension is reflected in the many provisions specifically targeting disadvantage, even if this means requiring unequal treatment. To this extent, the guide states that

> women must be allowed maternity leave if they are to have equal opportunity to work; people with disabilities may need special access to ramps; and marginalised groups may need special programmes to redress disadvantage and enable them to participate in the social, political and economic life of Kenya as equal citizens.[74]

Against this backdrop, I shall now consider the extent to which the equality guarantee in the Constitution advances transformative constitutionalism. This, along with the analytical framework developed, will provide the necessary background for the discussions in subsequent chapters on interpretation of different and interrelated conceptions of equality in the Constitution.

III. To What Extent Does the Constitution's Equality Guarantee Advance Transformative Constitutionalism?

The sub-sections of Article 27 and related equality provisions demonstrate a commitment to social transformation through the inclusion of equality guarantees that reflect the country's historical context of inequality. These are transformative

[72] ibid 7.

[73] C Murray, *Beginner's Guide to the Proposed Constitution: Chapter by Chapter* (2009) constitutionnet.org/sites/default/files/beginners_guide_to_proposed_const_chap_by_chap.pdf.

[74] ibid 24.

as they not only broaden the net of inclusion, but also dislodge the underlying social framework.[75] The former can be reflected in the more expansive and open list of grounds for non-discrimination, and the inclusion of special rights for various disadvantaged groups. The latter is echoed in the inclusion of affirmative action, which aims to redress past disadvantage through the equitable redistribution of power and resources. These equality provisions are mostly responding to past and ongoing inequalities and are thus all the more reason why an analysis of the impact and reference to context is essential, as argued in the analytical framework proposed in the previous section.

A. The Equality Guarantee as Broadening the Net of Inclusion

i. A More Expansive and Non-exhaustive List of Grounds for Non-discrimination

The transformative nature of the Constitution is reflected in Article 27(4), which includes a more expansive list of grounds for non-discrimination than those in section 82 of the previous 1963 Constitution. The previous Constitution only listed the grounds of race, tribe, place of origin or residence, political opinion, colour, creed or sex. The 2010 Constitution contains a broader list of grounds, including 'race, sex, pregnancy, marital status, health status, ethnic or social origin, colour, age, disability, religion, conscience, belief, culture, dress, language or birth', which highlight more accurately the history of inequalities in Kenya.

The list provided in Article 27(4) is non-exhaustive as it mandates that the State should not discriminate against *any* person on *any* ground, *including* those that are listed. Article 259(4)(b) of the Constitution explains that 'the word "includes" means, "includes, but is not limited to"'. This therefore means that the grounds listed are merely examples and are not meant to be exhaustive.

The acknowledgement that the list of grounds in Article 27(4) is not etched in stone, and that new grounds can be added in response to changes in society and individual circumstances, echoes the third principle of transformative constitutionalism, which recognises that change is constant. Grounds of non-discrimination are looked at extensively in Chapter 4.

ii. Inclusion of the Rights of Special Groups

Articles 53–57 of the Kenyan Constitution provide for the specific application of the rights of special groups. These groups include children, persons with disabilities, the youth, minority and marginalised groups, and the elderly.[76] The inclusion

[75] Albertyn (n 68) 254.
[76] Constitution of Kenya, 2010, Arts 53–57.

of these rights, in addition to the equality clause, can be viewed as an extension of Article 27. To the extent that these special provisions are about equality and affirmative action in favour of the aforementioned groups, their inclusion in Articles 53–57 means that the rights of special groups in the Constitution are equality rights.

These groups represent some of the most marginalised and disadvantaged individuals in Kenya, who needed to be recognised as noted in the justification given by the Committee of Experts on Constitutional Review for their inclusion in the Constitution.[77] The rights of special groups in Articles 53–57 are transformative as they reflect the multidimensional aspects of equality. For instance, the provisions in Article 54 provide for the rights of persons with disabilities to be treated with dignity and respect (the recognition dimension); to access educational institutions, facilities and public transport (the redistributive and transformative (accommodation of difference) dimensions); and state that at least 5 per cent of the members of the public in elective and appointive bodies be persons with disabilities (the participative dimension).

B. The Equality Guarantee as Eradicating Patterns of Systemic Disadvantage

Inequality and discrimination are said to be particularly harmful when they lead to patterns of systemic disadvantage or structural patterns of discrimination and domination. This notion is important in understanding the relationship between equality and transformative constitutionalism.

In her discussion on equality and groups, Young expounds on what patterns of structural or systemic disadvantage mean.[78] To interpret structural inequality she uses Frye's analogy of a birdcage.[79] In explaining the inhibition of a bird's flight because of the cage, Young states that an explanation as to why a caged bird is unable to fly would only make sense by looking at 'a large number of wires arranged in a specific way and connected to one another to enclose the bird'.[80] Applying this reasoning, Young explains that structural inequality relates to an account of 'someone's life circumstances [and] contains many strands of difficulty or difference from others that … when considered together … reveal a net of restricting and reinforcing relationships'.[81]

[77] See Committee of Experts on Constitutional Review, *Final Report of the Committee of Experts on Constitutional Review* (2011) 109; Constitution of Kenya Review Commission, *The Final Report of the Constitution of Kenya Review Commission. Approved for issue at the 95th Plenary Meeting held on 10 February 2005* (2005) 116–19.

[78] IM Young, 'Equality of Whom? Social Groups and Judgments of Injustice' (2001) 9 *Journal of Political Philosophy* 1, 5.

[79] M Frye, *Politics of Reality: Essays in Feminist Theory* (Trumansburg, NY, The Crossing Press, 1983).

[80] Young (n 78) 10.

[81] ibid.

To illustrate how systemic disadvantage occurs, Young uses Okin's[82] account of women's oppression. This account locates women's disadvantage within the gender roles society has set for men and women. Inevitably, such deeply ingrained social perceptions spill over from the family setting to social institutions. As a result, 'society continues to be organized around the expectation that children and other dependent people ought to be cared for primarily by family members [women] without formal compensation'.[83] These social stereotypes based on the view that a woman's place is in the home contribute to the 'systemic ways that result in disadvantage and vulnerability for many women'.[84] This is the understanding of patterns of systemic or structural disadvantage that is applied in the book.

Based on this definition, equality in the Kenyan Constitution can be said to require the eradication of patterns of systemic disadvantage in the following ways:

i. Inclusion of Gender Equality Provisions

Article 27(3) makes specific provision for equality between men and women, stating that 'Women and men have the right to equal treatment, including the right to equal opportunities in political, economic, cultural and social spheres'. The Constitution of Kenya Review Commission's final report noted that women's issues were very prominent in the submissions to the Commission, based on the fact that women held only 4.1 per cent of seats in Parliament at the time.[85] There was also the persistence of domestic and gender-based sexual violence against women, discrimination in inheritance and other matters of personal law, and low enrolment of girls in schools.[86] Keen on bringing to an end these past injustices, women were thus very active in the Constitution review process.[87] Women's claims for fair and equal treatment were said to demand a provision setting out their rights clearly, and which expressed the multiplicity of past injustices against them.[88] Therefore, although there would be an element of overlap with the general non-discrimination provision, it was felt that this was justified in the interests of ensuring a clear statement of the position of more than half of the population who are female.[89]

The gender equality guarantee in Article 27(3) can also be linked to other constitutional provisions addressing obstacles to women's empowerment and progress in the various spheres of life. In declaring unconstitutional cultural practices that are harmful to women, Article 60 requires that land policy, which has

[82] S Okin, *Justice, Gender, and the Family* (New York, NY, Basic Books, 1989).
[83] Young (n 78) 10.
[84] ibid.
[85] Constitution of Kenya Review Commission (n 77) 103–30.
[86] ibid.
[87] YP Ghai and JC Cottrell, *Kenya's Constitution: An Instrument for Change* (Nairobi, Katiba Institute, 2011) 49.
[88] Constitution of Kenya Review Commission (n 77) 103–30.
[89] ibid 108.

largely been based on customary laws that exclude women from land ownership, should include the elimination of gender discrimination.[90] In terms of challenging harmful practices such as forced marriages and unequal claims to matrimonial property upon divorce, Article 45 guarantees women equal rights to marry, during marriage and in the case of divorce. Also, unlike the previous Constitution, which discriminated against women on matters of citizenship, the 2010 Constitution includes equal rights for both women and men to pass citizenship to their children or have their spouse become a citizen.[91] Notably, under Chapter VI of the previous 1963 Constitution on citizenship, a woman could not pass on citizenship to her child or husband and also, upon marriage to a foreigner, she lost her own citizenship, adopting that of her husband.

Additionally, it is critical to note, as Ghai highlights, that most of the discrimination against women in Kenya comes from society and not the State.[92] Ghai's statement accurately reflects the patriarchal nature of Kenyan society, which views women as being subordinate to men. This perception has trickled down to social, political and economic structures and institutions in the country. The inclusion of gender equality provisions acts as a tool for social transformation as they intend to defeat deeply ingrained social values harmful to women, since these laws bind not only the State, but also individuals in their relationships with each other as stated earlier.[93]

ii. Recognition of Both Direct and Indirect Discrimination

Unlike the non-discrimination guarantee in section 82 of the previous Constitution, the 2010 Constitution recognises both direct and indirect discrimination. Article 27(5) provides that 'A person shall not discriminate directly or indirectly against another person on any of the grounds specified or contemplated in clause (4)'. Akin to the equal treatment requirement of treating people alike, direct discrimination outlaws differential treatment, especially when this is related to a person's individual characteristics.[94] However, on its own, direct discrimination is inadequate in eradicating systemic patterns of disadvantage. This is because of its symmetric application as it outlaws favourable treatment, irrespective of whether such treatment remedies or exacerbates disadvantage.[95] This highlights its inadequacy as a single principle aimed at dealing with inequalities in society, as in some scenarios certain vulnerable groups may require something more than just consistent treatment because of past and ongoing disadvantage.

[90] Constitution of Kenya 2010, Art 60.
[91] ibid Arts 14 and 15.
[92] YP Ghai, 'Analysis of Kenya's 2010 Proposed Constitution' www.katibainstitute.org/Archives/images/banners/Ghai-%20Analysis%20of%20Kenya's%202010%20proposed%20constitution.pdf.
[93] Text to nn 44–48.
[94] Fredman, *Discrimination Law* (n 4) 203.
[95] ibid 175.

Direct discrimination cannot outlaw invidious distinctions while at the same time recognising legitimate differentiations because of its insistence on consistent treatment.[96] Indirect discrimination intervenes, however, to remedy the inadequacies of direct discrimination.

Indirect discrimination recognises that facially neutral treatment can in practice perpetuate discrimination. Therefore, an inquiry into whether a person has been indirectly discriminated against requires an investigation of whether equal treatment in a particular case leads to unequal *impact* on a person or group based on their particular characteristics.[97] An example of this would be a mandatory requirement that all employees in a given company should work on Saturdays, which will have an unequal impact on Seventh Day Adventists or Jewish employees, whose religious beliefs require them not to work on Saturdays. Due to such an unequal impact, indirect discrimination recognises that equal treatment can lead to disparate results. This therefore means that indirect discrimination is an aspect of substantive equality. This is through its insistence on impact rather than an abstract view of equality as requiring sameness in treatment.

Indirect discrimination also allows justification, which helps to sieve out differentiations that are legitimate from those that impede structural transformation. For example, indirect discrimination would require proof that a job requirement for pilots to be of a certain height (which may exclude a disproportionately larger number of women applicants than men) is necessary for them to perform the job in question, instead of a mere assumption relating height to performance.

iii. Inclusion of Affirmative Action

The entrenchment of affirmative action in Article 27(6) and in several other provisions elsewhere in the 2010 Constitution, which were absent in the previous Constitution, holds much promise for the achievement of greater equality and transformative constitutionalism. Nonetheless, as stated earlier, there is a difficulty in reconciling affirmative action with equal treatment.[98] This is because affirmative action specifically mandates unequal treatment to redress pre-existing disadvantage experienced by a particular group.

However, the 2010 Constitution gives a justification for the use of affirmative action that is helpful in developing a solution for the difficult conceptual problem created by the tension between the two norms. Article 27(6) particularly states that affirmative action is meant to 'give full effect to the realisation of the rights guaranteed under [the] Article'. This means that affirmative action measures in the Constitution are viewed as being important in the achievement of full equality and are not a breach of it. Article 27(6) further mandates the State to

[96] ibid 154 and 167.
[97] ibid 203.
[98] Text to nn 63–65.

'take legislative and other measures including affirmative action programmes and policies designed to redress any disadvantage suffered by individuals or groups because of past discrimination'. This requirement protects affirmative action against claims of direct discrimination brought about by its unequal treatment in favour of disadvantaged groups. It does so by requiring that such measures be justified through the production of evidence that they are meant to redress disadvantage caused by past discrimination. Affirmative action provisions in the Constitution and the interpretive challenges they raise are extensively discussed in Chapter 5.

C. Exemption of Islamic Law from the Automatic Application of Equality Provisions in the Bill of Rights as a Drawback to Transformation

Article 24(4) of the Kenyan Constitution exempts Islamic law from the automatic application of equality provisions in the Bill of Rights, as applied by Kadhis' courts.[99] The jurisdiction of these courts is limited to 'the determination of questions of Muslim law relating to personal status, marriage, divorce or inheritance in proceedings in which all the parties profess the Muslim religion and submit to the jurisdiction of the Kadhi's courts'.[100] This exemption has the potential to affect the transformative nature of the equality guarantee and its harmonious interpretation. This is extensively discussed in Chapter 6, which recommends various ways of interpreting it to try and reduce its prima facie discriminatory nature or for courts to recommend its amendment or deletion.

IV. Conflicting Interpretations of Equality in Recent Case Law

Having considered the transformative nature of the equality guarantees in the Constitution, it is important to note that current judicial decisions do not provide clarity on the proper conceptualisation, interpretation and application of the competing conceptions of equality in the Constitution. Hence, this book hopes to fill in this lacuna.

There has been an increasing use of substantive equality principles, although some cases still use a formal equality approach. The High Court decision in *John Kabui Mwai & 3 Others v Kenya National Examination Council & 2 Others* is an example of a novel case where the Court, in recognising the transformative nature

[99] Kadhis' courts are established under Art 170 of the Constitution of Kenya, 2010.
[100] Constitution of Kenya 2010, Art 170(5).

of the Constitution and its emphasis on substantive equality, took a contextual and purposive approach to an equality analysis.[101] In the case, Gacheche, Dulu and Muchelule JJ affirmed a government policy affording less privileged children in public schools an opportunity to join prestigious national schools, even with lower examination grades than their assumedly better-off counterparts in private schools. The Court applied a contextual approach in its analysis of the equality questions before it, similar to the analytical framework referred to earlier, leading to a determination that the differential treatment resulted in equality.[102] In acknowledgement of the Constitution's emphasis on a substantive conception of equality, the judges held that

> [t]he special provisions of article 27(6) make it a unique set of constitutional provisions. When the Constitution was adopted, the framers knew, and clearly had in mind, the different status of persons in the society and the need to protect the weak from being overrun by those with ability. They had in mind the history of this country, both the differences in endowment either by dint of the region where one came from or as a function of other factors, which might necessitate special protection. Rightly or wrongly, and it is not for the courts to decide, the framers of the Constitution manifestly regarded as inadequate a blanket right to equal treatment, and their intention was to remedy the perceived societal inequalities thus recognizing the necessity of corrective measures, namely those envisaged in article 27(6), which were at the same time given the status of constitutional guarantee.[103]

The emphasis on a substantive conception of equality is also evident in the case of *Mohamed Fugicha v Methodist church in Kenya (suing through its registered trustees) & 3 Others*, discussed at length in Chapter 6.[104] In this case, the Court of Appeal recognised the right of Muslim female students to wear the *hijab* (a white headscarf and a pair of white trousers underneath the uniform skirts), it being a practice that was of exceptional importance to them. This demonstrates that the fourth dimension of substantive equality (the transformative dimension in terms of accommodating difference) has been applied by the courts.[105]

The Court of Appeal decision in *Fugicha* overturned the High Court decision in *Republic v Head Teacher, Kenya High School* (the *Hijab case*), where Githua J, at first instance, approached the interpretation of equality in a more conservative way.[106] The case revolved around the issue of equality in relation

[101] *John Kabui Mwai & 3 Others v Kenya National Examination Council & 2 Others* [2011] eKLR (HC) (*Kabui Mwai*).

[102] ibid 10; text to nn 66–69.

[103] *Kabui Mwai* (n 101) 9. Art 27(6) is the main affirmative action provision in the Constitution.

[104] *Mohamed Fugicha v Methodist church in Kenya (suing through its registered trustees) & 3 Others* [2016] eKLR. See also Ch 6, text to nn 58–63.

[105] See also *J.K (Suing on Behalf of CK) v Board of Directors of R School & Another* [2014] eKLR (HC) where Ngugi J stated obiter that the wearing of dreadlocks for cultural or religious reasons required protection under the Constitution and should be accorded reasonable accommodation.

[106] *Republic v Head Teacher, Kenya High School & Another Ex-parte SMY* [2012] eKLR (HC).

to religious freedom. The applicant sought on her own behalf, and on behalf of other Muslim students at the Kenya High School, an order compelling the Board of Governors as well as the Head Teacher to allow them to wear the *hijab* at the school. Githua J held that the equality clause was not violated and that the school had applied the principle of equality by treating all students in the same way.[107] From this finding, it is clear that the judge only looked at the concept of equality in terms of formal equality, which insists on sameness in treatment. The Court did not consider the context in relation to the need for protection of Muslim minorities in Kenya through substantive equality's requirement with regard to the accommodation of difference, as was done by the Court of Appeal in the *Fugicha* case.

The three judgments above highlight the positive approaches taken by Kenyan courts in analysing some of the equality cases so far, and the need for consensus on the correct judicial interpretation of equality. Nevertheless, none of the cases so far has comprehensively tackled the need to develop a principled approach to the conceptualisation and interpretation of the equality clause and the different understandings of equality therein. The *Kabui Mwai* case comes close to providing a principled approach to interpreting equality provisions in the Constitution. However, it says little, if anything, on how the various conceptions of equality in the Constitution conflict and should be harmoniously interpreted. In addition, no equality test or analytical framework like that advocated in this chapter has been developed so far.

V. Conclusion

As this chapter has shown, equality is a fundamental principle of the Constitution, and Article 27 contains the general understandings of equality. The chapter provides an analytical framework, which requires an analysis of the impact of an alleged discriminatory act in determining what treatment as an equal requires for different people. This analytical framework is important as it sets out a harmonious and coherent approach to interpreting the different conceptions of equality in Kenya's 2010 Constitution, something that has not been addressed by Kenyan courts so far.

This chapter has also shown that the equality guarantee in the Constitution can be said to be transformative, first, because of provisions that broaden the net of inclusion, and second, because of the various provisions that seek to eradicate patterns of systemic disadvantage, the core one being affirmative action. These transformative equality provisions, as was noted, are mostly responding to pre-existing inequalities, and thus all the more reason why a reference to context is essential in a discrimination analysis. However, the chapter has argued that

[107] ibid.

Article 24(4) of the Constitution acts as a drawback to transformation and the harmonious interpretation of the various conceptions of equality by exempting Islamic law from the automatic application of equality provisions in the Bill of Rights. It has therefore been suggested that either this provision should be amended to bring it into harmony with the Constitution's strong emphasis on equality, or novel interpretations of the article should be applied, as will be further interrogated in Chapter 6.

4

Grounds for Non-discrimination

Chapter 3 argued for a coherent understanding of the various conceptions of equality as seeking to answer the 'meta question' of what treatment as an equal means for different people, considering their context and whether the likely impact of an alleged discriminatory act is one that furthers equality or not. It propounded that in some cases treatment as an equal would mean sameness in treatment, and in other cases it would require differential treatment to remedy historical and ongoing patterns of disadvantage.

This chapter furthers the discussion in Chapter 3 and, to some extent, seeks to test the veracity of the conclusion made therein on the overarching conception of equality in the Constitution. It scrutinises underlying rationales behind the currently enumerated grounds for non-discrimination in Article 27(4) of the Constitution to establish whether there is a unifying coherent conception of equality that can be drawn on in adding unlisted analogous (similar) grounds. In tackling this central inquiry, the chapter interrogates two key questions: Is there a coherent conception of equality underlying the list of grounds for non-discrimination in Article 27(4), which can be drawn on in adding new analogous grounds? What does the list of grounds reveal about the overarching conception of equality in the Constitution? An analysis of these two questions in discussions throughout the chapter will provide a richer understanding of the overarching conception of equality in the Constitution and its application.

Courts around the globe have struggled to articulate a unifying coherent principle that can be applied in adding new grounds but have not been able to do so with any degree of precision. This is because the task of coming up with a watertight one-size-fits-all principle that can provide answers to questions relating to new grounds of discrimination over time, to 'reflect a political and social reality to which the law [should], belatedly, [give] recognition', is a difficult one.[1] A door has, therefore, been left open for further development of a watertight unifying principle(s), especially with regard to the 2010 Kenyan Constitution. Jurisdictions such as Canada and South Africa have considered factors such as human dignity, immutability, fundamental choice, personal autonomy, access to political power,

[1] See S Fredman, *Discrimination Law* (2nd edn, Oxford, Oxford University Press, 2011) 110–11; D Pothier, 'Connecting Grounds of Discrimination to Real People's Real Experiences' (2001) 13 *Canadian Journal of Women and the Law* 37, 41.

and a consideration of the history of disadvantage occasioned upon a particular group in expanding on the list of grounds. This chapter considers such comparative jurisprudence and the lessons that can be learnt from them. It then examines the applicability of all the principles identified in other jurisdictions to Kenya. This is done through a contextual analysis of the actual text of Kenya's 2010 Constitution, the Constitution's drafting history and current Kenyan cases in scrutinising whether a coherent approach to expanding the list of grounds in Article 27(4) can be found.

I. Laying the Background

A. Are All Distinctions Discriminatory?

As Fredman rightly notes, individuals and States classify people into different groups for various reasons that are legitimate.[2] As such, not every distinction made by individuals or created by legislation gives rise to discrimination. For instance, we as individuals make distinctions as to whom we will be friends with and the State creates different tax classifications for legitimate reasons, with those with higher income paying more tax than those with low income.[3] This covers everything and not just grounds for non-discrimination, which means that the State and courts do not want to review and reclassify all types of classifications under the prohibition of discrimination.

In general, therefore, classifications are legitimate as long as there is a rational connection between a classification and reasons for it, a relatively low standard. The focus of non-discrimination is not just on irrational classifications but on those distinctions which, even if rational, may be considered inherently suspect. Most especially, the concern is where a government and individuals are using a classification as proxy for stereotypical application of a person or group's personal characteristic so as to deny them equal protection and benefit of a right or advantage given to others. Along these lines, it has been stated that distinctions to be considered suspect and flagged as discriminatory are those that have 'the effect of imposing a burden or disadvantage not imposed on others and [that withhold] benefits or advantages which are available to others' without a good justification.[4]

On classifications that are inherently suspect, history bears witness to the fact that categorisations based on characteristics such as race, sex and ethnicity are mostly based on stereotypes and have had a discriminatory impact on these groups. Such harmful distinctions create and reinforce patterns of disadvantage

[2] Fredman (n 1) 8–9.

[3] See ibid and J Gardner, 'On the Ground of Her Sex(uality)' (1998) 18 *OJLS* 167, 167.

[4] *Egan v Canada* [1995] 2 SCR 513 (*Egan*) [131]. See also *Andrews v Law* [1989] 1 SCR 143 (*Andrews*); *Vriend v Alberta* [1998] 1 SCR 493 (*Vriend*) [70] and [92].

faced by these groups and send harmful messages that these groups are unworthy of equal concern and respect.[5] This further shows that the prohibition of discrimination is not meant to cover every classification but only suspect classes, requiring a heightened level of justification, beyond mere rationality. Hence, the establishment of grounds for non-discrimination is meant to set out the characteristics that the court should regard as suspect and therefore requiring a particularly intense degree of scrutiny or a strict level of justification.

Some countries do not have a list of grounds for non-discrimination, such as the US, which only has an open-textured right to equality in the Fourteenth Amendment, which simply states that the State should not 'deny to any person within its jurisdiction the equal protection of the laws'. This leaves it to the courts to decide which classifications attract judicial scrutiny.[6] Jurisdictions like the UK and the European Union anti-discrimination regime provide for an exhaustive list of grounds, which cannot be extended by courts but only through legislative and constitutional amendment.[7] This can be restrictive and tempts litigators to press the boundaries of existing grounds. For instance, it has been argued that 'sex' incorporates sexual orientation and transsexuality.[8] There is certainly greater value in recognition of these characteristics as independent grounds for non-discrimination, which can offer adequate protection for the said groups. The strength of a more specific ground (*lex specialis*), as opposed to a broad and general one (*lex generalis*), is that it is more tailored to the experience of the group in issue.

A third approach, which includes Kenya, is jurisdictions that have an open-ended list of grounds. At the same time, since there is already a long list of included grounds, there is less need for a comprehensive background analysis. However, where a ground is not mentioned, the question arises as to how to determine whether it can be considered an unenumerated ground analogous to those listed (the analogous grounds analysis). This is the chapter's main focus of inquiry.

B. Intersectionality: Should Determining Discrimination be Based on Individual Experiences or be Tied to Group-based Experiences?

A discussion on grounds for non-discrimination necessitates an interrogation of whether determining discrimination should be based on individual experiences or be tied to group-based experiences. Discrimination harms are best explained

[5] C McConnachie, 'What Is Unfair Discrimination? A Study of the South African Constitutional Court's Unfair Discrimination Jurisprudence' (DPhil thesis, University of Oxford, 2014) 156–58 and 189–90.

[6] Fredman (n 1) 118.

[7] ibid 113.

[8] ibid.

by looking at the overall resultant disadvantage caused by an alleged discriminatory act upon a group that an individual is a member of. However, as this section intends to show, this is a complex claim to make and has various demerits.

The desirability of a group aspect in conceptualising discrimination based on protected characteristics like race, gender and ethnicity is said to be in acknowledgement of 'the crucial role of interpersonal and community interaction in the formation of identity'.[9] As Chapter 3 argued, context is an important element to be taken into consideration in a discrimination analysis because 'Inherent in that context are the socio-economic circumstances and position of the individual in relation to his or her group and to group-based systemic disadvantage'.[10] Thus, in most cases, it is difficult to talk about a person's disadvantage without reference to the group(s) that he or she is a part of.

However, one valid concern about associating an individual's experience with the group they belong to is the danger of wrongfully collapsing an individual's circumstances to a group average, ignoring the many individual and intersecting differences between members within the group.[11] As Fredman rightly posits, 'groups may create oppressive internal hierarchies, including subordination of women, or be highly intolerant of those who do not conform to community norms, including gays and lesbians'.[12] Consequently, by failing to recognise that some people have more than one status, individual experiences of systemic inequalities because of other statuses are lost to the group average.[13] Hence, this is one of the core reasons why an appreciation of intersectionality theory has been said to be important as it considers the various intersecting grounds of discrimination that affect an individual based on the multiple statuses they have intensifying their disadvantage.[14]

Having noted the perils that bedevil a group-based approach to a discrimination analysis, it is important to also note the fact that avoiding the contextual group dimension of inequality may make an individual's experience of disadvantage seem merely incidental. As much as individuals differ in terms of their needs, wants and experiences of disadvantage, there are some inequalities that can only be better understood by looking at a person in his or her context. This would mean categorising the individual in a social group. Individuals may have diverse

[9] S Fredman, 'Redistribution and Recognition: Reconciling Inequalities' (2007) 23 *South African Journal of Human Rights* 214, 217 and 226.

[10] Ch 3, text to nn 66–74; C Albertyn and B Goldblatt, 'Facing the Challenge of Transformation: Difficulties in the Development of an Indigenous Jurisprudence of Equality' 14 *South African Journal of Human Rights* 248, 253. See also *Andrews* (n 4) [34].

[11] I Young, 'Equality of Whom? Social Groups and Judgments of Injustice' (2001) 9 *Journal of Political Philosophy* 1, 5. See also D Rae, *Equalities* (Cambridge, MA, Harvard University Press, 1981) 29–38 and 76–81.

[12] Fredman, *Redistribution and Recognition* (n 9) 226.

[13] Young (n 11) 6.

[14] See K Crenshaw, 'Demarginalizing the Intersection of Race and Sex: A Black Feminist Critique of Antidiscrimination Doctrine, Feminist Theory and Antiracist Politics' (1989) *University of Chicago Legal Forum* 139.

experiences of discrimination but, as Young opines, 'Evaluating inequality in terms of social groups enables us to claim that some inequalities are unjust … because such group-based comparison helps reveal important aspects of institutional relation and processes'.[15] Furthering this point, Loenen argues that interpretation of discrimination as a whole should begin with 'its historical genesis as a principle directed at protecting groups which have suffered from *structural* disadvantage, from *patterns* of exclusion, and not just from some incidental negative impact'.[16]

Drawing these points together, it can be said that in explaining people's disadvantage, it is hard not to connect them with a group(s) to better understand how they have suffered from structural disadvantage. However, an individual should not be bound to one group but should be situated in his or her context in considering all aspects of their personhood, including their various statuses that reinforce their disadvantage. Summarising the discussion on importance of using groups in explaining status-based discrimination, Young states that 'if we simply identify some inequality of condition or situation between individuals at a particular time we have no account of the causes of this unequal condition'.[17] A much fuller story is told by looking at an individual's situation in relation to his or her social group(s) and in the context of power relations within that group(s). Past or ongoing discrimination experienced by the group(s) as a whole can then also be said to be true of an individual member considering his or her other experiences that may reinforce or negate disadvantage.

Linking this to the definition of structural patterns of systemic disadvantage discussed in Chapter 3, using Young's exposition of Frye's analogy of a bird's cage, it is impractical to look at one wire at a time in explaining why a bird cannot fly out of its cage.[18] This can only be understood by considering all the wires which together form a pattern to enclose the bird, though the bird does not necessarily represent one category or group. Therefore, it is only by explaining the inequality experienced by an individual through the social experience of his or her group(s) that we can understand how they have been discriminated against and how this discrimination has affected them.[19] Groups are therefore essential in providing a fuller picture of how social relationships contribute to and reinforce the material disadvantage of some and not others.

At the same time, groups should not be regarded as rigid and essentialising. The cage metaphor also helps us see this. Each bird can have a unique cage with different sets of wires that enclose it. If each wire is a different group perimeter, then the result is to recognise the interaction between many groups in creating the subordinate relationship. Consequently, there should be awareness by

[15] Young (n 11) 2.

[16] T Loenen, 'The Equality Clause in the South African Constitution: Some Remarks from a Comparative Perspective' (1997) 13 *South African Journal of Human Rights* 401, 407.

[17] Young (n 11) 8.

[18] Ch 3, text to nn 78–84; Young (n 11) 5 and 10; M Frye, *Politics of Reality: Essays in Feminist Theory* (Trumansburg, NY, The Crossing Press, 1983).

[19] Young (n 11) 9–15.

courts, policymakers and other stakeholders that reference to one general group characteristic can collapse an individual group member's diverse experiences of discrimination to the group average of just one. So, for example, even though gender discrimination affects both an able-bodied woman from a dominant ethnic group and a poor disabled woman from a minority ethnic group, the way gender discrimination interacts with other group identities (poverty, disability and minority ethnicity) creates a unique cage of experience of disadvantage, and vertical, horizontal and diagonal power relations, for the latter group. Therefore, this book uses the term 'groups' with the underlying awareness of its capacity to collapse unique individual experiences of discrimination and thus what is really meant when referring to the term is *individual group-based discrimination on the basis of one or multiple grounds.*

II. The 2010 Constitution's Inclusion of a Non-exhaustive List of Grounds and the Court's Role in Expanding the List of Grounds

Article 27(4) of the Kenyan Constitution provides:

> The State shall not discriminate directly or indirectly against any person on any ground, *including* race, sex, pregnancy, marital status, health status, ethnic or social origin, colour, age, disability, religion, conscience, belief, culture, dress, language or birth (emphasis added).

This list of grounds is non-exhaustive. Such an interpretation of Article 27(4) was affirmed in the case of *Eric Gitari v Non-Governmental Organisations Co-ordination Board & 4 Others.*[20] In the case, it was held that grounds listed in Article 27(4) are not exhaustive since the term 'including' is defined in Article 259(4)(b) of the Constitution as meaning 'includes, but not limited to'. The Court interpreted this to mean that the list is not closed and that new grounds may be included as the context and circumstances demonstrate are necessary at a given point in time.[21]

The open-ended nature of the list of grounds leaves it to judges to decide on the inclusion of unenumerated grounds, bringing into play Article 259(1)(c) of the Constitution, which requires the Constitution to be interpreted in a manner that 'permits the development of the law'.[22] As Chapter 2 discussed, this means that judges will at various times be required to interpret and add to the list of grounds in Article 27(4) in a way that considers the changes in society and newly identified forms of discrimination. In doing this, judges are not to be guided by their own

[20] *Eric Gitari v Non-Governmental Organisations Co-ordination Board & 4 Others* [2015] eKLR (*Eric Gitari*).

[21] ibid [120] and [132].

[22] See Ch 2, text to nn 55–58.

personal opinions nor majoritarian opinion, but what the Constitution requires. The values and principles central to the Constitution act as the core guides to developing the law to recognise new grounds, as well as guides to limiting judicial discretion. These constitutional values and principles comprise human dignity, equity, social justice, inclusiveness, equality, human rights, non-discrimination and protection of the marginalised, among others.[23] The Kenyan High Court has particularly noted that 'the principle of equality, dignity and non-discrimination run throughout the Constitution like a golden thread'.[24] It has also been said that judicial discretion in the act of adding new and analogous grounds 'is shaped by the existence of enumerated grounds'.[25]

Such limits on judges' own personal value judgements and majoritarian opinion are especially important when it comes to issues such as sexual orientation, which were contentious during the Constitution's drafting process and which remain so. However, this is a challenging process since constitutional values and principles are drafted in an open-ended way. It is never wholly possible (or even desirable) to fully exclude judicial value judgements. This is particularly the case with open-textured conceptions such as dignity, equity and social justice. Nevertheless, as the cases show, it is possible to achieve judicial accountability for judges' value judgements by requiring them to scrupulously defend their position through well-reasoned judgments.

Current judicial decisions indeed bear this out. For instance, the three-judge bench in the *Eric Gitari* case stressed the difference between constitutional morality – values and principles entrenched in the Constitution which courts should safeguard and uphold – and popular morality. Regarding the latter, it stated that 'no matter how strongly held moral and religious beliefs may be, they cannot be a basis for limiting rights: they are not laws as contemplated by the Constitution'.[26] This is further backed by the holding in *John Harun Mwau & 3 Others v Attorney General & 2 Others* that judges are required to 'interpret the Constitution and uphold its provisions without fear or favour and without regard to popular opinion … [Their] undertaking is not to write or rewrite the Constitution to suit popular opinion', but 'to interpret the Constitution in a manner that remains faithful to its letter and spirit and give effect to its objectives'.[27] In both cases, the judges proceeded to separate views and opinions that they and a majority of Kenyans may consider undesirable or decadent, based on their moral or religious inclinations from actual constitutional tenets, even if the latter could be regarded as 'a document founded on deep political morality'.[28]

[23] The Constitution of Kenya, 2010, Arts 10(2) and 20(4)(a) and (b).

[24] *Eric Gitari* (n 20) [133].

[25] S Fredman, *A Comparative Study of the Anti-Discrimination and Equality Laws of the USA, Canada, India and South Africa* (European Communities, 2012) 32.

[26] *Eric Gitari* (n 20) [121]–[122].

[27] *John Harun Mwau & 3 Others v Attorney General & 2 Others* [2012] eKLR [109] and [185].

[28] *Eric Gitari* (n 20) [90] citing with approval this observation by the South African Constitutional Court in *National Coalition for Gay and Lesbian Equality & Another v Minister of Justice & Others* 1999 (1) SA 6 (CC) 6 (*National Coalition*) [136].

The facts and decision of the High Court in the *Eric Gitari* case show how these distinctions were made. The case concerned the registration of a non-governmental organisation (NGO) with the goal of addressing the discrimination, stigmatisation, violence and other human rights abuses suffered by LGBTI persons in Kenya and to advance their human rights.[29] The petitioner, Mr Gitari, had made at least three applications to the NGO's Co-ordination Board proposing the names Gay and Lesbian Human Rights Council, Gay and Lesbian Human Rights Observancy, and Gay and Lesbian Human Rights Organization, among others, all of which were rejected. In its defence, the Board stated that the rejections, although infringing on the petitioner's freedom of association, were justified because the Penal Code criminalises homosexual intercourse.[30] It based its decision to reject the registration request on regulation 8(3)(b) of the NGO Regulations of 1992, which states that the Director of a Board can reject registration applications if 'such name is in the opinion of the director repugnant to or inconsistent with any law or is otherwise undesirable'. This was despite the petitioner's efforts to distinguish the fact that his organisation sought to further LGBTI equality rights and not to further criminalised conduct.[31] The Board also argued that the proposed NGO would go against Kenyan cultural and religious values. On this, it specifically contended that 'homosexuality is largely considered to be a taboo and repugnant to the religious teachings, cultural values and morality of the Kenyan people'.[32]

Mr Gitari therefore sought a determination by the Court of whether he and gay and lesbian persons in Kenya are protected in Article 36 of the Constitution, which provides for freedom of association. He also contended that the refusal to register the proposed NGO violated human dignity and was tantamount to inhuman and degrading treatment, by attempting to ostracise the group and view gays and lesbians as criminals without rights to associate.[33] Further, he stated that the act was a violation of the right to equality before the law and it was a denial of freedom of expression and access to information, based on sexual orientation.[34]

In refusing to consider public opinion or popular morality, the three-judge bench quoted with approval the South African Constitutional Court's holding in *National Coalition for Gay and Lesbian Equality & Another v Minister of Justice & Others* that 'the dictates of the morality which [the court] enforces, and the limits to which it may go, are to be found in the text and spirit of the Constitution itself'.[35] The judges continued to state further that

> while the Constitution recognises the right of persons who for reasons of religious or other belief, disagree with or condemn homosexual conduct to hold and articulate such

[29] *Eric Gitari* (n 20) [1] and [19].
[30] ibid [4], [10] and [11].
[31] ibid [14].
[32] ibid [96].
[33] ibid [3], [26] and [28].
[34] ibid [29].
[35] See ibid [90]; *National Coalition* (n 28) [136].

> beliefs, it does not permit the state to '... **turn these beliefs – even in moderate or gentle versions – into dogma imposed on the whole society**'.[36]

The Court thus made it clear that its duty is not to substitute parties' views and beliefs with constitutional provisions, but to examine the issues and facts presented before it and determine the constitutionality or otherwise of the Board's refusal to register the proposed NGO.[37] The Court then proceeded to clarify that the petitioner did not seek to promote homosexual intercourse, same-sex marriage or paedophilia, as the Board and the third interested party argued and seemed to be concerned about, but the rights of LGBTI persons to associate in an NGO recognised by law in relation to the protection of their human rights.[38] Thus, it was held that no matter how reprehensible individuals may find other people's sexual orientation or sexuality, they must accord LGBTI persons their human rights as guaranteed to all persons by the Constitution in order to protect their dignity as human beings (Article 19(2)).[39]

The principles articulated in this case mean that, in determining whether to include an unenumerated ground, courts should uphold the letter and spirit of the Constitution as opposed to their own personal values or public opinion. Such an approach helps protect the rights of minority and vulnerable groups. Indeed, it is argued that an important way that a political community shows equal concern for all people living within its borders is by 'embedding certain individual rights in a constitution that is to be interpreted by judges rather than by elected representatives'.[40] As Ely argues, in instances where public opinion and representative government cannot be trusted, it is important for judges to use their discretion to protect the legitimate rights of minorities from the tyranny of the majority.[41] He notes further that inclusion of protected rights such as equality in a Constitution 'put side constraints on majority rule', which are imposed by the people themselves. Hence, 'judges do not check the people, the Constitution does, which means the people are ultimately checking themselves'.[42] This shows the strength of reliance on 'constitutional morality' or the letter and spirit of the Constitution rather than judges' own personal values and public opinion. The intervention of the courts in upholding the supremacy of 'constitutional morality' is also in line with the provision in Article 27(1) of the Constitution, requiring equal protection and benefit of the law. Regrettably, however, in the recent case of *EG & 7 Others v Attorney General; DKM & 9 Others (Interested Parties); Katiba Institute & Another*

[36] *Eric Gitari* (n 20) [91]. Highlighted in bold in the judgment.
[37] ibid [98].
[38] ibid [99] and [100].
[39] ibid [104].
[40] L McClain, 'Red Versus Blue (And Purple) States and the Same-Sex Marriage Debate: From Values Polarization to Common Ground?' (2008) 77 *UMKC Law Review* 415, 430.
[41] JH Ely, *Democracy and Distrust: A Theory of Judicial Review* (Cambridge, MA, Harvard University Press, 1980) 183.
[42] ibid 8.

(Amicus Curiae) – challenging the constitutionality of Kenya's sodomy laws – the High Court's decision was to the effect that the views of Kenyans on the issue cannot be ignored.[43] It is hoped that this undesirable position, which clearly fails to give primacy to 'constitutional morality', will be reversed on appeal.

The legitimacy of including sexual orientation as an unenumerated ground could nevertheless be challenged on grounds that it was deliberately omitted from the enumerated list as happened in the *EG* case.[44] This raises the question of the role of original intent in guiding judicial decisions as to whether to include unenumerated grounds. There are two responses to this argument. The first is to demonstrate that there was no clear intent at the drafting stage either to include or exclude sexual orientation as a ground. The second is to dispute the extent to which original intent should be an authoritative source of interpretation.

In relation to the first point, it is reported that the exclusion of sexual orientation as a ground was deliberate because the Committee of Experts on Constitutional Review (CoE) decided not to explicitly include it in the draft Constitution, 'citing fears that the draft would be rejected by a majority of Kenyans if it did so'.[45] However, there was also strong support at the time for its inclusion, with a push for greater liberties by the Gay and Lesbian Coalition of Kenya (GALCK) among other organisations, hoping to see the repeal of sodomy laws through the specific inclusion of sexual orientation as one of the grounds for non-discrimination.[46] As a result, the CoE seemed to have been deadlocked on the matter, with arguments for and against it, and chose to be silent on its inclusion, which, as argued in Chapter 2, means that they left it subject to judicial interpretation.[47] Second, it will be recalled that the discussion in Chapter 2 concluded that Kenyan courts are not tied to original intentions, which only act as interpretive guides since the Constitution embraces a living tree approach, allowing for the advancement of fundamental freedoms in the Bill of Rights and development of the law.[48]

Further to this, it could be argued that the deliberate omission means that courts should not add sexual orientation as a new ground or as an aspect of sex by its opponents. This was the argument before the Supreme Court of Canada in *Vriend v Alberta*.[49] In *Vriend*, attempts in 1984 and 1992 to include sexual orientation in the list of prohibited grounds of discrimination in Alberta's Individual's Rights Protection Act had been unsuccessful, with the proposed Bills not going through to second reading. The reasons for this were said to include the argument that 'sexual orientation is a "marginal" ground; that human rights legislation

[43] *EG & 7 Others v Attorney General; DKM & 9 Others (Interested Parties); Katiba Institute & Another (Amicus Curiae)* (Consolidated) [2019] eKLR (Aburili, Mwita and Mativo JJ) (*EG* case) [402]–[403].

[44] ibid [390]–[391].

[45] Equal Rights Trust and Kenya Human Rights Commission, *In the Spirit of Harambee: Addressing Discrimination and Inequality in Kenya* (London, Prontaprint Bayswater, 2012) 119.

[46] P Orengo, 'Kenya's Gay Movement Seeks Stamp of Approval', *The Standard* (Nairobi, 9 July 2013).

[47] Ch 2, text to nn 102–09.

[48] ibid.

[49] *Vriend* (n 4).

is powerless to change public attitudes; and that there [had] been few cases of sexual orientation discrimination in employment brought to the attention of the Minister'.[50]

In rejecting the argument that deliberate exclusion of sexual orientation meant that it could not be regarded as an unenumerated ground under the Canadian Charter of Rights and Freedoms (Canadian Charter), the Court's majority opinion came to two important conclusions. First, it held that 'the purpose of the Alberta Government in excluding sexual orientation was itself discriminatory'. This was because

> the purpose behind the deliberate choice of the Government not to include sexual orientation as a protected ground is to deny that homosexuals are or were disadvantaged by discrimination, or alternatively to deny that homosexuals are worthy of protection against that discrimination.[51]

On this point, the majority held that the Court can invalidate omissions that have an unconstitutional purpose or effect. The same can be said to debunk an argument that the deliberate exclusion of sexual orientation from explicitly listed grounds in the Kenyan Constitution means it should not be recognised at all by courts. Such a claim goes against the equality and non-discrimination guarantees in the Constitution.

Second, the majority opinion in *Vriend* observed that the legislation at issue was meant to 'provide comprehensive protection from discrimination for all individuals in Alberta'. Hence, selective exclusion of a group from that protection had a discriminatory effect.[52] This was because 'Persons who are discriminated against on the ground of sexual orientation, unlike others protected by the Act, are left without effective legal recourse for the discrimination they have suffered'.[53] The majority then proceeded to state that the discriminatory effects of the legislation were sufficient for it to establish that there was discrimination.[54] This would likewise mean that Kenyan courts denying protection against discrimination based on sexual orientation, because of the CoE's decision not to explicitly add it in Article 27(4), will be the antithesis of the constitutional goal set in Article 27(4)'s guarantee that there shall be no direct and indirect discrimination against 'any person'. The comprehensive protection of the Constitution applies to everyone and, as held in *Vriend*, there should not be selective exclusion.

Nonetheless, if the reaction to the *Obergefell v Hodges* US Supreme Court decision holding governmental bans on same-sex marriage unconstitutional is anything to go by, public opinion on recognition of controversial grounds may be persistent and refuse to die down quietly.[55] For instance, Boso observes that, after

[50] ibid [4].
[51] ibid [92].
[52] ibid [96].
[53] ibid [97].
[54] ibid [93].
[55] *Obergefell v Hodges* 576 US (2015).

Obergefell, legislation was enacted in North Carolina prohibiting 'local governments from including sexual orientation in laws barring discrimination'.[56] The reasons given were the need to afford 'equal dignity and liberty to those who are religious and do not wish to be complicit in sin'.[57] Boso therefore observes that 'the LGBTQ community has been largely successful in petitioning courts for redress, while its direct pleas to people and reliance on majoritarian politics have faltered'.[58] Such legislative pushbacks are, nevertheless, subject to judicial review as to their constitutionality, creating a continuous cycle of protection of the fundamental right to non-discrimination by courts.[59]

III. What Considerations are or Should be Taken into Account in Expanding the List of Grounds for Non-discrimination in Article 27(4)? Lessons from Canada and South Africa

The previous section discussed the more general principles and matters relating to unenumerated grounds. This section asks whether there are unifying themes in the existing grounds which can be drawn on to determine whether to include an unenumerated ground.

Substantial strides have been made by the Supreme Court of Canada and the South African Constitutional Court to develop unifying principles for adding unenumerated grounds for non-discrimination. Like the Kenyan Constitution, the Canadian Charter and the South African Constitution both have non-exhaustive lists of grounds for non-discrimination. This has left the task of expanding the list to judges, as in Kenya. An analysis of the jurisprudence from these two countries and philosophical literature on grounds will therefore be useful in pinpointing the already identified potential unifying principles, so there is no need to reinvent the wheel and rehash what has already been said in seeking to uncover such principles. The universal justification for referring to comparative jurisprudence set out in Chapter 1 also applies here. Fittingly, it can be said that Kenya 'shares patterns of inequality found all over the globe', meaning that developing criteria for adding unenumerated grounds would have to consider both Kenya's specific context and challenges which the country shares with the rest of humanity.[60]

[56] L Boso, 'Equality and Non-discrimination' in R Martin, S Areff and V Miyandazi (eds), *Global Perspectives on Human Rights: Oxford Human Rights Hub Blog* (3rd edn, Oxford, Oxford Human Rights Hub, 2016) ch 7.

[57] ibid.

[58] ibid.

[59] See Ch 2, text to nn 61–63.

[60] See Ch 1, text to n 7; *Prinsloo v Van der Linde* 1997 (6) BCLR 759 (CC) [20] (Ackermann, O'Regan and Sachs JJ).

However, it is important to first recognise the textual differences in the constitutional texts of Canada and South Africa from that of Kenya, before analysing the jurisprudence in these two countries on expansion of grounds and their application to Kenya. In the Canadian Charter, grounds for non-discrimination are encapsulated in section 15(1), providing that everyone 'has the right to the equal protection and equal benefit of the law without discrimination and, *in particular*, without discrimination based on race, national or ethnic origin, colour, religion, sex, age or mental or physical disability' (emphasis added). The use of the term 'in particular' in reference to grounds for non-discrimination in the Canadian Charter is the one that has been interpreted as opening the door for the addition of unenumerated grounds analogous to those listed in section 15(1).[61] The phrasing in the Kenyan Constitution is different from that of the Canadian Charter, with Article 27(4) using the term 'including'. Nevertheless, this term, as stated earlier, has been interpreted by Kenyan courts as creating an open-ended list of grounds – a similar approach to that taken in Canada.

In relation to the 1996 South African Constitution, section 9(3) on grounds requires the State not to 'unfairly discriminate directly or indirectly against anyone on *one or more grounds, including* race, gender, sex, pregnancy, marital status, ethnic or social origin, colour, sexual orientation, age, disability, religion, conscience, belief, culture, language and birth' (emphasis added). The use of the term 'including' and its interpretation as creating an open-ended list of grounds is similar to the position that has been taken by Kenyan courts.

Also, the South African Constitution explicitly provides different presumptions to be applied in relation to enumerated and unenumerated grounds. Accordingly, enumerated grounds raise a presumption of unfairness, with section 9(5) of the South African Constitution stating that 'Discrimination on one or more of the grounds listed … is unfair unless it is established that the discrimination is fair'. This contrasts with unenumerated grounds, whose unfairness should be proven by the claimant.[62] Like the South African approach, a different presumption for enumerated and unenumerated grounds can be implied in Article 27(4) of the Kenyan Constitution. Unlike enumerated grounds, which are automatically indicia of discrimination unless justified, discrimination based on unenumerated grounds should be proved. There is therefore a shift in presumption of discrimination.

Principles offered so far to be considered in adding unenumerated grounds include: (a) immutability, fundamental choice and autonomy; (b) access to the political process; (c) history of disadvantage; and (d) human dignity.[63] These four proposed unifying principles, to be discussed in the ensuing sub-sections, have

[61] *Andrews* (n 4) 145.

[62] See *Harksen v Lane NO* 1998 (1) SA 300 (CC) (*Harksen*) [46]–[47]; Fredman, *Discrimination Law* (n 1) 129.

[63] See Fredman, *Discrimination Law* (n 1) 129–39; R Wintemute, *Sexual Orientation and Human Rights: The United States Constitution, the European Convention, and the Canadian Charter* (Oxford, Clarendon, 1995); Gardner (n 3).

received significant attention in academic literature as to their meaning and value, particularly as they relate to the Canadian and South African jurisprudence. This analysis does not attempt to be an exhaustive account of all existing literature and cases touching on these principles. The main aim here is to provide a brief but succinct analysis of current Canadian and South African jurisprudence on grounds and core issues that Kenyan courts should take note of. The main findings from this discussion will then be applied to uncover whether a unifying principle exists in the Kenyan Constitution that can help identify new analogous grounds and what the underlying rationales behind grounds can tell us about the overarching conception of equality in the Constitution.

A. Immutability, Fundamental Choice and Autonomy

Arguments have been advanced that the listed grounds for non-discrimination consist of personal characteristics that are immutable, meaning that they cannot be changed by the holder of the said characteristics.[64] This leads us to the question of why grounds should be based on some sense of immutability. Distinctions on immutable statuses are said to be suspect because it seems unfair to subject someone to a detriment because of a characteristic they are unable to change. Behind this is a presumption that if you can change something and do not, you have not tried hard enough and do not merit better treatment. Distinctions based on immutable statuses therefore require strong justification when used to show that they are meant to fulfil a legitimate positive purpose.[65]

However, what if a characteristic can be changed? For instance, in the case of citizenship, where one can acquire a new one after a naturalisation process. In such instances, it is not sufficient to say that only characteristics which cannot be changed should be protected by discrimination law. Identities or characteristics which are chosen may also be protected. Fredman gives examples of long-accepted grounds for non-discrimination that can arguably be said to be a matter of personal choice. These include religion and pregnancy, which are protected from discrimination, even though they are in some circumstances a matter of personal choice, which fact is not usually relevant to their inclusion as protected characteristics.[66] For instance, in *Mandla & Another v Dowell Lee & Another*, a case concerning a school's 'no turban' rule, the UK House of Lords held, in relation to the words 'can comply', that the 'no turban' rule was not a requirement with which the applicant boy could, consistently with the customs of being a Sikh, comply and, therefore, the application of that rule to him by the headmaster was unlawful discrimination.[67]

[64] See Wintemute (n 63); Fredman, *Discrimination Law* (n 1) 131; C Albertyn and J Kentridge, 'Introducing the Right to Equality in the Interim Constitution' (1994) 10 *South African Journal of Human Rights* 149, 168.

[65] Wintemute (n 63) 16.

[66] Fredman, *Discrimination Law* (n 1) 131–32.

[67] *Mandla & Another v Dowell Lee & Another* [1983] 1 All ER 1062.

This leads to the question of why it is that we are so concerned about choice and the freedom of people to choose among valuable options. Of course, not all fundamental choices are protected from intervention by the State, and sometimes it is justifiable for the State to make a choice more costly in order to deter people from following a particular route, such as drug abuse. However, according to Wintemute, 'governments should not interfere with "fundamental choices (or rights or freedoms)", such as religion, political opinion, and choices protected by the "right to privacy" or the "right to respect for private life", without a special justification'.[68] Fundamental choice thus implies the importance of the choice to the person making it.[69] The principle requires respect for the personal identity chosen by an individual and it does not matter whether such identity is changeable or can be suppressed. Even if a characteristic can be changed, it is still unacceptable to expect people to change in order to get a benefit if it comes at great cost to their personal characteristic. Albertyn and Kentridge aptly point out that 'certain choices are so important to self-definition that these too should be protected'.[70]

Immutability and fundamental choice are said to have their foundations in the liberal idea of autonomy. As Raz argues, this notion views an autonomous person as being part author of their life, having a degree of control over their destiny, and having the freedom to choose between valuable options on how to fashion their life, including relationship choices.[71] Preconditions of the exercise of personal autonomy include possession of appropriate mental abilities, having an adequate range of valuable options to choose from, and independence from coercion and manipulation.[72] As long as these preconditions are satisfied, limiting a person's capacity to live out what their immutable personal characteristic dictates, which can be considered alongside their fundamental choice, unacceptably denies a person their right to live an autonomous life that they see as enabling them to flourish.[73] Gardner adds that, whether an immutable status remains so or has become changeable (eg by undergoing a sex change), this fact does little to affect the autonomy of a person possessing such a status and 'is no consolation to those who are discriminated against'.[74]

This brings us to how, in recent times, the line between immutability and fundamental choice has grown thinner by the day. For instance, some people today use skin-lightening creams to change their colour. Hence, it is not sufficient to say that since a status like pregnancy is in some circumstances a choice, depending on how one looks at it, we can discriminate against a person because of the choices they have made (eg dismissing a pregnant worker). It is still invidious to raise choice as a justification for discrimination. As Gardner points out, discriminating

[68] Wintemute (n 63) 16.
[69] ibid 17.
[70] Albertyn and Kentridge (n 64) 168.
[71] J Raz, *Morality of Freedom* (Oxford, Clarendon Press, 1986) 369–71.
[72] ibid 370, 372 and 373.
[73] Gardner (n 3) 168.
[74] ibid 172.

against people because of their fundamental choices 'tends to skew those choices by making one or more of the valuable options from which they must choose more painful or burdensome than others'.[75] It comes at an unacceptable cost to a person's personal identity and that is why such choices should be safeguarded.

Immutability and fundamental choice as markers of discrimination in expanding grounds have been adopted in Canada. Application of the notion of immutability can be traced back to the 1999 Canadian case of *Corbiere v Canada.*[76] The case concerned a challenge filed on behalf of all non-resident members of the Batchewana Band, which is part of Canada's Aboriginal Peoples. The petitioners claimed that section 77(1) of the Indian Act, which limited the right to vote in band elections to members who were 'ordinarily resident' on the reserve, violated section 15(1) (on equal protection and benefit of the law) of the Canadian Charter. It was estimated that only a third of the registered band members lived on the reserve. The Court established that Aboriginality-residence is a ground analogous to those stipulated in section 15 of the Canadian Charter. This was because the distinction was based on a personal characteristic essential to band members' personal identity. More so, it was stated that the distinction did not consider the fact that off-reserve band members also have important interests (eg by being co-owners of the band's assets) in their band's governance.[77] It was also pointed out in the case that living off reserve was the only choice for most of the off-reserve members, it being forced upon them or being a choice reluctantly made or at high personal cost 'because of the lack of opportunities and housing on many reserves'.[78]

Referring to immutability, the majority opinion observed:

> To identify a ground of distinction as analogous, one must look for grounds of distinction that are like the grounds enumerated in s. 15. *These grounds have in common the fact that they often serve as the basis for stereotypical decisions made not on the basis of merit but on the basis of a personal characteristic that is immutable or changeable only at unacceptable cost to personal identity.* This suggests that the thrust of identification of analogous grounds at the second step of the analysis is to reveal grounds based on *characteristics that we cannot change or that the government has no legitimate interest in expecting us to change to receive equal treatment under the law* (emphasis added).[79]

Two main tests for immutability are said to have been set in *Corbiere*. These show a move from just immutability to immutability plus unacceptable cost, which means that in certain contexts, identities chosen because they are regarded as fundamental should also be protected. The first is the narrow conception of immutability. This is the understanding that 'immutability includes characteristics that are actually immutable (that is, unchangeable)'.[80] However, as stated earlier, as much as

[75] ibid 171.
[76] *Corbiere v Canada* [1999] 2 SCR 203 (*Corbiere*).
[77] ibid 221.
[78] ibid 209.
[79] ibid 219.
[80] J Sealy-Harrington, 'Assessing Analogous Grounds: The Doctrinal and Normative Superiority of a Multi-Variable Approach' (2013) 10 *Journal of Law & Equality* 37, 37–38.

grounds like race and ethnic origin may fit well under this conception of immutability, grounds such as religion, citizenship, belief and culture do not.[81]

This has led to the application of the second test, constructive immutability. The second test is based on the Canadian Supreme Court's reference to 'grounds based on characteristics … that the government has no legitimate interest in expecting us to change to receive equal treatment under the law'.[82] The Court specifically mentioned religion, citizenship and Aboriginal band membership as constructively immutable, being only changeable at great cost.[83]

All in all, constructive immutability presupposes that a person should not be penalised for being who they are and choosing to be who they are – for example choosing to go to church on a Saturday, working part time to raise children, not having children or having children, which means that pregnancy as a choice should not lead to penalisation. Constructive immutability's strong reference to 'choice' means that it is closely akin to, if not the same as, the notion of fundamental choice. The Court's consideration of both immutability and fundamental choice in tandem supports the conclusion made earlier, that immutability is inadequate as the sole principle in explaining the rationale behind the inclusion of all the traditionally enumerated grounds. The main argument raised against its adequacy is that it is too limited as there are other grounds that are not immutable, but people have a right to exercise their power of choice and should not be penalised for such choices.

However, as discussed in the ensuing sections, these two notions are not and should not be the sole markers of discrimination, with the judges in the cases looked at in this section having considered other principles such as violation of human dignity.

B. Access to the Political Process – Discrete, Insular, Diffuse and Anonymous

According to this principle, grounds for non-discrimination should be employed to remedy the flaws of representative and majoritarian democracy. Ely, writing on the issue in the context of the role of judicial review in protecting minorities from unfair political processes (which is effectively an equality point), presents the flaws of representative democracy as being twofold: first, where 'the ins are choking off the channels of political change to ensure that they will stay in and the outs will stay out'; and second, situations whereby, 'though no one is actually denied a voice or a vote, representatives beholden to an effective majority are systematically disadvantaging some minority out of simple hostility or [prejudice]'.[84]

[81] Albertyn and Kentridge (n 64) 168.
[82] Sealy-Harrington (n 80) 37–38; *Corbiere* (n 76) 219.
[83] *Corbiere* (n 76) 220.
[84] Ely (n 41) 103.

Ely is thus concerned about minorities who will never have access to the political process or get traction because they face so much prejudice. Along these lines, the term 'discrete and insular minorities' has been used to refer to minority groups that are affected by the flaws of majoritarian democracy, being groups that lack political power, which largely leads to their interests being overlooked and their rights violated. The expression originates from a footnote in the 1938 US case of *United States v Carolene Products Co.*[85] In the case, Stone J alluded to the fact that where there is 'prejudice against discrete and insular minorities …, which tends seriously to curtail the operation of those political processes ordinarily to be relied upon to protect minorities'; this fact 'may call for a correspondingly more searching judicial inquiry'.[86] He therefore called for special protection of discrete and insular minorities from the political process, which has the capacity to be oppressive and prey on the powerless.

'Discrete' is said to refer to a situation whereby members of a group 'are marked out in ways that make it relatively easy for others to identify them' and is interpreted as referring to a group on the disfavoured side of politics.[87] On the other hand, 'insular' has been said to refer to a minority group whose members tend 'to interact with great frequency in a variety of social contexts' but is nevertheless a group that is not able to gather enough allies to defeat an unfavourable law.[88] Taken as a whole, the expression 'discrete and insular minorities' is said 'to identify those groups in society to whose needs and wishes elected officials have no apparent interest in attending'.[89] It therefore speaks to the need to challenge unfair power relations.

However, it has been argued, and rightly so, that the initial understanding of 'discrete and insular' as set out in the *Carolene* case needs a restatement. Ackerman, being the main proponent of this argument, sheds light on the fact that, as much as the description works well for racial or religious minorities, it locks out other groups that are also affected by the unfairness of representative democracy.[90] These include a politically ineffective majority such as women, who have been prevented from influencing legislative decision making because of organisational difficulties and systematic societal disadvantages.[91] Women are discrete, in the sense that they cannot hide that they are female. However, they are not insular but diffuse and are often numerical majorities in many polities. Despite not matching the 'insularity' or minority criteria, women still face systemic disadvantages and prejudice that

[85] *United States v Carolene Products Co.*, 304 US 144 (1938) (*Carolene Products*); Ely (n 41) 135–79.

[86] *Carolene Products* (n 85) fn 4.

[87] B Ackerman, 'Beyond Carolene Products' (1985) 98(4) *Harvard Law Review* 713, 729; Ely (n 41) 151.

[88] Ackerman (n 87) 726; Ely (n 41).

[89] Ely (n 41) 151.

[90] Ackerman (n 87) 717. See also D Farber and P Frickey, 'Is Carolene Products Dead – Reflections on Affirmative Action and the Dynamics of Civil Rights Legislation' (1991) 79 *California Law Review* 685.

[91] Ackerman (n 87) 718–19 and 724.

has led to their not having an effective political voice and hence also falling prey to the flaws of representative democracy.

Another example of a group that does not perfectly fit the *Carolene* 'discrete and insular minorities' criterion, but which deserves special protection because of its group members' lack of access to the political process, is homosexual persons. Gay and lesbian persons can conceal their sexuality from easy identification and hence Ackerman argues that, in contrast to 'discrete' minorities, they can be said to be 'anonymous' minorities.[92] Thus, this section supports a revision of the 'discrete and insular minorities' notion to also include 'diffuse' and 'anonymous' groups that also face prejudice and discrimination in accessing the political process. This larger conception of persons excluded from the political process enables us to add more unenumerated groups that 'suffer from systemic disadvantages in pursuing their interests' due to the unfairness of the political process in the circle of protection under grounds.[93] Aside from adding homosexual persons who are currently excluded from the list of grounds, it will also enable us to add poverty (the poor being diffuse and anonymous) as a ground and to explain the current protection of persons with disabilities (diffuse and discrete).

The discussion so far shows that access to the political process has a great capacity to be a tool for transformative change, and the lack of it is a key cause of disadvantage. Powerlessness renders one vulnerable to the whims of powerful 'gate-keepers' controlling the political process, and who determine which freedoms are deserving of legal protection and which ones are not. This echoes the assertion by Ely that 'No matter how open the process, those with most of the votes [or effective minorities] are in a position to vote themselves advantages at the expense of the others, or otherwise to refuse to take their interests into account'.[94] It is this fact that renders powerless groups susceptible to discrimination and hence why the task of safeguarding the rights of groups that cannot protect themselves politically is said to properly lie with the courts.[95] The courts, through the application of anti-discrimination law, hence become, and rightly so, the overall 'gate-keepers' that keep in check power wielders who can be oppressive in delineating or limiting rights of minorities and ineffective majorities.

That a decision or distinction is discriminatory because it adversely impacts on a discrete and insular minority group was considered by the Canadian Supreme Court in *Andrews v Law*.[96] The case concerned the rights of non-citizens, with citizenship not being a listed ground of non-discrimination under section 15(1) of the Canadian Charter. In the case, the respondent, Andrews, was a British citizen permanently resident in Canada. He met all the requirements for admission to the British Columbia bar apart from that of being a Canadian citizen. The case

[92] ibid 729.
[93] ibid 740.
[94] Ely (n 41) 135.
[95] ibid 151–52; text to nn 39–42.
[96] *Andrews* (n 4).

considered whether the citizenship requirement for one to be admitted to the British Columbia bar violated the equality rights guaranteed under section 15 of the Canadian Charter and, if so, whether that infringement was nevertheless justified by section 1 (on reasonable limitation of rights).[97] Recognising citizenship as an analogous ground to those enumerated in section 15(1), Wilson J, writing the main decision of the Court, stated that non-citizens permanently resident in Canada, like Andrews, form a kind of 'discrete and insular minority', which status entitles them to protection. This is because 'Relative to citizens, non-citizens are a group lacking in political power and as such vulnerable to having their interests overlooked and their rights to equal concern and respect violated'.[98]

She continued to hold that

> [a] rule which bars an entire class of persons from certain forms of employment, solely on the grounds of a lack of citizenship status and without consideration of educational and professional qualifications or the other attributes or merits of individuals in the group, infringes s. 15 equality rights.[99]

It would have been highly unlikely for non-citizens to face such a disadvantage because of the impugned law if they had access to political power. This would have enabled them to make their case against it during the legislation approval process.

Similar to the appeal by Ackerman and others for a broadening of the idea of discrete and insular minorities to include more groups, Wilson J noted how the range of groups that can be said to lack access to the political process has expanded with changes in political and social circumstances over time. She specifically noted that groups to be protected no longer included just the traditional listing of religious, national and racial minorities identified in *Carolene*, but that consideration should also be given to 'the difficulties experienced by the disadvantaged on the grounds of ethnic origin, colour, sex, age and physical and mental disability'. She therefore left space for the expansion of this notion.[100]

Citizenship is also an unlisted ground in section 9(3) of the South African Constitution. The South African Constitutional Court has, however, considered it as analogous to the listed grounds in *Khosa & Others v Minister of Social Development & Others, Mahlaule & Another v Minister of Social Development*.[101] In this case, the question before the Court was whether the right to social grants should be equally extended to permanent residents, to which the Court replied in the affirmative. Similar to the observation by the Canadian Supreme Court in *Andrews*, the South African Constitutional Court, in *Khosa*, recognised the vulnerability of permanent residents because of their minority status and lack of

[97] ibid 144.
[98] ibid 152.
[99] ibid 145 and 151.
[100] ibid 152–53.
[101] *Khosa & Others v Minister of Social Development & Others, Mahlaule & Another v Minister of Social Development* 2004 (6) BCLR 569 (CC) (*Khosa*) [69]–[71].

political muscle as necessitating their constitutional protection.[102] This was said to be especially so because, per Mokgoro J, 'both permanent residents and citizens contribute to the welfare system through the payment of taxes'. Hence, denying them benefits through social grants 'creates an impression that they are inferior residents and less worthy of social assistance'. This then has the capacity to relegate this group to the margins of society and deprive them of an essential right that would enable them to enjoy other constitutional rights.[103]

This discussion reveals that grounds for non-discrimination can be considered placeholders for the need to protect those who lack access to political power. The Canadian and South African cases cited also provide additional insights and lessons for Kenyan courts on what to look out for in making compelling arguments for the addition of unenumerated grounds to protect those whose lack of political power makes them prone to discrimination.

C. History of Disadvantage

Prohibited grounds of discrimination make clear society's seriousness in preventing discrimination against certain groups in society that have experienced a history of disadvantage. One of the most important lessons history has taught us is the capacity of human beings to try and impose upon others their values and views as to who is greater or lesser, and what is right and wrong. The repeal of laws that allowed slavery of black people and inhibited women from voting, to mention just a few, unmasked discriminatory social practices that had been legitimised by law.[104] The grounds for non-discrimination act as a reminder of this link to history and context.[105] Importantly also, it has been pointed out that 'Current or historic patterns of group disadvantage not only predict the effects of further unfavourable treatment but they also play a constitutive role in bringing about further group disadvantage'.[106] Hence, a major indicator that an unlisted ground is analogous to those listed, and should be recognised as a prohibited form of discrimination, is the fact that the people possessing the personal characteristic in question have experienced historical and ongoing disadvantage.

In the Canadian Supreme Court decision in *Andrews*, discussed earlier, it was stated that personal characteristics listed as grounds for non-discrimination 'reflect the most common and probably the most socially destructive and historically practiced basis of discrimination'.[107] Also in *Egan v Canada* on the unenumerated ground of sexual orientation, to be further discussed below,

[102] ibid [71] and [74] (Mokgoro J).
[103] ibid [74] and [77].
[104] McClain (n 40) 435–37.
[105] Pothier (n 1) 43.
[106] McConnachie (n 5) 285.
[107] *Andrews* (n 4) 175 (McIntyre J); text to nn 96–99.

it was held that 'from the evidence of historical, social, political and economic disadvantage suffered by homosexuals, it is apparent that … sexual orientation is an analogous and prohibited ground of discrimination'.[108] Therefore, in the Canadian context, a classification based on a group's unlisted personal characteristic that is tied to its members' history of disadvantage is considered analogous to listed grounds. This is more so because of the suspect nature of such a distinction based on past experience.

Similarly, the South African Constitutional Court stated in *Harksen v Lane NO* that 'What the specified grounds have in common is that they have been used (or misused) in the past … to categorize, marginalise and often oppress persons who have had, or who have been associated with, [certain] attributes or characteristics'.[109] This statement puts a stamp of approval on the use of history of disadvantage to identify unspecified grounds that are analogous to those listed.

In conclusion, the Canadian and South African cases discussed above attest to the fact that grounds are aimed at helping historically disadvantaged groups. An analysis of the history of disadvantage is therefore an important requisite for adding new grounds as it provides the historical context that helps us identify whether a distinction based on a personal characteristic perpetuates patterns of group disadvantage and should hence be considered a prohibited ground of discrimination. However, this requisite cannot be applied on its own. Using the history of disadvantage of LGBTI persons as an example, such disadvantage usually has its roots in unfavourable treatment because of a person's immutable status, socially unaccepted fundamental choice or because of prejudice against this group, which lacks access to political power to champion their rights. It is thus clear that this criterion does not work alone but is effectively applied in concert with the other identified principles.

D. Human Dignity

It is often argued that a shared feature of enumerated grounds is that the discriminatory nature of distinctions based on the listed characteristics is tied to human dignity, and that this principle is at the heart of identification of new additional grounds that are analogous to those listed.[110] Human dignity is also considered a self-standing right in many constitutions. For instance, the South African Constitution provides in section 10 that 'Everyone has inherent dignity and the right to have their dignity respected and protected'.

Dworkin points to two dimensions of human dignity that should be safeguarded and which are often violated by discriminatory practices. The first is the principle of intrinsic value, which holds that 'each human life has a special kind of

[108] *Egan* (n 4) [176]; text to nn 116–20.
[109] *Harksen* (n 62) [49].
[110] See *Egan* (n 4) 542–54 (L'Heureux-Dubé J); *Harksen* (n 62).

objective value … once a human life has begun, it matters how it goes. It is good when that life succeeds and its potential is realized and bad when it fails and its potential is wasted'.[111] By 'objective value', Dworkin explains that what he means is that it should matter to everyone whether a life succeeds or is wasted and that 'we should all regret an injustice, wherever it occurs, as something bad in itself'.[112] The second principle he gives is that of personal responsibility. This 'holds that each person has a special responsibility for realizing the success of his own life, a responsibility that includes exercising his judgment about what kind of life would be successful for him' free from coercion and manipulation.[113]

These two understandings of human dignity emphasise the need to respect both the intrinsic value of each person's life and their autonomy to live the kind of life they feel they are driven to lead, either by their intrinsic and innate characteristics or fundamental personal choice. These notions resonate with all the other principles highlighted above: immutability, fundamental choice, access to political power, and history of disadvantage. Human dignity can thus be said to be a vital constitutive element for all the other principles.

As much as human dignity is often implicated in the other principles, it is also an independent criterion for identifying new and analogous grounds of non-discrimination. This is best illustrated in the case law discussed below. Nonetheless, as will also be discussed, human dignity when used as a legal test is a malleable concept. Its application has particularly been problematic in cases where a claimant has to prove that a classification not only was based on a listed or unlisted ground for non-discrimination, but also amounts to a violation of human dignity.[114] Its malleability can additionally be seen in the clash between the two understandings of human dignity: the principle of intrinsic value (objective), involving what society sees as amounting to treatment of a person with equal concern and respect to enable them to flourish, and that of personal responsibility, which leaves it to an individual to decide the kind of life they find joy in. These two often conflict.

The idea of human dignity being a core value underlying the list of grounds for non-discrimination has its origins in the Canadian *Andrews* case on the unenumerated ground of citizenship, which recognised everyone's equal worth and right to equal concern and respect.[115] This was followed up in *Egan v Canada*, where the Canadian Supreme Court held that sexual orientation is a ground analogous to those listed in section 15 of the Canadian Charter.[116] L'Heureux-Dubé J's dissent and minority opinion in *Egan* applied human dignity as the main

[111] R Dworkin, *Is Democracy Possible Here? Principles of a New Political Debate* (Princeton, NJ, Princeton University Press, 2008) 9.
[112] ibid.
[113] ibid.
[114] Fredman, *A Comparative Study of the Anti-Discrimination and Equality Laws* (n 25) 51.
[115] *Andrews* (n 4) 152.
[116] *Egan* (n 4).

principle to be used in identifying unenumerated grounds analogous to those listed. She stated that

> [a] distinction is discriminatory within the meaning of s. 15 [Canadian Charter] where it is capable of either promoting or perpetuating the view that the individual adversely affected by this distinction is less capable, or less worthy of recognition or value as a human being or as a member of Canadian society, equally deserving of concern, respect, and consideration.[117]

In undertaking such an examination, L'Heureux-Dubé J emphasised that a 'subjective-objective perspective' be taken. By this, she meant that the assessment should be 'from the point of view of [a] reasonable person, dispassionate and fully appraised of the circumstances, possessed of similar attributes to, and under similar circumstances as, the group of which the rights claimant is a member'.[118] It is important to note, however, that L'Heureux-Dubé J took quite a different route from the majority, who focused on sexual orientation being 'unchangeable or changeable only at unacceptable costs' when adding it within the ambit of section 15 protection.[119]

In cases following *Egan*, the majority agreed with the view that discrimination was a violation of a person's dignity. L'Heureux-Dubé J's opinion therefore became mainstream.[120] In *Vriend*, for instance, the majority held that the denial of recourse to gays and lesbians for the making of formal discrimination complaints under Alberta's Individual's Rights Protection Act, which was the primary government statement of policy against discrimination, violated their human dignity.[121] This was because the distinction demeaned lesbians and gays, and strengthened and perpetuated the view that they are less worthy of concern and protection as Canadians.[122] It was further noted that this 'potential harm to dignity and perceived worth of gay and lesbian individuals constitutes a particularly cruel form of discrimination' as it was tantamount to suggesting that 'discrimination on the ground of sexual orientation is not as serious or as deserving of condemnation as other forms of discrimination'.[123]

The case of *Law v Canada*, which followed *Egan*, was not about the addition of unenumerated grounds (the same as *Gosselin v Quebec* and *R v Kapp* to be discussed below) which are the main focus of this chapter, but about whether a measure violated the substantive principle of discrimination.[124] However, the analytical process for establishing whether an unlisted personal characteristic is analogous to enumerated grounds, and should therefore be added within the same

[117] ibid [56] (L'Heureux-Dubé J).
[118] ibid.
[119] ibid [5] (La Forest J).
[120] See *Law v Canada* [1999] 1 SCR 497 (*Law*) 501–03; *Gosselin v Québec* [2002] 4 SCR 429 (*Gosselin*); *R v Kapp* [2008] 2 SCR 483 (*Kapp*) [22].
[121] *Vriend* (n 4); text to nn 49–54.
[122] ibid [102].
[123] ibid [100]–[102].
[124] *Law* (n 120).

ambit of protection, overlaps with a discrimination analysis. This is particularly because the process of adding new analogous grounds focuses on elements that make distinctions based on particular personal characteristics invidious, and hence discriminatory and requiring protection under grounds for non-discrimination.

Law concerned a claim by a 30-year-old woman, who had no dependent children or disability, that a pension plan which denied benefits to widows and widowers under 45 years of age, who, like her, had no dependent children or disability, was age discrimination. An open list of contextual factors for establishing discrimination based on a dignity violation was set out in the case.[125] Applying these factors, the Court held that, despite the distinctions in the pension plan, Ms Law's human dignity was not violated since, being a person under the age of 45, she was more capable of finding work and being financially independent than an older or disabled person.[126] This criterion for proving dignity violations has, however, created challenges for litigants in cases following *Law*. This is specifically because, aside from a claimant showing they had been disadvantaged by an unfair distinction, it created an additional hurdle by requiring them to prove that a distinction specifically violated their dignity.

The risks this extra requirement created are seen in the decision of the Canadian Supreme Court in *Gosselin v Quebec*.[127] As stated earlier, the case was not necessarily about an unenumerated ground, but its analysis of whether a measure breached the substantive principle of discrimination is still applicable to the addition of new grounds. The case concerned a challenge against a section of the Quebec 1984 Social Aid Act alleged to be discriminatory as it set the base amount of welfare for beneficiaries under 30 years old at about one-third of the base amount payable to those over 30. The benefits for those under 30 years old would only be increased if they participated in one of three remedial education programmes or skills training. The main applicant, Louise Gosselin, had a difficult life struggling with psychological problems and drug and alcohol addiction. This affected her attempts to work or participate in government programmes and led to her dependence on social assistance for most of her adult life.[128] The Court's majority opinion was that, save for the difference in the welfare benefits amounts, the applicant had to prove a denial of human dignity. It was, however, held that the applicant had failed to do this as she 'had not demonstrated that the government treated her as less worthy than older welfare recipients, simply because it conditioned increased payments on her participation in programs designed specifically to integrate her into the workforce'.[129]

The example of the approach in *Gosselin* shows how, in the Canadian context, the requirement for complainants to prove that an alleged discriminatory act

[125] ibid 501–03.
[126] ibid 556 and 562.
[127] *Gosselin* (n 120).
[128] ibid 454.
[129] ibid 431–32.

particularly offends their human dignity creates an additional burden on claimants. This was, however, corrected by the Canadian Supreme Court in the case of *R v Kapp*.[130] This case concerned a claim that the issuance of a communal fishing licence to three Aboriginal bands to fish for salmon one day in advance of the general fishing season in the mouth of the Fraser River and sell their catch was discriminatory against non-Aboriginal commercial fishers.

In its assessment of whether the licence was discriminatory, the Court acknowledged that considering human dignity independently, it being an abstract and subjective notion, 'has proven to be an *additional* burden on equality claimants, rather than the philosophical enhancement it was intended to be'.[131] The Court therefore moved away from using dignity as an independent legal test as set out in *Law* but affirmed that it is 'an essential value underlying the s. 15 equality guarantee' and that 'the protection of all the rights guaranteed in the *Charter* had as its lodestar the promotion of human dignity'.[132] The Supreme Court instead focused on an analysis of factors which identify impact amounting to dignity violations in establishing discrimination. These were compressed down to primary indicators that relate to identification of *distinctions that perpetuate disadvantage* and *stereotyping*.[133]

South African jurisprudence also recognises human dignity as the most integral element in identifying additional grounds analogous to those listed.[134] Human dignity is not only seen as an essential principle in adding new grounds, it is also applied as a self-standing right in section 10 of the South African Constitution. The case of *Prinsloo v Van der Linde* is particularly instructive on the application of human dignity to add an unenumerated ground.[135] The case related to a claim that a law which created a presumption of negligence in relation to fires spreading from non-controlled areas, and not those spreading from controlled areas, unfairly discriminated against owners and occupants of land who were not from fire-controlled areas.[136]

In seeking to establish the basis for adding an unenumerated ground, Ackermann, O'Regan and Sachs JJ stated that weight should be placed on the word 'discrimination' and in particular 'unfair discrimination'. It is in their description of these two terms that they invoked the principle of human dignity. They stated: 'In our view unfair discrimination … principally means treating persons differently in a way which impairs their fundamental dignity as human beings, who are inherently equal in dignity'.[137] It was thus concluded that 'Where discrimination

[130] *Kapp* (n 120).
[131] ibid [22].
[132] ibid.
[133] ibid [23].
[134] eg the landmark case of *Harksen* (n 62).
[135] *Prinsloo* (n 60).
[136] ibid [16] and [41].
[137] ibid [30]–[31].

results in treating persons differently in a way which impairs their fundamental dignity as human beings, it will clearly be a breach of section 8(2) [now section 9(3) of the current South African Constitution]'.[138] Based on this analysis, the Court held that the differentiation was a necessary regulatory measure and did not impair the dignity of owners and occupiers of land outside fire-controlled areas.[139] Essentially, based on this analysis, the distinction between owners and occupiers in fire-controlled and non-fire-controlled areas was not added as an unenumerated ground. The case shows both the use of dignity in the procedure for adding new grounds and the conflation of this process with a discrimination analysis.

Like the experience in the Canadian context, the application of human dignity as an independent legal test requiring independent proof of whether a distinction specifically violates it (in its abstract sense) has also shown its potential malleability in South African jurisprudence. This is clearly demonstrated by the minority opinion in *S v Jordan*.[140] The case concerned the constitutionality of section 20(1)(aA) of the South African Sexual Offences Act of 1975, which criminalised prostitution but had no similar offence for clients (patrons) of commercial sex workers. It was pointed out that the ground for differentiation between those who provide sex for reward, and those who purchased it, was not a specified ground in section 8(2) of the Interim South African Constitution. The appellants, however, argued that it could be considered indirect discrimination on the listed ground of gender or sex.[141] Thus, the issue before the Court was whether the distinction between sex workers and their clients was discriminatory on the basis of gender, prostitutes being 'overwhelmingly (though not exclusively) female, and patrons [being] overwhelmingly (though not exclusively) male'.[142] The decision of the Court was split, with Ngcobo J, writing for the majority, holding that the provision does not constitute unfair gender discrimination as it applies to both female and male sex workers and, additionally, that customers are liable to prosecution as accomplices to the offence committed by the prostitute.[143]

The minority opinion, written by O'Regan and Sachs JJ, however, found that the provision, making the prostitute the primary offender and the client liable at most as an accomplice, amounted to unfair indirect discrimination. This was because it reinforced a pattern of sexual stereotyping and double standards impermissible in a society dedicated to advancing gender equality.[144] Important to the discussion on human dignity, O'Regan and Sachs JJ upheld the constitutionality of the provision because it criminalised the commodification of the human body in a way that diminished the dignity of prostitutes. O'Regan and Sachs JJ specifically stated

[138] ibid [33].
[139] ibid [41].
[140] *S v Jordan* 2002 (6) SA 642 (CC).
[141] ibid [59] (O'Regan and Sachs JJ).
[142] ibid.
[143] ibid [8]–[11] (Ngcobo J).
[144] ibid [60], [63] and [64] (O'Regan and Sachs JJ).

that 'the dignity of prostitutes is diminished not by section 20(1)(aA) but their engaging in commercial sex work'.[145] This holding contrasted with what the appellants were arguing – that the impugned provision criminalising commercial sex work was a violation of their human dignity. This shows the malleability of human dignity because, at one end of the spectrum, acts like prostitution are seen as offending the dignity of commercial sex workers, while at the other end, commercial sex workers see their work as promoting their dignity by using their bodies in a way they see fit. The fact that these activities are also their source of livelihood is arguably a compelling factor for their participation in this type of work. However, in such a scenario, dignity does not really help to resolve the problem because of the clash between societal (or 'objective') perspectives on what amounts to dignity and individuals' views (subjective notion of personal responsibility) on the same.

This analysis has shown that, despite its potential malleability, human dignity, when factors are given for identifying its violation – either alone or in concert with the other requisites looked at for adding unenumerated grounds – is the golden thread that ties together the enumerated grounds. Hence, it is an integral element in the addition of new grounds.

IV. Do Kenyan Courts in Current Cases Apply the Identified Requisites When Considering Unenumerated Grounds? Should They?

Kenyan courts in recent cases on unenumerated grounds have, both explicitly and implicitly, recognised the above-identified requisites for adding new grounds. For instance, in *Republic v Kenya National Examination Council (KNEC) & the Attorney General Ex-parte Audrey Mbugua Ithibu*, Korir J applied both immutability (implicitly) and human dignity (explicitly) in considering the unenumerated ground of transsexuality.[146] In the case, the applicant, Audrey Mbugua Ithibu (previously known as Andrew Mbugua Ithibu) sought an order of mandamus for the Court to compel the respondent, KNEC, to carry out its statutory mandate by changing the particulars of her name on the Kenya Certificate of Secondary Education (KCSE) awarded to her by adding a 'no gender' mark to reflect her changed gender from male to female. The applicant had been diagnosed and treated for gender identity disorder and depression in 2008 and was in the process of undergoing sex-change surgery. She thus embarked on changing the particulars of her national identity card and academic papers to reflect this change.

Quoting the UK House of Lords decision in *Bellinger v Bellinger*, the judge noted that 'Transsexual is the label given … to a person … born with the anatomy

[145] ibid [74].

[146] *Republic v Kenya National Examination Council (KNEC) & the Attorney General Ex-parte Audrey Mbugua Ithibu* [2014] eKLR (HC) (*Audrey Mbugua*).

of a person of one sex but with an unshakeable belief or feeling that they are persons of the opposite sex'.[147] Alluding to the immutable nature of transsexuality – the fact that a person is born this way – Korir J stated that 'the Applicant has clearly demonstrated that he is different', being 'a person with the body of a man and a mind of a woman'. And further that his feminine mindset is so overwhelming that he even attempted to commit suicide because of his condition.[148]

Expounding on the human dignity requirement in Article 28 of the Kenyan Constitution as it applied to Audrey Mbugua, the judge stated that

> [h]uman dignity is that intangible element that makes a human being complete. It goes to the heart of human identity. Every human has a value. Human dignity can be violated through humiliation, degradation or dehumanisation. Each individual has inherent dignity which our Constitution protects. Human dignity is the cornerstone of the other human rights enshrined in the Constitution.[149]

The judge then proceeded to hold that the refusal to change the official KCSE examination certificates of the applicant and to leave blank the section on sex was discriminatory as it had the potential to impair the applicant's human dignity since she no longer identified herself as male. Hence, KNEC was ordered to issue the applicant with new KCSE examination certificates bearing no gender mark within 45 days.[150] This decision illustrates the willingness of the courts to apply both immutability and human dignity to bring unlisted grounds within the ambit of Article 27(4).

Nevertheless, aside from human dignity, should a transgender person's only other option be that of showing that this characteristic is an immutable aspect of their personhood for the court to add it as a ground? The recognition in the *Audrey Mbugua* case that KNEC's actions were discriminatory, having impaired the applicant's human dignity as she no longer identified as male, can also fall under the fundamental choice argument. This is because the non-recognition would also come at an unacceptable cost to the applicant's personal identity, whether we consider transsexuality as immutable or a fundamental choice. This shows us that immutability and fundamental choice are most effective when used together in the addition of an unenumerated ground.

The case of *Baby A (Suing through the Mother E.A) & Another v Attorney General & 6 Others* on intersexuality, an unenumerated ground in the Kenyan Constitution, is an example of instances where immutability may be applied on its own.[151] The Petitioners in the case sought, inter alia, the legal recognition of intersex persons in Kenya and that the term 'sex' under the Constitution should be interpreted to include 'intersex', terming its lack of recognition as inconsistent with

[147] *Bellinger v Bellinger* [2003] UKHL 21, [7]–[10].
[148] *Audrey Mbugua* (n 146) 10.
[149] ibid 11.
[150] ibid 12.
[151] *Baby A (Suing through the Mother E.A) & Another v Attorney General & 6 Others* [2014] eKLR (*Baby A*).

Article 27 of the Constitution. It was said that compliance with Article 27 would mean that intersex children should be registered at birth as intersex until they are able to have corrective surgery to create their dominant biological sex, and not to be identified, as happened in the case, by a question mark '(?)'.

In his decision, Lenaola J defined intersex as a condition whereby a baby is born with both male and female genitalia.[152] This therefore refers to immutability, although this fact was not explicitly mentioned. The judge stated that the disadvantages faced by intersex persons are 'symptomatic of the fact that a baby by societal expectation must be categorized as either male or female', which can be problematic.[153] To illustrate this, he cited an earlier decision of the High Court in *RM v Attorney General & 4 Others* before the 2010 Constitution came into force.[154] In the case, the High Court refused to recognise intersex as an aspect of sex, stating that this would be to erroneously add a 'third gender', while intersex persons, as the Court alleged, fall within one of the two categories of male and female gender included in the term sex. This left the plight of RM, an intersexual who had been socialised as male but exhibited more feminine features, including breasts slightly larger than those of an average male, to be incarcerated with male prisoners where he faced constant abuse, mockery, ridicule and inhuman treatment, unaddressed.[155] This particularly related to the Court in *RM* holding that different housing for intersex persons in prisons was unnecessary as they could be classified as either male or female, failing to recognise the plight of intersex persons in Kenya. Such plight includes the fact that they are usually assigned genders not of their own choosing and, like the applicant in the case, some intersex persons are unable to afford corrective surgery and to secure new or revised birth certificates, identity cards or any travel documents.

In *Baby A*, Lenaola J had two options as a judge. First, he could consider intersex as an aspect of sex, a 'third gender', or, second, he could recognise intersex as a new ground. On the first point, possibly due to the controversy of adding intersex as a third gender raised by the *RM* case, the judge held that the question whether there should be a third category of sex called intersexuals is to be addressed by clear legislation. Hence, he deferred the matter to the legislature.[156] On the second option, Lenaola J noted the possibility that a court can expand the list of grounds and extend the protection offered by the equality clause by reading in new grounds.[157] He then proceeded to recognise intersexuality as a prohibited ground of discrimination, meaning that 'intersexuals ought not to be discriminated against in any[]way including in the issuance of registration documents such as a birth certificate'.[158]

[152] ibid [51].
[153] ibid [52].
[154] *RM v Attorney General & 4 Others* [2010] eKLR (HC) (*RM*).
[155] ibid [7] (description of the treatment RM underwent while in prison).
[156] *Baby A* (n 151) [62].
[157] ibid [61].
[158] ibid.

The judgment in *Baby A* arguably applied the immutability marker in providing a compelling reason for adding intersexuality as a ground for non-discrimination. This characteristic does not straddle between immutability and fundamental choice like transsexuality. It is clearly one that solely falls under immutability, unless we are talking about the choice an intersex person should make about the gender they most prefer when undergoing corrective surgery.

However, the earlier-discussed *Eric Gitari* case on discrimination based on sexual orientation in registration of an LGBTI organisation shows the ambiguity created when the Court only looks at immutability and excludes fundamental choice in borderline cases.[159] The judgment only seemed to protect the immutable aspect of being gay or lesbian, and not the fundamental choice of sexual conduct among gays and lesbians. Accordingly, in response to submissions that homosexuality is prohibited under Sections 162, 163 and 165 of Kenya's Penal Code, which criminalise sexual acts between persons of the same gender, the three-judge bench held that the sections do not indicate that the Penal Code criminalises homosexuality or status as a homosexual. Rather it only prohibits certain acts 'against the order of nature', and the provisions are not clear because they do not define what acts against the order of nature are.[160] This holding brings into question the separation between the notion of immutability and fundamental choice, which is particularly murky in discussions of conceptual reasons behind the protection of sexual orientation and, within this broad category, sexual attraction and sexual conduct. Wintemute's work on the issue and Gardner's further exploration of his work is relevant to this discussion.

Wintemute's position is that both immutability and fundamental choice 'are valid and important [as markers of discrimination] and should be applied in tandem to decide whether discrimination on a given ground is wrongful'.[161] Using the example of sexual orientation, Wintemute argues that there are two ways of defining sexual orientation. The first relates to the term as referring to the direction of one's 'emotional-sexual attraction', and the second is the direction of one's 'emotional-sexual conduct' or activity.[162] He then argues that people are more sympathetic to sexual attraction and its immutable nature than to sexual conduct, which mainly implicates the notion of fundamental choice. Such a perspective ignores the interconnectedness of the two dimensions of sexual orientation, in that 'to deal with one is to tackle only half of the problem', as the sexual orientation of a person relates to both whom they are attracted to and with whom they are sexually active.[163]

The relatively easy acceptance of sexual attraction, but not of sexual activity, for lesbian, gay and bisexual persons overlooks the fact that the two almost always go

[159] Text to nn 29–39.
[160] *Eric Gitari* (n 20) 114.
[161] See Gardner (n 3) 169; Wintemute (n 63).
[162] Wintemute (n 63) 6–7.
[163] Gardner (n 3) 170.

hand in hand. Indeed, sexual attraction is usually coupled with the innate desire to express affection through sexual activity, except where one chooses to be celibate. This means that sexual attraction (immutable) and sexual activity (fundamental choice) are inextricably linked, and laying more weight on one and not the other amounts to an injustice. This fact was mentioned in the recent High Court case of *EG & 7 Others v Attorney General; DKM & 9 Others (Interested Parties); Katiba Institute & Another (Amicus Curiae)* challenging the constitutionality of Kenya's sodomy laws.[164] In the case, one of the expert witnesses, a psychiatrist, testified that human sexuality considers three interdependent elements: sexual orientation, sexual identity and sexual behaviour (activity). Hence, restricting one of the elements interferes with the functioning of normal human sexuality.[165]

Aside from being intuitively wrong, denying same-sex couples the right to partake in private sexual activity or public displays of affection that are allowed for opposite-sex couples is certainly an unfair intrusion into the authorship of the former group's lives, an authorship that is an essential aspect of their identity and happiness. This therefore makes the prohibition too costly for an individual, such that it would be hard for the State to prove that the limitation is nevertheless justified, there being a legitimate governmental interest in it. Thus, fundamental choice insists that there is a need to give people choice of values that are not burdened.

The opacity of using either immutability or fundamental choice as a marker of discrimination in borderline cases like sexual orientation, rather than the two of them being applied in tandem, is even more reason why the chapter concludes that it is not pragmatic to settle on one principle as the sole marker of discrimination. Indeed, other markers were applied in the *Eric Gitari* case. For instance, the history of disadvantage faced by homosexual persons in Kenya was said to necessitate their legal protection, to put to an end and avoid reinforcing the disadvantage already occasioned upon them. In the case, Lenaola, Mumbi Ngugi and Odunga JJ considered how the history of disadvantage occasioned to homosexual persons compounded their disadvantage. They specifically noted that lesbians and gays are 'not a popular or accepted group in Kenyan society … [and] even contemplating registering such an NGO [championing their rights] is perceived as bringing moral decadence into society, and as a herald of the breakdown of society'.[166] The judges used this historical and current context of unfavourable treatment to emphasise the need for protection of homosexual persons. They particularly observed that 'As a society, once we recognise that persons who are gay, lesbian, bisexual, transgender or intersex are human beings …, however reprehensible we may find their sexual orientation, we must accord them the human rights which are guaranteed by the Constitution to all persons, by virtue of their being human, in order to protect their dignity'.[167]

[164] *EG* case (n 43).
[165] ibid [39]–[44] and [50]–[52].
[166] *Eric Gitari* (n 20) [98].
[167] ibid [104].

The historical injustices faced by intersex persons were also referred to at length in the *Baby A* case, where it was specifically noted that

> the treatment of intersex persons by the Society raises important human rights issues because such persons have in the past been seriously stigmatized and have been subjected to a phenomenon referred to as 'intersex phobia' and invariably, 'trans phobia'. That the absence of public discussion and acknowledgement of intersexuality has therefore led to a lack of legal recognition for intersexuals as a distinct vulnerable group in need of protection by the law. Further, that the plight of intersexuals is exacerbated by the fact that there is no legal definition of intersexual persons and they have thus been exposed to discrimination since they remain unrecognized and unacknowledged.[168]

From this background, Lenaola J then proceeded to order that a report be filed in Court within 90 days on the progress made in creating a statute providing guidelines and regulations on the place of intersexuals as a sexual category and on the conduct of corrective surgery.[169]

Political powerlessness and vulnerability of groups whose characteristics are not listed in the grounds for non-discrimination has also been identified by Kenyan courts as necessitating the protection of such groups (discrete, insular, diffuse or an anonymous minority) from discrimination.

One important ground not listed in Article 27(4) is that of citizenship. This has particularly been a problem because Kenya is host to over 600,000 registered refugees from Somalia, South Sudan, Eritrea, Rwanda, Burundi and Democratic Republic of Congo due to the previous and ongoing political instability in these countries.[170] Amidst security challenges in the country, mostly posed by the Al Shabaab terror group from Somalia, there have been tendencies by various governmental actors to place a blanket label on refugees, particularly those of Somali origin, as a cause of insecurity. This claim led to a directive in 2016 to close refugee camps. This directive was, however, halted by the High Court in *Kenya National Commission on Human Rights & Another v Attorney General & 3 Others*.[171] The petitioners in the case argued that the directive was unconstitutional because it was discriminatory (Article 27), violated the right to fair administrative action (Article 47) by equating refugees to criminals, which went against the principle of 'individual criminality', and violated refugees' human dignity (Article 28). The government, on the other hand, argued that the closing of camps and return of refugees was justified because of 'overcrowding in the camps, [terrorist] attacks, huge economic costs, human trafficking, proliferation of arms, strained government resources and insecurity'.[172]

[168] *Baby A* (n 151) [22].
[169] ibid [71].
[170] *Kituo Cha Sheria & 8 Others v Attorney General* [2013] eKLR [2].
[171] *Kenya National Commission on Human Rights & Another v Attorney General & 3 Others* [2017] eKLR (*Refoulement of refugees*).
[172] ibid 3.

Importantly, Mativo J noted that Article 20 of the Constitution requires the Bill of Rights 'to be enforced in favour of *all persons* hence no distinction is made between nationals and non-nationals' (emphasis added) in holding the State accountable for its obligations under national and international laws ratified by Kenya.[173] The judge pointed out that 'Refugees are a special category of persons who are, by virtue of their situation, considered vulnerable', while Article 21(3) of the Constitution places an obligation on the State to protect the vulnerable.[174] He agreed with the petitioners that the government's directive was discriminatory and amounted to racial profiling, which was defined as 'the discriminatory practice by law enforcement officials of targeting individuals for suspicion of crime based on the individual's race, ethnicity, religion or national origin'.[175] This was said to be particularly the case because the directive referred to a particular community (refugees of Somali origin), and yet the country hosts refugees from several other countries. Thus, the judge stated that the notice amounted to discrimination and unfair treatment by purporting to condemn all refugees of Somali origin, which would arbitrarily and unjustifiably punish many innocents.[176] This holding shows that the Court arguably broadened the meaning of non-discrimination on the basis of ethnic origin to include refugees of Somali origin.

The judgment implicitly alludes to the discrete and insular minority status of refugees. First, they can be said to be 'discrete', being a group that can be easily identified because they mostly live in camps and can be identified by physical features tying them to their ethnic origin. Second, they are also 'insular' as they do not have any power to protect themselves through the vote because only citizens can vote. This decision therefore makes a case for the possible application of lack of access to the political process as a marker of discrimination.

From the above analysis it can be concluded that Kenyan courts have, in the various cases discussed, applied some aspects of the aforementioned requisites for adding new grounds. The controversy surrounding the use of dignity as a legal test, as highlighted in the Canadian and South African cases, has not been experienced in current Kenyan cases so far. It is also clear that there is still scope to effectively apply principles not exhaustively tackled so far, such as fundamental choice. This will be particularly valuable when courts are confronted with cases on the recognition of sexual orientation. As has been pointed out above, the High Court in the *Eric Gitari* case has only given recognition to homosexual attraction and not sexual conduct, which is still subject to sodomy laws. On the other hand, the High Court decision in the *EG* case was quite dismissive and basically referred the task of deciding the constitutionality of sodomy laws to the legislature.[177] The Court's judgment in the latter case largely failed to consider most of the arguments herein,

[173] ibid 5.
[174] ibid 16.
[175] ibid 15.
[176] ibid 15 and 21.
[177] See n 43.

mostly relying on a limitation of rights argument. It is hoped that the arguments in this chapter and the book at large will be helpful in guiding superior courts like the Court of Appeal and Supreme Court upon appeal.

This chapter has also shown that the interlocking nature of the requisites discussed, with each coming to the rescue when one falls short (for instance, how fundamental choice covers the demerits of immutability), means that Kenyan courts should apply a broad approach encompassing all these principles working in concert with each other. Courts could choose from these options the requisites that work best on a case-by-case basis. Such a broad approach would be the most workable in promoting substantive equality because of its capacity to cater for a variety of newly identified grounds of all shapes and forms, over a long period of time and across generations. It would also ensure the development of consistent jurisprudence.

V. What Do the Principles Unifying the List of Grounds Reveal About the Underlying Approach to Equality in the Constitution?

The analysis in this chapter reveals that most of the current cases on unenumerated grounds before Kenyan courts arise in instances where discrimination is said to have occurred in the context of other rights violations. These include the breach of administrative procedures, refusing to register and make changes to official documents, and infringement of the right to freedom of association. This goes to show the overarching importance of equality in the Constitution, illustrated by the requirements under each constitutional guarantee stipulating that they should be applied to 'everyone' or 'all persons' as discussed in Chapter 3.[178]

The requisites for adding unenumerated grounds also incorporate both a formal and substantive conception of equality. On the one hand, requisites like immutability and fundamental choice in the context of characteristics like race and sex speak to the invidious nature of differential treatment on the basis of these statuses – especially when they are irrelevant to the benefit in issue or not tied to merit – insisting instead on sameness in treatment, which is a formal conception of equality. On the other hand, requisites like access to political power and history of disadvantage, when applied in the context of grounds such as disability, gender and ethnicity, point to the adverse effects that facially neutral treatment may have in instances where these groups have faced historical and ongoing patterns of disadvantage. It thus mandates a more substantive approach to equality, requiring the accommodation of difference and appreciation that neutrality in treatment may in fact have discriminatory effects, where there are salient differences in people's

[178] Ch 3, text to nn 44–49.

contextual situation. This validates the conclusion in Chapter 3 on the overarching conception of equality in the Constitution, seeking to answer the 'Meta question' of what treatment as an equal requires for different people, with substantive equality being the central principle and formal equality derivative.

VI. Conclusion

Noting that there are some important grounds that are unenumerated in the open-ended list provided in Article 27(4) of the Kenyan Constitution, such as citizenship, intersexuality, transsexuality and sexual orientation, this chapter has considered how Kenyan courts could consider such unenumerated grounds in a discrimination claim. This chapter has provided clarity on the common themes that can be drawn from enumerated grounds to make up the criteria that can be used for identifying new grounds or stating that they fit within an existing ground. It has shown that there is scope for adding unenumerated grounds, analogous to those listed, on the basis of a set of principles including immutability, fundamental choice, access to the political process, history of disadvantage and human dignity. Accordingly, it has been concluded that the application of a broad approach, where all these principles work in concert with each other and act as a basket of tools from which courts can pick, depending on the case in issue, is the best way forward to comprehensively cover a wide range of new grounds.

This chapter has also shown that grounds incorporate both a formal and substantive conception of equality, which are applied depending on the matter in issue, further proving that the overarching conception of equality in the Constitution is one that considers what treatment as an equal requires.

5

Conceptualisation and Application of Affirmative Action

This chapter aims to provide a restatement of the importance of affirmative action in Kenya, noting the conceptual challenges and impassioned debates surrounding its implementation so far. It also makes recommendations on the most workable approaches to interpreting and applying the various affirmative action measures in the Constitution.

Affirmative action in the 2010 Constitution is unusual among equivalent constitutions as it is a duty upon the State and not just permitted. This is because Article 27(6) mandates that 'the State *shall* take legislative and other measures including affirmative action programmes and policies designed to redress any disadvantage suffered by individuals or groups because of past discrimination' (emphasis added). This provision also specifies what the Constitution requires the main aim of affirmative action to be – *to redress disadvantage caused by past discrimination*.

However, 10 years on, the implementation of affirmative action measures has been slow and, from the very start, raised a lot of controversy. At one end of the continuum, there is the slow pace in implementing affirmative action measures that seek to redress the disadvantage faced by persons with disabilities, minorities and marginalised groups. This is coupled with little public debate and litigation to bring duty bearers to task in meeting the constitutional affirmative action guarantees for these groups.[1] At the other end of the divide are the many impassioned debates surrounding the implementation of gender quotas in elective and appointive State bodies, both as to their legitimacy and the best approach to their application.[2] As a result of this, a law giving force to constitutional affirmative action provisions in favour of disadvantaged groups (Articles 54–56) and the general rule that not more than two-thirds of members in elective and appointive bodies should be of the same gender (Article 27(8)), is yet to be enacted.

These setbacks to the implementation of affirmative action measures mark a fundamental departure from earlier consensus on their importance. Notably, inclusion of

[1] L Thuo, 'Is the two-thirds gender rule discourse engendering double invisibility in public life for other vulnerable groups in Kenya?' (Oxford Human Rights Hub Blog, 19 August 2016) ohrh.law.ox.ac.uk/is-the-two-thirds-gender-rule-discourse-engendering-double-invisibility-in-public-life-for-other-vulnerable-groups-in-kenya/.

[2] ibid.

different types of affirmative action measures in the 2010 Constitution was not considered a controversial issue during the constitutional drafting period.[3] Up until the Constitution's promulgation, there was widespread consensus as to their necessity and value. This is further evidenced by a review of seven Regional Constituency Reports representing some of the major regions in the country and what the people in these areas wanted to be included in the equality provisions. All seven reports (Westlands, Lamu, Nakuru, Mandera, Kisumu, Likoni and Molo) highlight the desire for affirmative action measures in favour of women, persons with disabilities, minorities and marginalised groups, among other disadvantaged groups.[4]

This necessitates a reappraisal and restatement of affirmative action in Kenya, its value, importance and applicability. In this pursuit, the chapter interrogates the following questions: What are the aims of affirmative action in the 2010 Constitution, as evident from the different types of affirmative action measures included therein? On determination of beneficiaries, does the fact that a person is a member of a historically disadvantaged group meant to benefit from an affirmative action measure automatically entitle that person to such benefits? Or should all those who are to benefit prove that they are 'genuinely in need' of the benefits? Are affirmative action measures mandatory and immediate or should they be progressively realised? What is the role of courts and judicial scrutiny in giving effect to affirmative action measures in the Constitution through judicial interpretation? These are the main questions the chapter interrogates in seeking to answer the central question of how to conceptualise, interpret and apply *competing and interrelated conceptions of equality* in the Constitution.

Noting the breadth of affirmative action debates in Kenya and globally, this chapter only discusses key themes arising in the constitutional text, academic commentaries, emerging cases and general jurisprudential debates in Kenya.

I. Affirmative Action Measures in the Kenyan Constitution

This section discusses the various affirmative action measures in the Constitution and what necessitated their inclusion. It also flags some of the current challenges to their implementation to be discussed in greater depth in subsequent sections.

[3] Committee of Experts on Constitutional Review, *Final Report of the Committee of Experts on Constitutional Review* (2011) 62–79. The 2010 Constitution's Committee of Experts on Constitutional Review, like the Constitution of Kenya Review Commission before it, did not consider affirmative action a contentious issue during the drafting of the Constitution. The contentious issues that they identified excluded affirmative action.

[4] Constitution of Kenya Review Commission, *Report of the Constitution of Kenya Review Commission, Volume four Constituency Constitutional Forum Reports: Constituency No. 6, Westlands; Constituency No. 24, Lamu East; Constituency No. 136, Nakuru Town; Constituency No. 40, Mandera East; Constituency No. 185, Kisumu Town West; Constituency No. 11, Likoni; and Constituency No. 138, Molo. Approved for issue at the 66th Meeting of the Commission held on 20 March 2003* (2003).

A. General Affirmative Action Provision

Article 27(6) is the general affirmative action provision in the Constitution. It states that affirmative action is meant to 'give full effect to the realisation of the [equality] rights guaranteed under [the] Article'. This clarifies that affirmative action measures further equality and are not a breach of it. This forecloses the complex debates in other jurisdictions, such as in the US, as to whether affirmative action breaches equality or furthers it.[5] Since this position is clear in the Kenyan context, we therefore need not look extensively into viewpoints that categorise affirmative action as not falling under equality, more substantively conceived.

The Kenyan High Court has acknowledged the fundamental role that affirmative action plays in the achievement of greater equality. This was in the *John Kabui Mwai* case, which was extensively discussed in Chapter 3.[6] The Court, recognising the centrality of affirmative action in realising full equality, stated:

> The special provisions of article 27(6) make it a unique set of constitutional provisions. When the Constitution was adopted, the framers knew, and clearly had in mind, the different status of persons in the society and the need to protect the weak from being overrun by those with ability. They had in mind the history of this country, both the differences in endowment either by dint of the region where one came from or as a function of other factors, which might necessitate special protection … the framers of the Constitution manifestly regarded as inadequate a blanket right to equal treatment, and their intention was to remedy the perceived societal inequalities thus recognizing the necessity of corrective measures, namely those envisaged in article 27(6), which were at the same time given the status of constitutional guarantee.[7]

The above quote demonstrates that affirmative action is at the heart of the equality provisions in Article 27 of the Constitution. It is an essential part of the equality clause that promotes the right to equality in the substantive sense. The Kenyan Constitution, through its inclusion of extensive affirmative action measures, has therefore taken a similar stand to that of Canada, India and South Africa. The courts in these countries 'have stressed that affirmative action is a facet of the principle of non-discrimination rather than an exception, a possible means of achieving equality rather than a breach'.[8] The significance of affirmative action

[5] See S Fredman, *A Comparative Study of the Anti-Discrimination and Equality Laws of the USA, Canada, India and South Africa* (European Communities 2012) 64–68; D Sabbagh, 'Affirmative Action' in M Rosenfeld and A Sajó (eds), *The Oxford Handbook of Comparative Constitutional Law* (Oxford, Oxford University Press, 2012) 4.

[6] *John Kabui Mwai & 3 Others v Kenya National Examination Council & 2 Others* [2011] eKLR (HC) (*Kabui Mwai*); Ch 3, text to nn 101–03.

[7] *Kabui Mwai* (n 6) 9.

[8] Fredman (n 5) 10. See also Equal Rights Trust, *Declaration of Principles on Equality* (London, Equal Rights Trust, 2008) 5.

in achieving full equality is aptly captured in a speech by former US President Lyndon Johnson. He states:

> Freedom is not enough. You do not take a person who for years has been hobbled by chains and liberate him, bring him up to the starting line of a race and then say, 'you are free to compete with all the others,' and still justly believe that you have been completely fair.[9]

These perspectives buttress the argument in Chapter 3 that equality in the Kenyan Constitution is multifaceted, constituting varying but mutually reinforcing principles of equality that form a workable whole in addressing different types of injustices.[10]

Article 27(6) further mandates the State to 'take legislative and other measures including affirmative action programmes and policies designed to redress any disadvantage suffered by individuals or groups because of past discrimination'. This provision protects affirmative action against claims of direct discrimination arising from unequal treatment in favour of disadvantaged groups. It does so by requiring that such measures be justified through production of evidence that they are meant to redress disadvantage caused by past discrimination. Reference to the disadvantage suffered by both individuals and groups means that group membership is an important aspect in framing affirmative action measures. This coincides with the views of commentators such as Khaitan who point out that affirmative action measures are usually 'designed to benefit any members of one or more protected group(s) qua such membership'.[11]

As noted in Chapter 4, discounting the contextual group dimension of inequality may make an individual's experience of disadvantage seem merely incidental. But, when particulars are given about discriminatory practices that have contributed to the disadvantage faced by a certain group, we can better understand what led to the need for an affirmative action measure that seeks to redress it.[12] However, as was also discussed, we should not focus on the group dimension of disadvantage to such an extent that we lose sight of the individual experiences of disadvantage because of possession of multiple statuses. Take, for example, the multiple disadvantages faced by a physically disabled woman from a minority group because of her gender, disability and belonging to a minority group. Khaitan rightly notes that such cases 'may necessitate tailor-made tools that address the specific patterns of disadvantage they face'.[13] Indeed, as will be further discussed, one key strength of the 2010 Constitution is its inclusion of different types of affirmative action

[9] LB Johnson, 'Commencement Address at Howard University: "To Fulfill These Rights"' (Howard University, 4 June 1965) www.brown.edu/Departments/Economics/Faculty/Glenn_Loury/louryhomepage/teaching/Ec%20137/Ec%20137%20spring07/President%20Lyndon%20B%20Johnson%27s%20Howard%20University%20Speech.pdf.

[10] Ch 3, text to nn 57–74.

[11] T Khaitan, *A Theory of Discrimination Law* (Oxford, Oxford University Press, 2015) 217.

[12] Ch 4, text to nn 9–20.

[13] Khaitan (n 11) 219.

measures for various groups (eg women, persons with disabilities, the youth, marginalised groups and the elderly).

The broad repertoire of affirmative action measures that have been adopted by the State to implement the general affirmative action requirement in Article 27(6) also attests to this broad net of inclusion. For instance, in 2015 the National Government Affirmative Action Fund was set up under the Ministry of Public Service, Youth and Gender Affairs. It is meant to support affirmative action measures to redress past disadvantage through enhancing access to financial facilities for the socio-economic empowerment of women, the youth, persons with disabilities, needy children and elderly persons.[14]

Another example is the directive by President Uhuru Kenyatta in 2013 that government procurement rules be amended to ensure that 30 per cent of contracts are given to the youth, women and persons with disabilities without competition from established firms.[15] This process is currently under way. Regrettable, however, is the lack of spelt-out measures specific to groups that are disadvantaged because of two or more of their statuses, such as disabled women. More so, the effective implementation of the measures currently in force is obstructed by corruption.[16]

In addition, amid concerns that affirmative action measures may be over-inclusive – protecting both members of a disadvantaged group who really need protection and those within the group who have not experienced disadvantage – Article 27(7) sets the record straight.[17] It seeks to correct the over-inclusiveness problem of affirmative action by describing the persons who should benefit. It elucidates that measures taken under the general affirmative action provision in Article 27(6) 'shall adequately provide for any benefits to be on the basis of genuine need'. The provision thus gives rise to the principle of genuine need in the selection of affirmative action beneficiaries. This will be further discussed in the later section on the principle of genuine need.[18]

B. Affirmative Action Provisions on Gender Representation

Article 27(8) sets the principle that 'not more than two-thirds of the members of elective or appointive bodies shall be of the same gender' ('the two-thirds gender rule' or 'gender quotas'). This mandate is a *strong-form* affirmative action measure because it intends 'to increase the likelihood that target group members … will be

[14] Kenya Gazette Legal Notice No. 52 of 2016 sets out the Public Finance Management (National Government Affirmative Action Fund) Regulations, 2016 and the National Government Affirmative Action Fund.

[15] See Access to Government Procurement Opportunities (AGPO), 'Access to Government Procurement Opportunities' www.agpo.go.ke.

[16] See Ch 8, text to nn 130–38.

[17] C Murray, *Beginner's Guide to the Proposed Constitution: Chapter by Chapter* (2009) 25, constitutionnet.org/sites/default/files/beginners_guide_to_proposed_const_chap_by_chap.pdf.

[18] Text to nn 96–118.

admitted, hired or promoted'.[19] It does so by putting in place preferential policies that give an advantage to the sex whose representation in political and appointive bodies is less than a third. It is also a gender-neutral quota because 'neither men nor women may constitute a majority of more than two-thirds'.[20]

The two-thirds gender rule is reiterated in Article 81(b) as a principle that should guide the electoral system in elective public service bodies. Women being the under-represented gender in Kenya's Parliament, in addition to the two-thirds gender rule, the Constitution sets certain numerical requirements for the election and nomination of women to the National Assembly and Senate.

These numerical requirements aim to help meet the quota set in Articles 27(8) and 81(b) that at least one-third of parliamentarians should be women. In this respect, Article 97(1) stipulates that there should be at least one elected woman representative for each of the 47 counties in Kenya in the National Assembly. Since the overall number of members in the National Assembly should be 349,[21] to meet the one-third gender requirement, the gender with the least members (women) should have at least 117 seats. Hence, if no additional women were elected on top of the 47 required women representatives, and the two women nominated to represent persons with disabilities and the youth (raising the total to 49), there would be a gender deficit of 68 members that would need to be addressed.

For the Senate, Article 98(1) provides that on top of the elected members, there should be an additional 16 women nominated to the Senate by political parties, two nominated youth representatives (being one man and one woman) and two nominated persons with disabilities (being one man and one woman). The total number of members in the Senate should be 67.[22] The gender with the least numbers would thus need to have at least 23 members. Women are also under-represented in the Senate. Thus, in addition to the 18 Senate seats reserved for women (16 nominated women Senators, one female representative for the youth and one female representative for persons with disabilities), five more seats will have to go to women for the one-third requirement to be met.[23]

A significant challenge that has raised controversy in the implementation of the two-thirds gender rule is the fact that Articles 81(b), 97(1) and 98(1) do not provide a mechanism for appointing the additional women parliamentarians or Senate members needed to meet the one-third requirement in the National Assembly and Senate. The controversy surrounding the implementation of the

[19] J Nickel, 'Strong Affirmative Action' (1990) 17(1) *Journal of Ethnic and Migration Studies* 49, 49–50.

[20] K Owino, D Owiro, M Marchant and S Jairo, *Implementing the Constitutional Two-Thirds Gender Principle: The Cost of Representation* (2015) 18.

[21] Kenya's 2010 Constitution, Art 97. The 349 members of the National Assembly consist of 290 members elected by constituencies, 47 elected women representatives and 12 nominated members to represent the youth, persons with disabilities and workers.

[22] ibid Art 98. Of the 67 members, 47 are elected by counties, 16 nominated women senators, 2 nominated youth representatives and 2 representatives for persons with disabilities.

[23] Owino et al (n 20) 7–9.

rule in these two houses of Parliament led to its non-application in the 2013 and 2017 general elections, even though the Constitution was already in force. This contrasts with the application of the rule in County Assemblies, where, in addition to the general principle under Article 81(b), Article 177(1)(b) further provides that County Assemblies should consist of 'the number of special seat members necessary to ensure that no more than two-thirds of the membership of the assembly are of the same gender'. This therefore provides a mechanism for the immediate implementation of the rule in County Assemblies. This challenge is further discussed in the later section on affirmative action and gender quotas.[24]

C. Affirmative Action Provisions on Persons with Disabilities

Articles 54–56 of the Constitution provide for specific affirmative action measures for certain vulnerable groups. As Chapter 3 stated, this can be viewed as an extension of the Article 27 equality clause.[25] Article 54 focuses on persons with disabilities. Article 54(1) provides for reasonable accommodation of persons with disabilities by requiring the State to ensure that they can have reasonable access to all places, especially educational institutions and facilities, public transport and information. It additionally provides that the State should ensure that those who are visually impaired, deaf or hard of hearing have access to Braille devices and materials or sign language facilities, respectively. Also, generally, depending on a person's disability, it entitles them to have access to materials and devices that will help them overcome the barriers they encounter as a result of such disability.

The reasonable accommodation requirement, as it relates to persons with disabilities, introduces another dynamic to the analysis. There are ongoing debates as to whether it is a form of affirmative action or goes beyond it in certain respects. Befort and Donesky interrogate this matter extensively.[26] They draw most of their examples from the US context, but the conclusions they arrive at are nevertheless relevant and persuasive to the Kenya milieu, as will be further illustrated using the provisions of Article 54(1).

They rightly note that reasonable accommodation in the context of persons with disabilities is indeed a form of affirmative action to a certain extent. They support Karlan and Rutherglen's view that 'Reasonable accommodation is affirmative action, in the sense that it requires an employer [or State organs] to take account of an individual's disabilities and to provide special treatment to him for that reason'.[27]

[24] See text to nn 125–58.

[25] Ch 3, text to nn 76–77.

[26] S Befort and T Donesky, 'Reassignment under Americans with Disabilities Act: Reasonable Accommodation, Affirmative Action, or Both' (2000) 57 *Washington and Lee Law Review* 1045.

[27] ibid 1081–82; P Karlan and G Rutherglen, 'Disabilities, Discrimination, and Reasonable Accommodation' (1996) 46(1) *Duke Law Journal* 1, 14.

However, reasonable accommodation is distinct from traditional forms of affirmative action like gender quotas in various ways. First, reasonable accommodation has an individualised character to it.[28] Unlike traditional forms of affirmative action, reasonable accommodation does not set predetermined numerical targets or quotas to increase representation of a historically under-represented group *qua group membership*. It instead identifies the type of disability of a person in question who is qualified to get a position at a school or workplace but requires special needs or adjustments to function at their optimum level.

Disabilities vary and the type of reasonable accommodation required may be quite individualised. For instance, a workplace which employs one visually impaired person will be required to provide Braille devices and materials to that one person under Article 54(1)(d) of the Constitution. Article 54(1)(e) further emphasises the largely personalised character of reasonable accommodation by mandating that, generally, a person with any disability is entitled to access materials and devices that will help in overcoming the barriers that the person encounters because of such disability. Hence, using the example of a workplace scenario, an employer is obliged to accommodate the individual physical or mental impairments of a disabled applicant or employee capable of performing the essential functions of the job. However, Befort and Donesky point out that such accommodation should not pose an undue hardship on the employer, to be assessed on a case-by-case basis.[29]

Second, Befort and Donesky argue that 'from a policy standpoint, the "perceived fairness" of reasonably accommodating the known impairments of disabled individuals simply may be greater than in other affirmative action contexts'.[30] They make a fitting observation that the perceived fairness is most likely because, unlike affirmative action measures on race and gender, the consideration of a qualified disabled person's disability has an inherent relationship with the ability of the person to do the job. In this sense, 'Reasonable accommodation thus ensures that disabled persons are not deprived of job opportunities to which they otherwise might not have access under a disability blind statute'.[31]

It is because of these unique features that the reasonable accommodation of a disability requirement is usually discussed separately from traditional affirmative action measures. However, the core idea behind it – the differential treatment of persons with disabilities by the taking of affirmative steps to make facilities and workplaces accessible and usable by them – makes it a form of affirmative action. Hence the reason why it is discussed alongside traditional affirmative action measures in this chapter.

Article 54(2) then goes on to require the State to 'ensure the progressive implementation of the principle that at least five percent of the members of the

[28] See Befort and Donesky (n 26) 1084–85; Karlan and Rutherglen (n 27) 14–16.
[29] Befort and Donesky (n 26) 1084–85.
[30] ibid 1085–86.
[31] ibid.

public in elective and appointive bodies are persons with disabilities'. This rule applies to both representation-based measures (elective quotas) and redistributive measures (jobs). There is a related requirement in section 13 of Kenya's Persons with Disabilities Act 2003, which requires the National Council for Persons with Disabilities 'to secure the reservation of five per cent of all casual, emergency and contractual positions in employment in the public and private sector for persons with disabilities'.[32] This provision is more expansive than that in Article 54(2) as it applies the 5 per cent requirement to the private sector.

However, despite these positive constitutional and statutory provisions, the situation of persons with disabilities on the ground is generally very different.[33] A survey done by the Public Service Commission reveals that, as of 2014, less than 1 per cent of members appointed in the public sector were persons with disabilities. This was despite Article 54(2)'s requirement that the State should ensure that the numbers do not go below 5 per cent.[34] In terms of reasonable accommodation, it is also reported that the public transport sector still poses a big challenge to persons with disabilities as most of the public service vehicles are privately owned and are not disability friendly.[35] This contravenes the Article 54(1)(c) requirement that persons with disabilities are entitled 'to reasonable access to all places, [and] public transport'.

Such situations show that the constitutional entrenchment of affirmative action provisions alone cannot be the panacea for many of the inequality problems in Kenya without constitutionalism, the need to internalise and live by the dictates of the Constitution.[36] There is therefore a need for positive intervention by Parliament, the judiciary and other stakeholders in championing the implementation of laws and policies that advance these affirmative action measures so that they do not become mere pipedreams. This includes a need for proper management and disbursement of the National Development Fund for Persons with Disabilities so that it caters for a diverse range of those who need it. One positive step is the recent policy developed by the Public Service Commission in complying with Article 54(1)(a) on ensuring access to facilities for persons with disabilities. This policy requires all public service institutions to 'Advertise available job vacancies in a format accessible to persons with disabilities including using

[32] Persons with Disabilities Act No. 14 of 2003, Laws of Kenya.

[33] See *Union of Domestic, Hotels, Educational Institutions, Hospitals and Allied Workers v Association for the Physically Disabled of Kenya* [2015] eKLR.

[34] Public Service Commission, *Diversity Policy for the Public Service* (Nairobi, The Government Printer, 2016) 3.

[35] See PA Nyagudi, 'Overview of the Current Policies, Legislation and Programmes for Persons with Disabilities in Kenya' in *Launch of PWD Web Portal and e-Accessibility Workshop for Persons with Disabilities* (Laico Regency, Nairobi: National Council for Persons with Disabilities, 2012); and Kenya National Bureau of Statistics, *Kenya National Survey for Persons with Disabilities – Main Report* (2008) xvi.

[36] HWO Okoth-Ogendo, 'Constitutions without Constitutionalism: Reflections on an African Political Paradox' in D Greenberg, S Katz and S Wheatley (eds), *Constitutionalism and Democracy: Transitions in the Contemporary World* (Oxford, Oxford University Press, 1993) 66.

established Government channels, print, large print, Braille, television, radio and the internet'.[37] Such facilitative measures ensure that job openings or educational opportunities reach diverse persons with disabilities, such as the visually impaired and hard of hearing.

D. Affirmative Action Provisions on the Youth

Article 260 of the Constitution defines the youth as all individuals in Kenya who are aged between 18 and 35 years. Article 55 recognises the youth as a special group requiring protection. It obliges the State to take affirmative action measures touching on the youth to ensure that they

(a) access relevant education and training;
(b) have opportunities to associate, be represented and participate in political, social, economic and other spheres of life;
(c) access employment; and
(d) are protected from harmful cultural practices and exploitation.

Article 55 confronts the reality that the youth in Kenya have numerical strength but are not adequately represented in the national, political and socio-economic development processes in the country. Kenya also has a high rate of youth unemployment.[38] During the Constitution drafting stages, a summary of people's submissions observed that the youth get a raw deal in governance, being 'represented by old people who do not understand their problems'; hence the need for reserved seats for the youth in Parliament.[39] This has been realised in Article 98(1)(c) of the Constitution, which provides that the Senate should consist of, inter alia, 'two members, being one man and one woman, representing the youth'. Article 97(1)(c) also reserves seats for youth representatives in the National Assembly. Article 100(a) then provides a general principle, similar to that in Article 55(b), requiring the government to enact legislation to promote the representation of the youth alongside other marginalised groups in Parliament.[40]

In terms of affirmative action measures to ensure that the youth access relevant education and training, the aforementioned National Government Affirmative Action Fund provides bursaries and scholarships for the youth.[41] In relation to representation in the economic field, the Youth Enterprise Development Fund

[37] Public Service Commission (n 34) 10.

[38] Y Ghai and J Cottrell, *Kenya's Constitution: An Instrument for Change* (Nairobi, Katiba Institute, 2011) 61.

[39] Constitution of Kenya Review Commission, *The Final Report of the Constitution of Kenya Review Commission. Approved for issue at the 95th Plenary Meeting held on 10 February 2005* (2005) 103, 161 and 396.

[40] These include women, persons with disabilities, ethnic and other minorities, and marginalised communities.

[41] See n 14.

managed by the Ministry of Public Service, Youth and Gender Affairs provides loans and business development support to youth-owned businesses. The fund was adopted in 2007, before the promulgation of the 2010 Constitution, but is seen as a furthering of affirmative action mandates in the Constitution.[42] However, this fund, like the others mentioned, is still marred by corruption.[43]

E. Affirmative Action Provisions on Ethnic Minorities and Other Marginalised Communities

Article 56 specifically obliges the State to put in place affirmative action programmes for minorities and marginalised groups designed to ensure that they

(a) participate and are represented in governance and other spheres of life;
(b) are provided special opportunities in educational and economic fields;
(c) are provided special opportunities for access to employment;
(d) develop their cultural values, languages and practices; and
(e) have reasonable access to water, health services and infrastructure.

The affirmative action programmes stipulated above are meant to ensure the participation of previously excluded minorities and marginalised groups in governance and other spheres of life. In terms of political representation, Article 100(d) and (e) additionally oblige Parliament to enact legislation to promote representation of ethnic and other minorities and marginalised communities in Parliament. Further, Articles 174(e) and 177(1)(c) put protection and promotion of the interests and rights of minorities and marginalised communities as part of the key objects of devolved county government.

In addition to the requirement in Article 56(b) that special opportunities be given to minorities and marginalised communities in the economic field, and in Article 56(e) that they be given access to basic services, Article 204 creates an Equalisation Fund for marginalised areas. The fund is meant to provide basic services including water, roads, health facilities and electricity to marginalised areas to the extent necessary to bring the quality of those services in these areas to the level generally enjoyed by the rest of the nation, so far as possible.

On employment in the public service sector, Article 232(1)(h) and (i) require the representation of Kenya's diverse communities and the affording of equal opportunities for appointment, training and advancement for members of all ethnic groups. The same is required in the allocation of political parties' seats (Article 90(2)(c)), composition of the Defence Forces (Article 241(4)), National Police Service (Article 246(4)), National Executive (Article 130(2)), and in appointments to Commissions and Independent Offices (Article 250(4)). These provisions

[42] www.youthfund.go.ke.
[43] Jipeshughuli, 'Why Aren't Kenya's Affirmative Action Funds Working?' *Jipeshughuli* (Nairobi, 6 March 2017).

complement the Article 56(c) mandate that minorities and marginalised groups be given special opportunities in access to employment.

Nevertheless, as with the other affirmative action provisions, implementation of the above provisions touching on minorities and marginalised groups is still a challenge. For instance, the National Cohesion and Integration Commission's 2011 survey reported that ethnic inequalities are still prevalent in the public sector, and particularly that

> [o]ver 50 per cent of Kenya's ethnic groups are only marginally represented in the Civil Service – the country's largest employer. Only 20 out of over 40 listed Kenyan communities are statistically visible in the Civil Service. Some 23 communities have less than one per cent presence in the Civil Service.[44]

In its 2016 report, the position remained largely unchanged, with the six biggest ethnic communities in the country (the Kikuyu, Kalenjin, Luhya, Luo, Kamba and Kisii) making up 79.9 per cent of government parastatal employment, leaving only 20.1 per cent of opportunities to the over 36 other ethnic communities.[45]

The need for affirmative action to ensure inclusion of persons from minority and marginalised communities in governance was considered in *John Mining Temoi & Another v Governor of Bungoma County & 17 Others*.[46] In the case, the petitioners contended, inter alia, that the selection process of chief officers in Bungoma County, one of Kenya's 47 counties, failed to apply the requirements in Articles 56 and 232 of the Constitution that appointments in public service should reflect the ethnic diversity of the people of Kenya. The petitioners specifically complained that members of the Bongomek community, a marginalised ethnic group in Bungoma County, were not included in the list of nominees despite one candidate who hailed from this community having been shortlisted and interviewed. Thus, they stated that the County's Public Services Board failed to apply Articles 56 and 232 of the Constitution, which, they rightly observed, require the application of 'affirmative action measures to ensure representation of marginalized communities in appointive posts'.[47]

It was averred that the Bongomek community was one of the five main tribes residing in Bungoma County but was a minority ethnic group since it consisted of only 3,704 individuals out of a county population of 2 million. Yet, while other ethnic communities were adequately represented in the governance of the County, there was not even a single representative from the Bongomek tribe.[48] The matter had been raised before the Bungoma County Assembly but was not tabled for debate.[49] Mabeya J agreed with the claimants that the respondents' actions were

[44] Quoted in Public Service Commission (n 34) 2.

[45] National Cohesion and Integration Commission (NCIC), *Ethnic Audit of Parastatals in Kenya* (Nairobi, NCIC, 2016) 24.

[46] *John Mining Temoi & Another v Governor of Bungoma County & 17 Others* [2014] eKLR.

[47] ibid [10] and [11].

[48] ibid [66].

[49] ibid [79].

an affront to constitutional guarantees in relation to non-discrimination in public appointments, affirmative action, and the obligation to reasonably accommodate marginalised communities. He held that the Bongomek is a marginalised group in Bungoma County and should be given due consideration in County governance appointments. Mabeya J thus ordered the Bungoma County Public Services Board to appoint the shortlisted and interviewed member of the Bongomek community.[50] This case shows that, to some extent, Kenyan courts are on the right track in applying affirmative action to ensure inclusion of persons from minority and marginalised groups in governance.

II. Aims of Affirmative Action as Evident from Constitutional Provisions

The constitutional provisions discussed above explicitly and implicitly reveal the various aims that affirmative action measures in the Constitution hope to achieve. Article 27(6) of the Constitution is instructive as to the principal aim of affirmative action. It requires the State to come up with 'affirmative action programmes and policies designed to *redress any disadvantage suffered by individuals or groups because of past discrimination*' (emphasis added). Article 260 of the Constitution emphasises the ameliorative aim of affirmative action by stating that it 'includes any measures designed to overcome or ameliorate an inequality or the systemic denial or infringement of a right or fundamental freedom'. This aim can also be found in the Final Report of the Constitution of Kenya Review Commission, which preceded the Constitution. In the report, the Commission noted that during the review process, affirmative action was seen as a direct response to historical injustices and prevailing concerns of inequality. These included the need for inclusion of disadvantaged groups that had been excluded in one way or another from the social, political and economic spheres.[51]

The report states that such inequalities demanded affirmative action measures that were capable of dealing with a wide range of interrelated issues: 'remedying historical injustices; providing level playing ground and equal opportunities to all; promoting inclusive participation by all in decision making; [and] providing special assistance to the marginalized areas and communities'.[52] These aims, reflected in the various types of affirmative action provisions in the Constitution, can fittingly be categorised under Fredman's four-tier dimensions of equality.[53] First, the recognition dimension which relates to respect for human dignity and worth in addressing stigma and stereotyping against a certain group. Under this

[50] ibid [72] and [84].
[51] Constitution of Kenya Review Commission (n 39) 100.
[52] ibid.
[53] S Fredman, *Discrimination Law* (2nd edn, Oxford, Oxford University Press, 2011) 25–33.

heading we can include aims like providing role models for members of disadvantaged groups. This helps remove hidden obstacles to their advancement, which manifest in the form of clouded perceptions of what they can or cannot do because of societal stigma and stereotyping.

Second, the redistributive dimension, whose main goal is to break the cycle of disadvantage through an egalitarian distribution of jobs, elective positions and resources, among other things. This includes measures such as numerical targets and quotas in public service jobs. Third, the participative dimension, which relates to granting marginalised groups a political voice and, to a large extent, seeks to advance social inclusion. Affirmative action measures guaranteeing seats in public elective and appointive bodies to women, persons with disabilities, persons from marginalised communities and the youth fall under this dimension. And fourth, the transformative dimension, whose purpose is to dismantle systemic inequalities and accommodate difference. It goes beyond affirmative action changing the gender or ethnic composition in various fields as it requires 'substantial change in the economic, social and cultural model which is at the root of the inequalities'.[54] This includes aims such as making reasonable adjustments for persons with disabilities and social inclusion through the granting of social funds for the economic empowerment of disadvantaged groups.

These aims can be further collapsed into three broader categories of affirmative action as: (i) a corrective measure; (ii) providing role models; and (iii) aiming to achieve social inclusion. These are further discussed below.

A. Affirmative Action's Corrective Aim

Ideally, because Article 27(6) requires the application of affirmative action measures to redress past disadvantage, this could be taken as implying that such measures are a bridge from the past. From this perspective, affirmative action can be interpreted as a form of restorative justice, restitution or a way of granting reparations for past injustices. However, there is a need to unpack and clarify how this aim should be understood in the Kenyan context. To be clear and critical of this aim, some of the US literature is helpful and apt in illuminating the underlying assumptions and shortfalls of this rationale. Taylor, for example, refers to the corrective aim of affirmative action as backward looking.[55] Such a backward-looking reparation-focused approach requires difference consciousness to address prevailing inequality, whether gender, ethnic or age related. Conceptualising affirmative action measures in this way means that they will principally fall under substantive equality's approval of differential treatment to show equal concern and respect.

[54] *Kalanke v Freie Hansestadt Bremen* [1995] IRLR 660 (ECJ), 665.
[55] R Taylor, 'Rawlsian Affirmative Action' (2009) 119(3) *Ethics* 476, 478.

The converse assumption is that formal equality is static and presumes that the initial starting point was fair, which makes it a static approach that assumes the past is invisible and does not have ongoing effects. This explains its insistence on ethnic and gender blindness.

Nevertheless, the use of a backward- and forward-looking dichotomy can be quite confusing. If we insist that affirmative action is strictly backward looking, we leave it open to criticism such as the one pointed out by Ackerman, that reparations only apply to generations affected by past discrimination before the playing field was levelled, and not subsequently.[56] This would, for instance, lead to the view that if the new generation of women are no longer explicitly denied the right to run for leadership positions, they can freely and equally participate in democratic politics.

When this type of backward-looking stance is solely considered, the conclusion would then be that gender quotas should not be applied. If we conceive of affirmative action in this way – as compensation to specific individuals or groups from a certain generation alone – we move back to a delictual or tort idea of wrongfulness, which affirmative action has been moving away from. This is quite a narrow and simplistic view of the situation that fails to consider the actual reality on the ground. In Kenya, de facto social practices are still far from translating equality laws and policies to reality. Hence, in these recent times, Taylor observes that affirmative action's corrective aim rightfully recognises that ethnic bias or sexist legacies may 'continue in the form of systematic discrimination sustained by hateful doctrines and stereotypes'. These then 'act to further disadvantage historically burdened groups and make a mockery of "strict compliance"'.[57]

The legacies of past discrimination are particularly enduring in the private domain and act as obstacles to the social, political and economic participation of affected groups. In many instances, the crude reality is that, despite a change in the law to guarantee equality of opportunity, the achievement of, for instance, de facto gender equality in practice takes time to achieve.[58] Hence the need for a conceptualisation of affirmative action corrective measures that is not tied to the strictly backward-looking approach explained here. This fact has been acknowledged by Wilfred Lichuma, the previous chairperson of the Kenyan National Gender and Equality Commission, a quasi-governmental body created under Article 59 of the Constitution to oversee the inclusion and non-discrimination of disadvantaged groups. In relation to the continued legacies of sexism and patriarchy in Kenya, she observes that 'Change of mindset is a long-term strategy for our society to appreciate that women have equal capacities in leadership as men'.[59] Women continue

[56] B Ackerman, 'Beyond Carolene Products' (1985) 98(4) *Harvard Law Review* 713, 744.

[57] Taylor (n 55) 482 and 486. See also J Rawls, *A Theory of Justice* (Cambridge, MA, The Belknap Press of Harvard University Press, 1971) 215.

[58] F Raday, 'Gender and Democratic Citizenship: The Impact of CEDAW' (2012) 10(2) *International Journal of Constitutional Law* 512, 515, 517 and 527.

[59] Sunday Nation Team, 'Ask your Question: Wilfred Lichuma', *The Daily Nation* (Nairobi, 4 May 2017).

to be inhibited from participating in politics and other spheres of life because of stigma and socially ingrained stereotypes of what they can or cannot do, which then create obstacles for them.[60]

An example of this are the reasons behind the failure of Parliament to pass the Two-Thirds Gender Rule Laws (Amendment) Bill 2015. This bill was meant to, inter alia, give effect to the rule in Article 27(8) of the Constitution that not more than two-thirds of members in elective and appointive bodies should be of the same gender. It is reported that 'Political intrigue, chauvinism and apathy contributed to the shooting down [of the] bill', which would rightly grant women more seats in Parliament.[61] Many of the male parliamentarians boycotted voting and gave patriarchal and sexist reasons for their refusal to vote. Some of the sentiments included claims that other politicians would nominate their 'girlfriends', that women would be given 'free seats' diminishing quality of representation, and that women representatives are just 'flower girls' and the positions are a waste of money, insinuating that female politicians do not contribute much to parliamentary business.[62] These sentiments show that patriarchy and sexism are still pervasive and so are gender stereotypes which continue to disadvantage women, despite clear provisions on gender equality in the Constitution.

Moreover, as stated in Chapter 4, women in Kenya can be referred to as a politically ineffective majority. This is because, despite making up almost 51 per cent of the population, women's political participation has been encumbered by 'structural impediments that unconstitutionally impair [their] bargaining position in the ongoing pluralist process'.[63] The 21 per cent representation of women in Parliament after the 2017 general election means that female politicians are largely ineffective in voting against proposed legislation disadvantageous to women, as well as voting in laws that aim to redress women's disadvantage.[64] Yet, as Young propounds, the most effective way to both block discrimination and redress disadvantage caused by past discrimination is through political participation.[65] Indeed, 'the political branches of government are the prime movers of policy change through law'.[66]

Thus, affirmative action's corrective aim seeks to dislodge women's disadvantage by putting in place policies for their effective representation in politics.

[60] United Nations General Assembly, *Convention on the Elimination of All Forms of Discrimination Against Women*, 18 December 1979, United Nations Treaty Series, vol 1249, 13.

[61] W Ayaga and J Ng'etich, 'Why Kenyan MPs shot down gender bill', *Standard Digital* (Nairobi, 6 May 2016).

[62] See ibid; F Oluoch, 'As Kenya election approaches, two-thirds gender rule hands over parliament', *The EastAfrican* (Nairobi, 28 April 2017).

[63] Ackerman (n 56) 721; Ch 4, text to nn 91–93.

[64] F Oluoch, 'More women elected in Kenya, but the numbers still fall short', *The EastAfrican* (Nairobi, 12 August 2017).

[65] See IM Young, 'Equality of Whom? Social Groups and Judgments of Injustice' (2001) 9 *Journal of Political Philosophy* 1, 4; IM Young, *Justice and the Politics of Difference* (New Jersey, Princeton University Press, 1990) 56.

[66] M Carcien, 'Rawls and Reparations' (2010) 15 *Michigan Journal of Race and Law* 267, 269.

Women's presence in Parliament can then lead to structural change. Accordingly, by having an effective political voice, women parliamentarians can use this power to champion the removal of discriminatory policies and the putting in place of legislation that will have a positive impact on the lives of all women, for instance in relation to favourable policies on maternal health and childcare.[67]

In the Kenyan context, affirmative action's corrective aim should thus be broadly conceived and the best way to go about this is by first doing away with the strict backward- and forward-looking approaches. The corrective aim should not only apply to individuals who were directly affected by the previous discriminatory status quo but should also apply to those who continue to feel the effects of such disadvantage because of the slow pace of achieving de facto social change.[68]

B. Affirmative Action's Aim of Providing Role Models

It is hard to explain the low numbers of women parliamentarians in Kenya because, absent obstacles, the eligibility requirements for contesting a seat in national elections are fairly achievable. Section 22(1)(b) of the Elections Act provides that a person is qualified if he or she 'holds a certificate, diploma or other post secondary school qualification acquired after a period of at least three months study, recognized by the relevant Ministry'.[69] Additionally, a person must have a degree from a university that is recognised in Kenya for election as 'President, Deputy President, county Governor or deputy county Governor'.[70] According to 2014 statistics, the percentage of boys and girls pursuing secondary education was 53.6 per cent and 46.4 per cent respectively, and for those in universities (both national and private) 59.9 per cent and 40.5 per cent.[71] The numbers are not so disproportionate, especially for secondary education. These statistics therefore illustrate that if this trend is an enduring one, there is a 'critical mass' of women with secondary and university education who qualify for elective political seats. Yet there are still only a few women politicians. The inequality of outcome through the under-representation of women shows that 'something is blocking the way'.[72] In Kenyan society this has been largely attributed to the patriarchal nature of society, which devalues the voice of women.

Stroud observes that affirmative action measures like gender quotas are a helpful remedy to this state of affairs.[73] She rightly argues that affirmative action helps do away with 'the regrettable tendency to place blinkers on one's own

[67] Fredman, *Discrimination Law* (n 53) 264.
[68] See Raday (n 58).
[69] Elections Act No. 24 of 2011, Laws of Kenya.
[70] ibid s 22(2).
[71] Kenya National Bureau of Statistics, *Kenya Facts and Figures 2014* (2014) 11.
[72] A Phillips, 'Defending Equality of Outcome' (2004) 12(1) *Journal of Political Philosophy* 1, 8.
[73] S Stroud, 'The Aim of Affirmative Action' (1999) 25(3) *Social Theory and Practice* 385, 386.

career aspirations'.[74] This challenge occurs when an excluded disadvantaged group starts internalising social stereotypes of it and ends up accepting rather than challenging such 'false consciousness'. To explain this further, Stroud uses the example of gender stereotyping on girls' aspirations. She puts it thus:

> [F]or years many girls interested in the medical field never truly contemplated the option of striving to become a doctor: girls are *nurses*, not doctors. Such failures genuinely to consider a whole range of career options deemed appropriate only for men have severely constrained the horizons of many girls and young women over the years.[75]

The 'blinkers condition' is a helpful analogy in the Kenyan context that elucidates how social stereotypes relating to various disadvantaged groups have affected these groups' participation in various fields. It also helps us understand the value of role models created through affirmative action measures like reserving political seats for persons from under-represented groups. Ensuring that historically under-represented groups have representatives in various public roles and fields creates role models that individuals from that group can look up to. It makes them see that it is possible to enter a profession they were previously made to think they cannot. This can hasten the purging of harmful narratives inculcated in our society that a certain group of people are not suited for a particular profession. This argument is supported by Fredman, who points out that 'the provision of role models operates on the self-perception of excluded groups, piercing stereotypes and giving them the self-confidence to move into non-traditional positions'.[76]

Illustrating the gains of this aim of affirmative action in Kenya so far, the 2017 general elections were a trendsetter and full of many firsts. The number of women vying for elective seats was substantially higher than in previous years and several female contenders beat their male opponents.[77] In the National Assembly, the number of elected female parliamentarians increased from 16 in 2013 to 22 in 2017, with some counties electing women for the first time in the history of Kenyan elections. In the Senate, no women were elected in 2013, but 2017 saw three women clinching the highly competitive Senate seats. This was also the case in the gubernatorial race, where three women were elected governors, whereas none was elected in the 2013 elections.[78] This shows that gender quotas, which were first applied in the 2013 general elections, might have played a role in emboldening women to vie for competitive and highly coveted political seats. This example shows the importance of role models in doing away with the blinkers condition.

[74] ibid 389.

[75] ibid 386, 388 and 389.

[76] Fredman, *Discrimination Law* (n 53) 268.

[77] See E Wainaina, '22 women for Parliament as regions elect first female MPs', *The Daily Nation* (Nairobi, 11 August 2017); A Shiundi, 'Factsheet: Kenya's new parliament numbers' africacheck.org/factsheets/factsheet-kenyas-new-parliament-numbers/.

[78] ibid.

C. Affirmative Action's Aim of Social Inclusion

An example of affirmative action measures that aim to achieve social inclusion are those in Article 232(h) and (i) of the Constitution. These provisions require the representation of Kenya's diverse communities and afford equal opportunities for appointment, training and advancement for men and women, members of all ethnic groups, and persons with disabilities in all levels of public service. The aim of social inclusion justifies redistribution-oriented affirmative action measures meant to redress 'disadvantages that arise from being excluded from shared opportunities enjoyed by others'.[79] Such social exclusion is said to be mainly attributable to unequal power relations in social relations, which lead to poverty; deprivation; exclusion from political participation, receiving credit, or employment; or some other form of disadvantage.[80]

The socially excluded in Kenya include women, persons with disabilities, ethnic minorities, indigenous peoples and the poor. These groups are often discriminated against because of their status and under-represented in the social, political and economic fields. This dovetails with the argument that discrimination frequently results in some form of social exclusion;[81] more so because those who are discriminated against 'are denied the opportunity to participate in the mechanisms offered by society through which they may establish meaning for their lives, the connections of a community, and a sense of self-respect'.[82]

Indeed, one proposed definition of social exclusion refers to it as 'the exclusion of individuals due to their membership of particular groups that suffer discrimination'.[83] The World Bank also notes that 'Discrimination on the basis of gender, ethnicity, race, religion, or social status can lead to social exclusion and lock people into long-term poverty traps'.[84] These definitions show that discrimination is a key cause of social exclusion. In recognition of the need for social inclusion of the excluded groups listed above, the 2010 Constitution makes them the main beneficiaries of affirmative action, with the addition of the elderly and the youth, as pointed out earlier. Such measures provide an excellent framework to confront the legacy of social exclusion and marginalisation in the country.

Collins defines social inclusion as 'a theory of how society can be integrated and harmonious …, the theory is that if everyone participates fully in society, they are

[79] A Sen, *Social Exclusion: Concept, Application and Scrutiny* (Manila, Asian Development Bank, 2000) 44.

[80] See ibid; S Khan, E Combaz and E Fraser, *Social exclusion: Topic guide* (Revised edn, Birmingham, University of Birmingham, 2015) 3; S Hickey and A du Toit, *Adverse Incorporation, Social Exclusion and Chronic Poverty* (Working Paper No. 81, Chronic Poverty Research Centre, University of Manchester, June 2007) 4–5.

[81] H Collins, 'Discrimination, Equality and Social Inclusion' (2003) 66(1) *MLR* 16, 21.

[82] ibid 29.

[83] Khan, Combaz and Fraser (n 80) 3.

[84] World Bank, *World Development Report 2000/01: Attacking Poverty* (Washington DC, Oxford University Press for the World Bank, 2000) 117.

less likely to become alienated from the community and will conform to its rules and laws'.[85] Hence, aside from seeking to grant justice for the socially excluded, social inclusion also seeks to create a stable society.[86] This was recognised by Ngugi J in *Centre for Rights, Education and Awareness (CREAW) v Attorney General & Another*.[87] In the case, she observed that at the core of Kenya's 2010 Constitution

> is the belief that there can only be real progress in society if all citizens participate fully in their governance, and that all, male and female, persons with disabilities and all hitherto marginalised and excluded groups get a chance at the table.[88]

All in all, the aim of social inclusion is important in legitimising the application of affirmative action in three ways. First, as Collins argues, it is valuable because of its insistence 'that wherever the line is drawn [on the minimum acceptable level for material and non-material goods], everyone should be raised to that level'.[89] This offers a strong justification for affirmative action's deviation from the equal treatment principle. Social inclusion necessitates affirmative action policies where it is established that 'preference or priority [is] to be given to members of a particular group, if the group can be classified as socially excluded' from social goods or opportunities enjoyed by others.[90] Therefore, social inclusion justifies differential treatment through application of affirmative action measures that can effectively remedy disadvantage caused by social exclusion.

Second, the aim of social inclusion is helpful in applying affirmative action as it does not require comparators, which has been a problematic aspect of anti-discrimination laws. Let us take, for instance, a restitution argument that gender quotas in favour of women are desirable because women have historically been treated less favourably than men in politics, due to discriminatory laws and patriarchal societal norms. This claim could be opposed by men from indigenous communities who may argue that they are also comparably disadvantaged politically, leading to what some have called 'Oppression Olympics'.[91] This describes 'intergroup competition and victimhood', pitting one disadvantaged group against another in a zero-sum game kind of ideology, rather than a solidarity approach – we can all seek representation or benefits.[92]

Invoking social inclusion would not encounter such contestations because it does not require comparators. According to Collins, it only 'asks for proof that the rule or practice tends to reinforce the exclusion of an individual member of an excluded group or most members of the excluded group',[93] adding that, in this case

[85] Collins (n 81) 24.
[86] ibid.
[87] *CREAW v Attorney General & Another* [2015] eKLR (HC) [112].
[88] ibid [1].
[89] Collins (n 81) 24.
[90] ibid 40.
[91] See Ange-Marie Hancock, *Solidarity Politics for Millennials: A Guide to Ending the Oppression Olympics* (New York, NY, Palgrave-Macmillan, 2011).
[92] ibid 3–6.
[93] Collins (n 81) 32.

also, 'comparison can supply evidence of exclusionary effect, but it is not essential to proof'.[94]

Hickey and du Troit add that the language of social inclusion 'can help to socially embed the analysis of … discrimination and show how social exclusion based on identity is linked not simply to "prejudice" and "attitudes" but to broader political and political economy processes'.[95] It therefore makes a strong and more watertight case for the application of affirmative action measures like gender quotas to promote inclusion rather than justification using comparators.

Third, the aim of social inclusion legitimises the application of affirmative action measures as it promotes diversity in the workplace, educational institutions and decision-making bodies. This then brings together viewpoints and outlooks from people with diverse perspectives and experiences, enriching interactions and enabling decision making to be truly conscious of the experiences of all groups of people in the polity, particularly the socially excluded.[96]

These three broad aims derived from affirmative action measures in the Constitution therefore attest to their legitimacy and importance.

III. Determining the Beneficiaries – Principle of Genuine Need

Having set out the constitutional provisions on affirmative action and their aims, which legitimise their application, this section interrogates the question of how to delineate beneficiaries. There have been concerns that affirmative action measures can be over-inclusive – helping persons in a stipulated vulnerable beneficiary group not disadvantaged by past discrimination – and under-inclusive – excluding individuals outside a stipulated beneficiary group who have nevertheless suffered disadvantage. Therefore, it is important to determine where the line should be drawn in delineating beneficiaries. However, 'while drawing the line, it should be ensured that it does not result in taking away with one hand what is given by the other'.[97] This involves being able to distinguish between different types of need and the diverse approaches that should be taken to ensure that the affirmative action measure applied truly corresponds with the *need* being addressed. Hence, in determining beneficiaries, we also need to interrogate whether there is a difference in delineating beneficiaries for affirmative action measures that grant monetary or material benefits, and those that seek to achieve social inclusion by enhancing representation. These are the issues that this section analyses.

[94] ibid.
[95] Hickey and du Toit (n 80) 18.
[96] Fredman, *Discrimination Law* (n 53) 266–67.
[97] *Indra Sawhney v Union of India* AIR 1993 SC 477 [86] (*Indra Sawhney*).

A. What Does the Principle of Genuine Need Mean?

As already pointed out, Article 27(7) of the Constitution establishes the principle of genuine need.[98] This principle requires that an affirmative action measure should *only* benefit those within a disadvantaged group who really need it. For instance, Murray explains that real need in this case would mean 'Even if a student belongs to a marginalised community, if he or she comes from a wealthy family or went to an excellent school, there is no genuine need and affirmative action is not justified'.[99] Therefore, this principle creates a workable corrective approach to the over-inclusiveness and under-inclusiveness problem of affirmative action.[100]

The concept is similar to the 'creamy layer' principle developed by the Indian courts. Khaitan explains that 'The metaphor alludes to the layer of cream that floats to the top when boiled milk begins to cool down, with a consistency different enough from the remaining milk to be easily separable'.[101] This concept has been largely developed by the Indian courts in the context of reservations for 'socially and educationally backward classes of citizens' (OBCs).[102] For example, in *Ashoka Kumar Thakur v Union of India*, the then Chief Justice of India, KG Balakrishnan, stated in relation to this concept that 'To fulfil the conditions and to find out truly what is socially and educationally backward class, the exclusion of "creamy layer" is essential'.[103] This had been explained earlier in *Indra Sawhney v Union of India*.[104] Here, the Court observed that where some of the members of a backward class 'are far too advanced socially (which in the context, necessarily means economically and, may also mean educationally) the connecting thread between them and the remaining class snaps … [their] exclusion benefits the truly backward'.[105] This meant, as Fredman opines, that 'the definition of the beneficiary class must correspond with the purpose of the provision, namely to advance those who are disadvantaged'.[106]

[98] Text to nn 17–18.

[99] Murray, *Beginner's Guide* (n 17) 25.

[100] C Murray, 'Kenya's 2010 Constitution' (2013) 61 *Neue Folge Band Jahrbuch des öffentlichen Rechts* 747, 764–65.

[101] Khaitan (n 11) 224, fn 16.

[102] See Constitution of India, Art15(5) which provides:

> Nothing in this article or in sub-clause (g) of clause (1) of article 19 shall prevent the State from making any special provision, by law, for the advancement of any socially and educationally backward classes of citizens or for the Scheduled Castes or the Scheduled Tribes in so far as such special provisions relate to their admission to educational institutions including private educational institutions, whether aided or unaided by the State, other than the minority educational institutions referred to in clause (1) of article 30.

[103] *Ashoka Kumar Thakur v Union of India*, Writ Petition (civil) 265 of 2006 (Date of Judgment 10/04/2008) [149].

[104] *Indra Sawhney* (n 97).

[105] ibid [86]. However, this does not apply to Scheduled Castes and Tribes.

[106] Fredman, *A Comparative Study of the Anti-Discrimination and Equality Laws* (n 5) 68.

However, according to Murray, besides the exclusion of the 'creamy layer' approach taken by Indian courts, the principle of genuine need in the Kenyan Constitution has other functions:

> One assumes that the provision is a response to the widespread phenomenon of the 'creamy layer', a problem common to affirmative action programmes but particularly evident in India where a small elite in disadvantaged groups is believed to reap most of the benefits. The question is whether a reference to need is the appropriate corrective to these problems of affirmative action. It is, for instance, unclear whose or what need it refers to. At first blush it may be taken to mean that individuals who are not personally disadvantaged should not benefit from affirmative action. Thus[,] children of wealthy members of a disadvantaged group should not be eligible for special consideration in university admissions. Another reading, however, would simply require affirmative active [*sic*] to be genuinely required (needed). This reading would turn the provision into a form of necessity clause, heightening the bar for special programmes but it would, for instance, allow an affirmative action programme that gave access to the bench to individuals from minority groups who are not themselves 'needy' in the usual social and economic sense but whose presence on the bench would fill a social need for a representative judiciary.[107]

Three conclusions as to the meaning of genuine need can be extracted from Murray's statement. The first meaning is in relation to the 'creamy layer' phenomenon, where 'need' is taken to implicate an element of economic or material disadvantage. This reading of genuine need in Article 27(7) is supported by Ghai and Cottrell, who point out that 'almost every group that is generally disadvantaged has some members who have done well – often called "the creamy layer"'.[108] Emphasising the desirability of economic disadvantage in proving genuine need, they state that 'It is not fair if scholarships and training programmes are monopolised by these people [those who are economically well off] – and the Constitution tries to prevent this from happening'.[109]

Murray, however, seems to give a word of caution that the notion of genuine need should not be interpreted as defeating a legitimate (genuinely required) affirmative action programme aimed at filling a non-material social need. An example is the *need* to achieve social inclusion by enhancing representation of marginalised groups or creating role models from under-represented groups. Hence, the second meaning of genuine need is that an affirmative action measure should fill a social gap such as guaranteeing social inclusion to a group that has been excluded because of past discrimination. One example Murray alludes to is a measure aimed at increasing representation of persons from minority groups on the bench, even if they are not 'needy' in the economic sense. This points to the different aims of affirmative action discussed in the previous section, such as social inclusion, representativeness and supplying role models from minority groups,

[107] Murray, 'Kenya's 2010 Constitution' (n 100) 764–65.
[108] Ghai and Cottrell (n 38) 45.
[109] ibid.

which are socially needed but are not necessarily based on economic disadvantage. Thus, the aim of an affirmative action programme and the type of disadvantage (need) it seeks to redress will determine whether it should be checked by the concept of genuine need.

The third possible meaning that Murray identifies is that, in selecting an affirmative action programme, the government should ensure that the programme is genuinely needed, requiring a high justification threshold.

B. Is there a Difference in Delineating Beneficiaries for Material and Non-material Affirmative Action Benefits?

In determining genuine need, there is clearly a difference in delineating beneficiaries for affirmative action measures that grant material benefits like economic assistance and those that give non-monetary benefits such as social inclusion or representation. In the former instance, especially when dealing with affirmative action measures like education bursaries, which are mostly based on economic need, it is relatively easy to determine what genuine need is. However, in the latter case, when it comes to the distribution of socially valued positions, it becomes harder to determine what this is.

Indeed, under non-monetary affirmative action benefits, some issues are easier to navigate than others, depending on the rationale. Two scenarios best explain this argument. The first scenario relates to affirmative action measures to fill the social *need* for female role models in higher education. In Kenya this is being achieved through the setting of lower secondary school national examination cut-off points required to join universities for female students.[110] The determination of beneficiaries for this non-material affirmative action benefit is largely uncontroversial but we should not discount the possibility of it facing the dilemmas discussed below.

The second scenario is, however, more complicated. It touches on the need for diversity, and regional and ethnic balance as criteria in the distribution of public service jobs in Kenya. In appointments to public service, alongside the consideration of fair competition and merit in Article 232(1)(g) of the Constitution, Article 232(1)(h) requires that such appointments consider the 'representation of Kenya's diverse communities'. Article 232(1)(i) further provides that selection should afford equal opportunities for appointment to men and women, members of all ethnic groups and persons with disabilities. The *need* here is to give individuals from disadvantaged groups equal opportunities to thrive and participate actively in public life by putting in place affirmative action measures that promote

[110] See Advance Africa, *Kenya Universities and Colleges Central Placement Service* (KUCCPS) (2015). The Joint Admissions Board in Kenya set the cut-off point for placement to degree programmes at B (60 points) for male candidates and B minus (58 points) for female candidates.

diversity and representativeness. This is in recognition of the illegitimate exclusion they may have faced in the past, arising from circumstances beyond their control.[111] Such circumstances include having a physical disability or belonging to a marginalised ethnic group.

However, determining the persons to benefit from a broad non-material affirmative action measure that applies to different disadvantaged groups is a challenging exercise because there will often be conflicting demands. For example, the *need* to grant equal opportunities to various disadvantaged groups gives rise to the dilemma as to whether to appoint a rural man or an urban woman, both of whom are from groups that have suffered past inequalities but such disadvantage has affected them differently.[112] The same applies to individuals from different marginalised ethnic groups.

The various difficulties in applying the non-material *need* for diversity and representativeness can be seen in the case of *Community Advocacy and Awareness Trust & 8 Others v Attorney General*.[113] It involved a dispute over appointments made to the National Gender and Equality Commission established under Article 59 of the Constitution. The main contention was that the President and Prime Minister wrongly and erroneously assigned to some of the nominees for appointment ethnicities and regions to which they were not ordinarily affiliated for the purposes of disqualifying them from appointment.

The selection panel recommended to the President and Prime Minister at the time a list of six interviewed and ranked persons for appointment. The person who was ranked fourth on merit and suitability was selected based on the *need* for regional balance besides competence. The first nominee was bypassed, as the permanent secretary to the Cabinet, concluding that she was Kikuyu, stated that there were three other members of the Commission with the same ethnic background. However, Professor Maria Nzomo (the first-ranked nominee) argued that, even though her mother was Kikuyu, because Kenyan society is patrilineal, she was in fact a Kamba, as this was her father's ethnicity. She further stated that she had since become a Luhya by marriage because her husband was a Luhya from Kenya's Western province, and her normal residence for purposes of determining regional balance was Nairobi.

On the issue of merit, Majanja J rightly held that the President and Prime Minister are not obliged to appoint the first-ranked person nominated to them for appointment as there are other values guiding appointment that need to be considered besides merit.[114] Article 232 of the Constitution lists the other values to be considered as including diversity, regional and ethnic balance, and the need to afford equal opportunities for appointment to men and women, members of

[111] Phillips (n 72) 2 and 4.
[112] See *Federation of Women Lawyers Kenya (FIDA-K) & 5 Others v Attorney General & Another* [2011] eKLR (HC) (*FIDA v AG*) 30.
[113] *Community Advocacy and Awareness Trust & 8 Others v Attorney General* [2012] eKLR (HC).
[114] ibid [93].

all ethnic groups and persons with disabilities. Moreover, according to the Court, all nominees were competent and suitable for appointment apart from the ranking, and thus it was held that the meritocracy argument lacked merit.[115] On the wrongful assignment of ethnicities, Majanja J found that Professor Nzomo could objectively be said to be Kikuyu because of her ethnic parentage, though mixed.[116] He also stated that assigning ethnicities as criteria for selection is a controversial but necessary task in dealing with the deep-rooted ethnic disadvantage in the country.[117] Thus, Majanja J concluded that the choices made were rational, satisfied all the values and achieved the purposes set in the Constitution. He therefore found no discrimination prohibited under Article 27.[118]

The case raises several problems that are encountered in determining who the beneficiaries of affirmative action based on non-material *need* are. In such a case, for example, once a lack of ethnic representation has been identified, should the appointing committee target their advertisement to members of minority ethnic groups only? What about fair competition and merit? Is one's ethnicity patrilineal or matrilineal? What about a cross-ethnic married woman, how is her ethnicity determined? There is also a question as to whose need should be satisfied, is it the need of those who require role models, or the need of the individual beneficiaries? Without a definitive and widespread understanding of issues surrounding ethnicity and representativeness, determining ethnic affiliation raises many complex cultural and political questions. Nevertheless, the concept of genuine need is important as it would require legislation to be as detailed as possible. It can thus be used to advocate for a more targeted distribution plan, which takes into consideration a multiplicity of factors to assess genuine need within the target class(es).

This point implicates the rights of non-beneficiaries and shows us why a justification analysis is essential for affirmative action measures developed under Article 27(6). This is looked at below.

C. The Justification Analysis – Interests of Non-beneficiaries

Affirmative action measures need to be narrowly tailored and well crafted to avoid claims of being overly discriminatory to non-beneficiaries. The principle of genuine need in Article 27(7) ensures that a delicate balance is struck between the rights and interests of beneficiaries and those of non-beneficiaries. This is because it requires that an affirmative action measure be genuinely needed, requiring a high justification threshold as highlighted in the preceding sub-section. Compelling evidence will therefore have to be adduced to prove this, which helps protect the rights of non-beneficiaries.

[115] ibid [96] and [97].
[116] ibid [127].
[117] ibid [124] and [133].
[118] ibid [134].

The Kenyan High Court in *John Kabui Mwai* acknowledged the need for justification of affirmative action measures and added that such justification should be done by examining the larger societal context. It specifically noted that

> [i]t is only by examining the larger context that a court can determine whether differential treatment results in equality or whether, on the other hand, it would be identical treatment which would in the particular context result in inequality or foster disadvantage.[119]

In addition to a consideration of context, the Constitution of Kenya Review Commission (CKRC) in its final report further stated that affirmative action programmes should be 'justified by full data and using appropriate means and goals, be transparently operated, limited by time, adequately monitored' and 'should not amount to unfair discrimination'.[120] This means that positive discrimination measures in favour of a particular disadvantaged group require justification and should only be taken when strictly necessary. Also, going by the CKRC's observation that such measures should be limited by time, they should only last until the situation causing the disadvantage is satisfactorily addressed, which means that they should have sunset clauses, depending on how the measure is crafted.

McCrudden, emphasising these points, suggests several principles to be considered in the implementation of affirmative action measures that mitigate their effects on non-beneficiaries.[121] These principles mirror the above suggestion by the CKRC. The first principle is that preferences should be taken only as a measure of last resort when it has been determined that there is 'no reasonable alternative … available, or all have already been exhausted'. Second, McCrudden argues that preferential measures should be temporary, having a time limit on their applicability or 'a withdrawal of the availability of the exception where an identified proportion has been achieved'. This, however, depends on how the affirmative action measure is crafted. For instance, the rule in Article 27(8) of the Kenyan Constitution that not more than two-thirds of the members in elective and appointive bodies should be of the same gender is 'timeless'. It can apply to both men and women whenever their representation in elective or appointive bodies is below a third.

Third, such programmes should take into consideration the effect of preferences to innocent third parties. This is the hard question, how to balance the effects of affirmative action measures to non-beneficiaries against their benefits. Thus, even more reason why such programmes should be temporary or not be applicable once the required proportion is reached. Fourth, McCrudden argues that no one should be 'compulsorily removed from employment as part of [an affirmative action] programme' and lastly that the procedures employed to implement such programmes 'should be open and fair'.[122]

[119] *Kabui Mwai* (n 6) 10.
[120] Constitution of Kenya Review Commission (n 39) 104.
[121] C McCrudden, 'Rethinking Positive Action' (1986) 15 *Industrial Law Journal* 219.
[122] ibid 242.

An example of a temporary corrective measure is the Equalisation Fund established under Article 204 of the Constitution. The fund is meant to enable marginalised regions in the country to catch up in development with the rest of the nation. It is, however, a temporary measure as it is meant to lapse 20 years after the promulgation of the Constitution (2030).[123] It is hoped that 20 years will be enough time to address the development inequality faced by these regions in comparison to the rest of the country. Nevertheless, if the objective is not achieved by that time, the fund is subject to extension by Parliament (Article 204(7)). This accentuates McCrudden's point on the need for data-informed decision making and the idea of ending an affirmative action programme once the desired proportion of equality is achieved.[124]

IV. Are Affirmative Action Measures Mandatory and Immediate or Should They be Progressively Realised?

As argued in the Introduction, affirmative action was not considered a controversial issue during the drafting and promulgation of the Constitution.[125] However, its implementation, specifically when it comes to gender quotas, has raised many debates as to its legitimacy and how it should be implemented. The debates mainly relate to whether implementation of affirmative action measures should be mandatory and immediate or progressively realisable. There also seems to be a difference in implementing representation-enhancing measures and those aimed at resource redistribution. The latter is largely said to be progressively realisable while the former has been immediately implemented in almost all cases. This section focuses on gender quotas. It interrogates whether gender quotas in Kenya's 2010 Constitution, as a representation-enhancing measure, are mandatory and immediate or progressively realisable, considering their aims.

The root of the controversy in implementing gender quotas is the fact that Articles 27(8), 81, 97 and 98 of the Constitution, as expansively discussed above,[126] provide for the two-thirds gender rule but do not offer a mechanism for its implementation. This omission is what has given rise to the debate as to whether the implementation of gender quotas under the two-thirds gender rule should be immediate or progressively realisable. Fuelling this debate was the provision in the Fifth Schedule of the Constitution, prescribing time frames for the enactment of legislative measures to give effect to the two-thirds gender principle. For the National Assembly and Senate seats, the deadline for implementation of such legislation was set as 27 August 2015. Therefore, the argument by proponents of

[123] The Constitution of Kenya 2010, Art 204(6).
[124] McCrudden (n 121) 225–26 and 242.
[125] See n 3.
[126] Text to nn 19–24.

progressive realisation was that the deadline meant the implementation of the two-thirds gender rule was mandatory but progressively realisable in the period before 27 August 2015. They further posited that the rule would only become immediately realisable on or after this date. The deadline therefore acted as a form of structural interdict that gave the State flexibility to act as long as implementation was concluded by a certain date.

The lack of clarity as to the immediate or progressive realisation of gender quotas led to contradictory High Court decisions. An example is the decision in *Federation of Women Lawyers Kenya (FIDA-K) & 5 Others v Attorney General & Another* (*FIDA v AG*).[127] The case concerned the application of the two-thirds gender rule in appointments made by the Judicial Service Commission with respect to inaugural judges of the Supreme Court, upon its creation under the 2010 Constitution. A three-judge bench held that the issues raised by the applicants concerning the rule under Article 27(8) were not yet ripe for judicial adjudication. This was because the State had not yet taken legislative or other measures to implement the two-thirds gender rule. According to the justices, these measures and policies required progressive realisation. However, they had to be put in place by the 27 August 2015 deadline given in the Fifth Schedule of the Constitution. The petition was filed in June 2011, which meant that four years remained for the enactment of legislation on the two-thirds gender rule.

However, a contrary decision was given by the three-judge High Court bench in *Milka Otieno & Another v Attorney General & 2 Others*.[128] In contrast to the decision in *FIDA v AG*, the Court held: 'We … are of the view that the provision of the Constitution [Article 27(8)] gives the [State] and public officers other steps and measures to be undertaken whether legislation is in place or not'.[129] The case related to the enforcement of the two-thirds gender rule under Article 27(8) in the composition of the Kenya Sugar Board. The Court held that the composition of the Board should respect the two-thirds gender rule, even if there was no legislation in place enforcing it.

Various questions emerged from issues raised in the two cases and general debates on the two-thirds gender rule. These can be summarised into four key points. First, there was the issue of whether constitutional rights requiring legislation in order to be implemented can be crystallised in the absence of such enabling legislation, especially where there is a constitutional deadline for the enactment of such legislation. Second, there was the question of progressive realisation of Article 27(8) and whether this formulation by the courts contradicts the way equality is understood. Third, as a matter of constitutional interpretation, there were questions as to the effect of the use of the word *shall* in Article 27(8) and whether it connotes a mandatory obligation. And fourth, there

[127] *FIDA v AG* (n 112) (Mwera J, Warsame J and Mwilu J).
[128] *Milka Otieno & Another v Attorney General & 2 Others* Petition 33 of 2011 (HC) (Ali-Aroni J, Chitembwe J and Chemitei J).
[129] ibid 10.

was the issue of how the different provisions touching on gender quotas, whether for the National Assembly, Senate, County Assembly or public appointive positions, can be harmoniously interpreted considering the rule that the Constitution should be interpreted as a whole.[130]

These questions are interrogated below in an analysis of the Supreme Court Advisory Opinion that sought to deal with these issues. The analysis also considers how the position arrived at by the Supreme Court affects conceptualisation and harmonious interpretation of the equality guarantee and the aims of affirmative action.

A. The Supreme Court Advisory Opinion on the Two-thirds Gender Rule

Following debates on how to implement the two-thirds gender rule before the 2013 general election, the former Attorney-General, Githu Muigai, requested an advisory opinion from the Supreme Court raising the arguments pointed out in the preceding sub-section. This was *In the Matter of the Principle of Gender Representation in the National Assembly and the Senate* (Gender Representation Advisory Opinion).[131] The crux of the matter before the Court was whether the two-thirds gender rule in the Constitution required progressive realisation or if it required the same to be implemented immediately and applied in the March 2013 general election.

The Attorney-General argued that in addition to the 47 seats set aside for women parliamentarians in Article 97(1) of the Constitution, if the electorate fails to elect enough women to meet the one-third limit, 'the only way to comply with prescribed equity-fractions would be through *nominations*'.[132] However, he stated that this move would be unconstitutional as it would increase the membership figure of the National Assembly and Senate over and above the constitutional limits. Moreover, the Attorney-General contended that such a move would place an undue financial burden on taxpayers and thus urged the Court to hold that the rule should be progressively realised with regard to elective representation.[133] Conversely, there were also concerns that not fulfilling the two-thirds gender rule in the 2013 general election would be an affront to the Constitution.

Other interested parties and the amici curiae insisted that the rule should be implemented immediately.[134] On the issue of progressive realisation of

[130] This rule is comprehensively discussed in *Centre for Rights Education and Awareness (CREAW) & 7 Others v Attorney General* [2011] eKLR (HC).

[131] *In the Matter of the Principle of Gender Representation in the National Assembly and the Senate* Advisory Opinion No 2 of 2012 (SC).

[132] ibid [30].

[133] ibid.

[134] ibid [31].

Article 27(8), the interested parties and amici curiae objected to the application of this principle to gender equity. They argued that the principle is only provided for in Article 43 on the implementation of socio-economic rights, and in Article 54 on the progressive realisation of the principle that at least 5 per cent of the members of the public in elective and appointive bodies should be persons with disabilities.[135] The progressive realisation of socio-economic rights is related to available resources, which distinguishes it from the gender representation rule. In addition, it was stated that the failure to put in place legislation to implement the rule amounted to gender discrimination under Article 27(1) on the right to equal protection and equal benefit of the law, and Article 27(3) on equal treatment and equal opportunities for both men and women.[136]

The Supreme Court's majority opinion referred to progressive realisation as a non-legal term that was coined from international human rights instruments. They gave the example of the International Covenant on Economic, Social and Cultural Rights (ICESCR), which under Article 2 provides for progressive realisation by State Parties of the rights contained therein.[137] Arguing that the 2010 Constitution draws inspiration from international human rights instruments, the Court defined progressive realisation as 'the gradual or phased-out attainment of a goal which by its nature, cannot be achieved on its own, unless first, *a certain set of supportive measures are taken* by the State'.[138] However, the judges omitted to mention the link between progressive realisation and available resources, which is central to the concept in the ICESCR.

The majority held that where the Constitution provided for clear gender quota figures, gender equity was immediately realisable but where this was absent, the attainment of the one-third gender requirement was progressively realisable since it was 'dependent on the State's *further action*'.[139] In terms of their understanding of progressive realisation, the majority stated that

> the expression 'progressive realization', as apprehended in the context of the human rights jurisprudence, would signify that there is no mandatory obligation resting upon the State to take *particular measures*, at a *particular time*, for the realization of the gender-equity principle, save where a time-frame is prescribed. And any obligation assigned in mandatory terms, but involving *protracted measures*, legislative actions, *policy-making* or the *conception of plans* for the attainment of a particular goal, is not necessarily inconsistent with the progressive realisation of a goal.[140]

Therefore, the judges argued that the use of the word 'shall' in Article 27(8) does not call for immediate action but for 'faithful and responsible discharge of a

[135] ibid [36].
[136] ibid [39].
[137] ibid [49]–[51].
[138] ibid [53].
[139] ibid [57] and [58].
[140] ibid [61].

public obligation'.[141] Furthermore, in the opinion of the majority, Article 81(b) was merely a principle that would 'inspire the development of concrete norms of specific enforcement'. The majority opinion therefore referred to Article 81(b) as a 'soft gender quota'. To be immediately realisable, it required an additional concrete normative provision that would transform it into a specific right. However, in the case of County Assemblies, they observed that Article 177 had transformed Article 81(b) into a specific enforceable right that was immediately realisable. Hence, they referred to Article 177 as providing for 'hard gender quotas'.[142]

Since there was no such concrete normative provision for National Assembly and Senate seats in addition to Article 81(b), the Court held that implementation of the rule for these seats was subject to progressive realisation. This was because it was dependent on the enactment of enabling legislation. Nevertheless, the majority noted that the Fifth Schedule of the Constitution prescribed time frames for the enactment of legislative measures to give effect to the two-thirds gender principle. As highlighted earlier, for the National Assembly and Senate seats, the deadline for implementation of such legislation was set as 27 August 2015.[143] The case was being heard between November and December 2012, which means that around three years were left to this deadline.

In contrast to the majority opinion, former Chief Justice Willy Mutunga, in his dissenting opinion, rejected the idea of progressive realisation of the two-thirds gender rule. This was for four reasons. First, he acknowledged the point raised by the applicants that the two-thirds gender rule in Article 27(8) and Article 81(b) uses the word *shall*, which assumedly meant that it required immediate realisation. He nevertheless opted to go with a holistic approach to interpretation in determining whether the rule was immediately or progressively realisable.[144]

Second, in light of the context and drafting history, Mutunga CJ opined that denying women the right to representation in the National Assembly and Senate based on the two-thirds gender rule in the 2013 general election would be inimical to the equality guarantee and was hence unconstitutional. He argued that it was also against the concept of transformative constitutionalism in breaking down the structural inequalities occasioned to women. This, he said, was because Kenyans, particularly women, on voting for the new Constitution, had in mind the continuous and consistent struggle 'for their equity and equality in all spheres of life'.[145] Third, he noted that since Article 177(1)(b) was held to require immediate realisation of the two-thirds gender rule in relation to the election of County Assembly representatives, refusing the same principle for the National Assembly and Senate elections would discriminate against women running for these seats.[146] Hence, he essentially argued for a harmonious understanding of the Constitution.

[141] ibid.
[142] ibid [77].
[143] ibid [79].
[144] ibid Dissenting Opinion [9].
[145] ibid Dissenting Opinion [11.4].
[146] ibid Dissenting Opinion [11.5].

Lastly, the former Chief Justice recognised the fact that equality under the Constitution 'is not the traditional [formal equality] view of providing equality before the law'. Equality in the Constitution was substantive. It involved 'undertaking certain measures, including affirmative action, to reverse negative positions that have been taken by society'. Therefore, he posited that 'where such negative exclusions pertain to political and civil rights, the measures undertaken are immediate and not progressive'.[147]

B. Critical Analysis of the Supreme Court Advisory Opinion on the Two-thirds Gender Rule

The issues raised in the case were difficult to navigate but the majority opinion was positive to the extent that it recognised the constitutional timeline for implementing the two-thirds gender rule. This was a middle ground in acknowledging that, first, the two-thirds gender rule required careful thought on the best way it could be implemented considering the unclear wording of the Constitution. Second, the recognition of the constitutional deadline meant that the rule would not become obsolete because of its indeterminate nature.

As much as it is clear that affirmative action measures cannot be implemented overnight, the assessment made here is that the Court's use of the term *progressive realisation* is problematic. First, it is argued that the Court used the wrong terminology as, by stating that legislation on implementation of the two-thirds gender rule needs to be implemented by the 27 August 2015 deadline, the solution they gave was more of a structural interdict and had little to do with progressive realisation. This is because, rather than saying that realisation should be over an undefined period, the Court required realisation (by adopting legislation) by a given date. The Court's holding is effectively a structural interdict which is 'a remedy in terms of which the court orders an organ of state to perform its constitutional obligations and to report to the court on its progress in doing so' or, the court can also come up with a time frame within which the order must be complied with.[148] The latter approach was applied in the case.

Second, as much as the Supreme Court gave what it felt was a clear solution – for the State to implement a law by 27 August 2015 – it left open the question of whether legislation to be put in place should be subject to immediate application in the next general election or progressively realisable in subsequent elections. Therefore, it is unclear whether, once reasonable plans are put in place for progressive realisation of the rule, such steps should automatically be taken to be in accordance with the Constitution no matter the time frame provided for

[147] ibid Dissenting Opinion [11.7].

[148] See RJ de Beer and S Vettori, 'The Enforcement of Socio-Economic Rights' (2007) 10(3) *Potchefstroom Electronic Law Journal* 1, 10.

their implementation. Thus, there is a gap in the Supreme Court's decision, which affects current debates on implementation of the rule.

The majority opinion similarly failed to consider the impact that an interpretation of the clause, as requiring the progressive realisation of gender quotas, would have on its aims and the Constitution's transformative nature, as considered in Mutunga CJ's dissenting opinion. This is particularly in relation to the application of affirmative action to address the deep-rooted gender inequality in Kenya. It is also difficult to reconcile the unclear claim of progressive realisation of the two-thirds gender rule with the way the whole equality clause should be understood. As expansively discussed in Chapter 3, the equality clause should be viewed in the substantive sense.[149] Also, it is usually mandatory and immediately realisable after a determination is made on whether equal treatment or difference in treatment should be applied, depending on what showing equal concern and respect would mean in different contexts. To this extent, the Court failed to consider the harmonious interpretation of the Constitution.

Moreover, although the use of the principle has been defined in the majority opinion as a mandatory requirement that is dependent on further action, it can still inordinately delay the attainment of rights envisioned in the Constitution to be immediately guaranteed. Progressive realisation has come to be seen as an excuse by States for the non-implementation of indeterminate rights, in particular socio-economic rights. These rights, which mostly give rise to positive duties, are usually viewed as requiring progressive realisation, stagnating their implementation because of the recognition that the State might not have all the available resources to immediately realise the right in full. However, it does have an immediate obligation to have a plan, not to discriminate and to take the first steps. This was the main reason why the Committee on Economic, Social and Cultural Rights (CESCR) adopted the minimum core concept in their third General Comment.[150]

Thus, the claim that a constitutionally entrenched equality provision requiring gender equity in representation should be progressively realised, without giving a detailed explanation of what this claim actually entails, makes it open to misinterpretation. Current debates on the implementation of the rule buttress this argument, as discussed below.

C. Current Debates on Application of the Two-thirds Gender Rule

There has been continued fascination with the notion of progressive realisation of the two-thirds gender rule. Some parliamentarians even made proposals to the

[149] Ch 3, text to nn 60–74.

[150] CESCR, *General Comment No. 3: The Nature of States Parties' Obligations (art. 2, para. 1, of the the Covenant)*, 14 December 1990, E/1991/23 (CESCR 1990). See also Ch 7, text to nn 13–17; Ch 8 text to nn 75–76.

effect that the constitutional deadline for implementing the two-thirds gender rule be removed and substituted with the requirement that the rule should be implemented progressively. This is because of the claims by the government that '[the] rule is too costly to implement in full'.[151] This was proposed in a Constitutional Amendment Bill that was taken before Parliament on 30 April 2015 by the chairperson of the National Assembly Justice and Legal Affairs Committee.[152]

Various women's organisations and human rights institutions have fiercely contested the proposed amendment, calling it unconstitutional.[153] The claim that the rule is too costly to be immediately implemented has also been disputed by a study conducted by the National Women's Steering Committee and the Institute of Economic Affairs.[154] The study shows that in total, implementing the rule for the National Assembly and Senate seats would amount to an estimate of Ksh 2.4 billion (US$24 million). This would require each citizen to pay 1 shilling per week for a year, which is not such a heavy burden on taxpayers.[155] Thus, Owino, one of the authors of the study, argues that 'the speaker of the National Assembly and the press were wrong to promote the impression that this spending is inordinately large without comparing it to total spending'. Hence, he argues that '[it is] a lie to continue opposing the "two-thirds rule" on claims of unaffordability'.[156]

This raises the question whether a claim of affordability is a legitimate reason to limit a constitutional right. The assumption made here is that the claim may be valid subject to a proportionality analysis, which in this case is not met as the study on the cost for implementing the rule suggests. Efforts to inordinately delay implementation of the rule are therefore an affront to the spirit of the Constitution and the aspirations of the electorate, which voted overwhelmingly for the 2010 Constitution and were in favour of the enforcement of the two-thirds gender rule.

The courts are still keen on pushing for the implementation of the rule in light of the Constitution's transformative vision. In a 2015 decision of the High Court, Ngugi J, noting the laxity of Parliament in implementing the two-thirds gender rule, ordered the Attorney-General and the Commission for the Implementation of the Constitution to prepare a bill on gender representation within 40 days from the pronouncement of the court orders.[157] This application of a structural interdict by Ngugi J supports the argument made herein that progressive realisation is not the relevant interpretive approach to adjudicating the implementation of the two-thirds gender rule; more so because a deadline for its implementation was already

[151] K Owino, 'The "two-thirds" gender rule can be implemented – affordably', *The Daily Nation* (Nairobi, 14 May 2015).

[152] Two-Third Gender Rule Laws (Amendment) Bill 2015, s 3.

[153] See CREAW, *Respect the Rule of Law – On the Implementation of the Constitutional Principle on the 'Not More Than Two Thirds Gender' Principle* (2015); R Nyagah, 'KEWOPA wants gender balance provision implemented now', *Kenyan Woman* (Nairobi, 1 June 2015).

[154] Owino et al (n 20).

[155] See Owino (n 151).

[156] ibid.

[157] *CREAW v Attorney General & Another* (n 87) [112].

given in the Constitution. It is yet to be seen how the rule is to be implemented but the challenges show that the road to transformation implicates many other actors than just the courts.

Considering the above-cited shortfalls in implementing the various affirmative action provisions in the Constitution, there is a need to go back to the drawing board and revisit the reasons why affirmative action measures were necessary in the first place. The aims of different affirmative action provisions in the Constitution, as discussed earlier, remind us of their importance and the urgency and immediacy with which they should be implemented. Over and above the need for a restatement of the aims and legitimacy of affirmative action measures in such debates is the challenge of the lack of political goodwill. This is particularly in relation to the male-dominated Parliament's tardiness and opposition to implementing gender quotas, which they obviously view as a challenge to their hold on power.[158] Hence the reason why courts, as guardians of the Constitution, need to be more proactive in giving innovative orders that breathe life into the dictates of the Constitution.

It is, however, acknowledged that the authority granted to the judiciary is limited. Consequently, when political goodwill interferes with the enforcement of court orders, civil society needs to step in. The role of the courts in implementing affirmative action measures through judicial interpretation is discussed below.

V. Role of Courts and Judicial Scrutiny in Affirmative Action Cases

As highlighted throughout the chapter, the 2010 Constitution requires the application of affirmative action measures to ameliorate the disadvantage suffered by individuals and groups because of past discrimination (Article 27(6)). However, when a non-beneficiary challenges the legitimacy and applicability of an affirmative action measure, a balancing test will have to be applied by the court. In the 2010 Constitution, this balancing test is in the form of a proportionality analysis guided by the provisions in Article 24, the limitations clause. The guidelines set out in Article 24(1)(a)–(e) require that a limitation must serve a pressing and substantial purpose; there should be a rational connection between the means used and goal to be achieved; it should lead to a minimum impairment of a fundamental right; and, lastly, that it should be shown that there are no other less restrictive means available.

These criteria indicate that affirmative action measures, to the extent that they limit the rights of non-beneficiaries to equality by excluding them from benefits granted, should be narrowly tailored to meet their legitimate aims. Put another way, there should be a close fit between the means (affirmative action measures put

[158] See Thuo (n 1).

in place) and ends (eg affirmative action's corrective aim, provision of role models, the need for diversity and social inclusion).[159]

Let us apply this test to the highly contested rule in Article 27(8) of the Constitution that not more than two-thirds of the members in elective and appointive bodies should be of the same gender. The first question to be addressed is whether the measure hopes to achieve a legitimate aim. As noted by Mutunga CJ, the aim of this measure is to ensure that women are adequately represented in public bodies. The measure is also meant to do away with the long-term and systemic discrimination women have faced, leading to their minimal representation, if not complete exclusion, in Parliament since the birth of the nation in 1963.[160] This affirmative action measure is therefore based on a legitimate aim, to guarantee women's adequate representation by eradicating their continued exclusion because of past discrimination. Without preferential treatment in elective and appointive bodies in favour of women, the enduring effects of past discrimination may not disappear on their own.[161]

The second question to be analysed is whether the provision is narrowly tailored to meet its aims. Looking at how the two-thirds rule is crafted, it is a flexible measure as it only applies when either gender fails to attain one-third representation in elective and appointive bodies. The flexibility in the application of this measure means that it is narrowly tailored to meet its aims. It also minimally impairs the rights of non-beneficiaries because of this flexibility and the fact that the basic qualification for one to be elected or appointed to these posts remains.

As highlighted by Fredman, further questions emerge when applying the affirmative action 'means and ends test' that courts should look out for.[162] These questions have been addressed in various sections of this chapter and will be consolidated here. The first question is, what aims are legitimate? This has been discussed in Sections I and II. The second is how close should the 'fit' be between the affirmative action measure and the identified aim? This question has been answered in the discussion on the principle of genuine need in Section III. The principle requires that those who are to benefit from affirmative action measures should be those who are *genuinely in need of the benefit*. This therefore necessitates a close fit between affirmative action means and ends. It also answers the third question of how the class of beneficiaries should be delineated. A corresponding issue accompanying this third question is whether such delineation can include individuals within the beneficiary group 'who have not themselves suffered disadvantage (over-inclusiveness)' or exclude persons outside the beneficiary group who have nevertheless been disadvantaged (under-inclusiveness).[163] The principle

[159] Fredman, *Discrimination Law* (n 53) 232.
[160] *Gender Representation Advisory Opinion* (n 131) dissenting opinion [11.1]–[11.4].
[161] See Brennan J's opinion in *United States v Paradise et al.*, 480 US 149 (1987) 165.
[162] Fredman, *Discrimination Law* (n 53) 233.
[163] ibid.

of genuine need requires that the chosen beneficiaries should match the affirmative action aim being advanced.

The example of providing education bursaries to children from marginalised regions, whose dire economic situation is a result of past discrimination, helps to explain this supposition. The affirmative action aim in this scenario is the amelioration of the economic disadvantage that inhibits access to education for children from marginalised areas, where such disadvantage is because of past discrimination. In this case, the principle of genuine need will require that the affirmative action measure be crafted in a way that ensures those who benefit are children in *genuine need* of it. Hence, children from marginalised regions who are nevertheless well off, and can comfortably access education without a bursary, should be excluded from such benefits. The principle of genuine need thus helps to ensure that the affirmative action measures applied correspond with the aims that they hope to achieve. This means that, as stated earlier, affirmative action measures should be as clear and detailed as possible.

The fourth question relates to the evidence that needs to be adduced to demonstrate that the affirmative action measure can achieve the identified aim. As highlighted earlier, the CKRC stated that necessity of affirmative action programmes should be evidenced by full data on the issue.[164] This can include data on the success that an affirmative action measure has achieved in jurisdictions whose context is quite similar to that of Kenya. For instance, in his *Gender Representation Advisory Opinion* dissent, Mutunga CJ referred to the success of gender quotas in Kenya's neighbouring countries, Tanzania and Rwanda.[165]

The last question that Fredman highlights is whether there should be a 'sunset' clause when it is believed that an affirmative action measure has achieved its aim. As has also been discussed, affirmative action measures should be temporary so as not to unduly over-burden non-beneficiaries when the required target is achieved.[166] However, this depends on how the measure is crafted. As was pointed out, a measure like the two-thirds gender rule is somewhat 'timeless' as it applies whenever either gender fails to achieve one-third representation in elective or appointive public bodies.

The application of this balancing test, which receives its legitimacy from Article 24 of the Constitution, will be a helpful guide to courts in conducting proper scrutiny in affirmative action cases. The 'means and ends fit' test is comprehensive and, if properly applied, will avoid unclear holdings like that of the majority in the Supreme Court *Gender Representation Advisory Opinion*.[167] This decision failed to align the aims of the two-thirds gender rule with the means for its application. This was by stating that the measure should be progressively realised, which does not correspond with its aims, which gesture towards immediate realisation.

[164] Text to n 120.
[165] *Gender Representation Advisory Opinion* (n 131) Dissenting Opinion [11.3].
[166] Text to nn 120–24.
[167] Text to nn 131–50.

VI. Conclusion

This chapter has analysed the various affirmative action provisions in the Constitution, their different aims and how to delineate beneficiaries. Four key points have been made. First, affirmative action, as it is framed in the Kenyan Constitution, is to be viewed as part of substantive equality and is aimed at achieving full equality; it is not a breach of it. The chapter has shown that it is possible to apply the analytical framework developed in Chapter 3 on how to harmoniously apply competing conceptions of equality, such as equal treatment and affirmative action, by considering what treatment as an equal requires for different people. Second, the various aims of affirmative action provisions in the Constitution have clarified their importance, which helps debunk challenges as to their legitimacy and restate the urgent need for their implementation. Third, by applying the different aims of affirmative action provisions in the Constitution, the chapter has clarified that measures like the two-thirds gender rule require immediate as opposed to progressive realisation. However, politics, above all else, has proven to be a great inhibitor to the application of the different aims of affirmative action.

Lastly, this chapter has set out the fact that, under Article 24 of the Constitution, a proportionality test should be applied to judicial scrutiny of affirmative action cases, and the measures applied should be narrowly tailored to meet their legitimate aims. The question of disappointed third parties in the application of affirmative action has not yet come up in the form discussed in the chapter. However, if such a question arises in future cases, the chapter has argued that courts can address it by asking what the aim of the affirmative action measure in question is, whether the means provided for its enforcement fit the aim, and the timeline for its application (which stops when the disadvantage identified is remedied).

6

Competing Equalities: Religion, Culture and Gender Equality

The question of how to resolve the tensions that exist between cultural and religious accommodation, on the one hand, and gender equality, on the other, has been a perennial issue in Kenya, but one that lacks resolution.[1] The same tensions subsist between culture and religion at one end of the spectrum, and sexual orientation on the other, as discussed in Chapter 4. As can be recalled from the analysis in Chapter 4, those who oppose the recognition of lesbian and gay persons in Kenya usually assert that homosexuality goes against 'Kenyan cultural and religious values'.[2]

This tension and how to resolve it has been confronted by the Kenyan High Court, which has stressed the need to separate constitutional morality – consisting of values and principles that courts should safeguard and uphold, such as the individual right to non-discrimination – and popular morality. In this regard, the High Court authoritatively stated that 'no matter how strongly held moral and religious beliefs may be, they cannot be a basis for limiting rights: they are not laws as contemplated by the Constitution'.[3] It is the aim of this chapter to provide more clarity on how to resolve the tensions between culture/religion and gender equality. This contributes to the overall aim of the book, namely the harmonious conceptualisation, interpretation and application of competing and interrelated conceptions of equality. Such competing conceptions are evident in the clash between the need to grant cultural and religious equality and the reality that some cultural and religious norms violate and conflict with gender equality.

Culture and religion are central practices in the lives of millions of Kenyans. Recent statistics show that nearly 85.53% of Kenyans are Christian (33.42% Protestant, 20.6% Catholic, and 31.51% other Christian groups), 10.9% Muslim, 0.13% Hindu, 0.68% traditionalist, 0.99% some other religion, 1.6% atheist and around 0.17% have unknown affiliations.[4] Culture and religion, as practised in

[1] MN Wangila, *Female Circumcision: The Interplay of Religion, Culture, and Gender in Kenya* (Maryknoll, NY, Orbis Books, 2007) chs 1 and 2.

[2] Ch 4, text to nn 31–32; *Eric Gitari v Non-Governmental Organisations Co-ordination Board & 4 Others* [2015] eKLR (*Eric Gitari*) [120] and [132].

[3] *Eric Gitari* (n 2) [120] and [132].

[4] Kenya National Bureau of Statistics, *2019 Kenya Population and Housing Census Volume IV: Distribution of Population by Socio-economic Characteristics* (Nairobi, Kenya National Bureau of Statistics, 2019) 422.

Kenya, are dealt with together in this chapter because, as much as they are fairly distinct concepts,[5] they are closely linked. This is particularly so with regard to their approach to gender, which is the focus of this chapter. Both concepts are underpinned by patriarchal notions where power and authority are male identified and 'institutions in a given society are structured in such a way as to give men relative control over critical aspects of women's lives'.[6]

The relationship between culture and religion is two sided. On the one hand, religion and religious attitudes influence the cultural way of life of communities.[7] In this sense, religious dictates are seen as the beliefs behind culture. Indeed, historically, culture in Kenya is closely connected to religious beliefs, with stories of tribal origin often attributing their coming into being to a superhuman force which rules the world and the life of all persons in the community.[8] For instance, in the tribal legend of the Kikuyu of Kenya, Kenyatta narrates that in the beginning of all things there was the first man called Gikuyu, the founder of the tribe, who was called by the Mogai (the divider of the universe) and given lands and shown how to communicate with Mogai if he needed anything.[9] Ways of life of the Kikuyu were then, traditionally, organised around beliefs touching on the worship of the Mogai. For instance, initiation rites were conducted alongside purification ceremonies, where initiates sought protection and guidance from their ancestral god.[10] Thus, because of the connection of these rites to religious beliefs, it was considered both a taboo and an evil deed not to undertake such rites, many of which are still practised to this day.

This old story, similar to legends on the origins of various other tribes in Kenya,[11] illustrates that religion is at the heart of many cultural practices in the country. The cultural life of the community is then ordered around such religious precepts. The religious basis of the cultural practices of most, if not all, tribes in Kenya therefore makes it hard to eliminate certain inhumane practices. This is because of a fear of the wrath that will be unleashed by the superhuman force which members of the community are believed to be answerable to. Such negative repercussions (eg going to hell) are felt to be of a higher order of justice than secular law.

On the other hand, culture also influences the approach to religion. For instance, in recent times, the adoption of theistic religions like Islam and Christianity by

[5] A Mazrui, *The Politics of Gender and the Culture of Sexuality: Western, Islamic, and African Perspectives* (E Anwar ed, Lanham, MD, Rowman & Littlefield, 2014) 189.

[6] Wangila (n 1) 23; A Ousseina, *Muslim Women in Postcolonial Kenya: Leadership, Representation, and Social Change* (Madison, WI, University of Wisconsin Press, 2013) 5 and 142.

[7] C Dawson and GJ Russello, *Religion and Culture* (Washington, DC, Catholic University of America Press, 2013) 43.

[8] ibid, 36–47.

[9] J Kenyatta, *Facing Mount Kenya* (New York, NY, Vintage Books, 1965) 3.

[10] ibid, 130–37.

[11] BA Ogot, *History of the Southern Luo* (Vol 1, Nairobi, East African Publishing House, 1967) 142–43; W Ng'ang'a, *Kenya's Ethnic Communities: Foundation of the Nation* (Nairobi, Gatundu Publishers Limited, 2006).

indigenous Kenyan communities has led to an intermingling or merging of culture and religion to evolve new ways of life. For example, many Christians usually have 'pre-wedding' ceremonies observing the customary marriage rites of their tribe before formally celebrating their marriage in a church. Also, Mazrui observes that 'many African Christian males have practiced polygamy despite the disapproval of the church'.[12] This overlap and interrelationship between culture and religion in Kenya, particularly their approach to gender, informs the decision to look at them together in this chapter.

Culture and religion are certainly essential in the formation of one's identity. However, there are negative, retrogressive and discriminatory aspects of culture and religion that are profoundly invasive of women's right to equality. Baraza rightly observes that in Kenyan society, the greatest challenge to gender equality, particularly in marriage and family affairs, is patriarchy, which is very much grounded in deep-rooted cultural and religious norms that subordinate women to men.[13] This is the same in many other polities across the globe. As Raday aptly notes, almost all religions and traditional cultures 'rely on norms and social practices formulated or interpreted in a patriarchal context'.[14] Sullivan adds that 'Many gender-specific human rights violations are grounded in cultural and religious practices'.[15] Yet since claims for cultural and religious freedom are mostly anchored on the right to personal autonomy, there has been reluctance by human rights advocates in the past to interrogate and question discriminatory customary and religious norms.[16]

However, with the coming into force of the 2010 Kenyan Constitution, which has multiple gender equality provisions,[17] the tensions between these rights needs to be confronted and addressed. This need is further reinforced by several regional and international human rights instruments, emphasising gender equality and renewing efforts to challenge discriminatory cultural and religious practices.[18] By virtue of Article 2(6) of the Constitution, 'International Treaties, and Conventions that Kenya has ratified, are imported as part of the sources of the Kenyan Law'.[19] This means that the country is bound by conventions it has ratified and acceded to and should refrain from acts that go against the object and purpose of such

[12] Mazrui (n 5) 189.

[13] N Baraza, 'Family Law Reforms in Kenya: An Overview' (Heinrich Böll Foundation's Gender Forum, Nairobi, 30 April 2009) 2.

[14] F Raday, 'Culture, Religion, and Gender' (2003) 1(4) *International Journal of Constitutional Law* 663, 664–65.

[15] DJ Sullivan, 'Gender Equality and Religious Freedom: Toward a Framework for Conflict Resolution' (1992) 24 *New York University Journal of International Law and Politics* 795.

[16] ibid 796; NK Modirzadeh, 'Taking Islamic Law Seriously: INGOs and the Battle for Muslim Hearts and Minds' (2006) 19 *Harvard Human Rights Journal* 191, 193.

[17] eg the Art 27(3) requirement that women and men have a right to equal treatment and equal opportunities in all spheres of life.

[18] eg Protocol to the African Charter on Human and Peoples' Rights on the Rights of Women in Africa, CAB/LEG/66.6 (13 September 2000); UN General Assembly, Convention on the Elimination of All Forms of Discrimination Against Women, 18 December 1979, United Nations Treaty Series, vol 1249, 13.

[19] *Re the Matter of Zipporah Wambui Mathara* [2010] eKLR (HC) [9].

international instruments. This includes the Convention on the Elimination of All Forms of Discrimination Against Women (CEDAW), which Kenya entered into without any reservations.[20]

This chapter offers a critical analysis of the cultural and religious norms that conflict with gender equality and makes proposals on how to resolve this conflict. These proposals are then applied to the final analysis of the exemption given to Islamic law as exercised in Kadhis' courts from the application of the equality clause.

I. Culture, Religion and Gender Equality in the 2010 Constitution

The equality guarantee in Article 27(4) of the 2010 Kenyan Constitution explicitly includes non-discrimination, directly or indirectly, against any person on grounds of sex, culture and religion. Article 27(3) lays greater emphasis on the importance of gender equality by providing that women and men should be treated equally and granted equal opportunities in all spheres of life. Before embarking on the tensions between culture/religion and gender equality, this section interrogates in greater detail the meaning, significance and constitutional provisions on culture, religion and gender equality.

A. Culture

There is no set definition of culture in Kenya under the 2010 Constitution. However, the definition given to it by the African Commission on Human and People's Rights (the Commission) in the *Centre for Minority Rights Development (Kenya) and Minority Rights Group International (on behalf of Endorois Welfare Council) v Kenya* case gives a fitting and compelling description of it that is relevant to the Kenyan context.[21] The Commission stated that 'culture' under Article 17 of the African Charter on Human and Peoples' Rights (African Charter) is understood to mean

> that complex whole which includes a spiritual and physical association with one's ancestral land, knowledge, belief, art, law, morals, customs, and any other capabilities and habits acquired by humankind as a member of society – the sum total of the material and spiritual activities and products of a given social group that distinguish it from other similar groups.[22]

[20] See indicators.ohchr.org.

[21] *Centre for Minority Rights Development (Kenya) and Another on behalf of Endorois Welfare Council v Kenya* Communication 276/2003 (ACHPR) (*Endorois*).

[22] ibid [241]. See also R Murray and S Wheatley, 'Groups and the African Charter on Human and Peoples' Rights' (2003) 25(1) *Human Rights Quarterly* 213, 224.

The definition is succinct but broad enough to cover the areas focused on in this chapter. Importantly, the Commission goes on to state that Article 17 of the African Charter also understands cultural identity as encompassing a group's religion.[23] This captures the close relationship between culture and religion.

Notable, also, is the relationship between culture and customary law. Customary law has been defined as 'customs and usages traditionally observed among the indigenous African peoples … and which form part of the culture of those people'.[24] From this definition, it is clear that customary law is derived from unique and significant long-established cultural practices of a group, which solidify and give rise to rules that are then considered customary law.[25] Customary law is therefore an aspect of culture.

Interrogating the cultural way of life of various tribes in Kenya, Wangila observes that culture is always changing 'given the ongoing adaptation of new values – both secular and religious'.[26] This means that customary law is also not static. Indeed, Shadle's examination of transcripts of proceedings from the courts set up for native Africans during colonialism, situated in Kenya's Nyanza region during the colonial period, reveal that 'elders followed a much more nuanced customary law in the courts than the one spelled out in the colonial texts'. This illustrates that customary law changed to accommodate changes in society, with the common view being that codification of customary law would stifle evolution.[27]

The broad definition of culture given by the African Commission is affirmed by Mazrui, who expounds on the characteristics highlighted in his espousal of the seven core functions of culture in Kenya and Africa in general.[28] The first function is culture as a lens of perception, in terms of how people view themselves and their environs. He gives the example of how the African cultural conception of immortality – the belief that 'no person is really dead for as long as the person's blood flows in the veins of the living' – has led to parents having many children to improve chances of immortality.[29] The second function involves culture as a spring of motivation that influences patterns of behaviour such as work ethic. This function contributes to common stereotypes about people from the various ethnic groups in Kenya. For instance, people from the Luhya tribe are usually stereotyped as being farmers and cooks, and those from the Kikuyu tribe as being business oriented.

[23] *Endorois* (n 21) [241].

[24] TW Bennett, 'Re-Introducing African Customary Law to the South African Legal System' (2009) 57(1) *American Journal of Comparative Law* 1, 27; South African Recognition of Customary Marriages Act 120 of 1998, s 1(ii).

[25] Bennett (n 24) 26–29.

[26] Wangila (n 1) 13.

[27] BL Shadle, 'Changing Traditions to Meet Current Altering Conditions: Customary Law, African Courts and the Rejection of Codification in Kenya, 1930–60' (1999) 40(3) *Journal of African History* 411, 414–15.

[28] Mazrui (n 5).

[29] ibid 154.

The third function is culture as a standard of judgement for what is right or wrong, beautiful or ugly. For instance, Mazrui describes how taking a chicken to a chief in African traditional society was an acceptable form of salutation but is rejected in modern society as amounting to bribery.[30]

The fourth is culture as a basis of stratification, the most predominant being gender stratification.[31] Mazrui describes how, culturally, African women were (and still are in many households in Kenya) considered custodians of fire (collecting firewood and cooking), water (ensuring water supply for the home), and earth (fertility of the womb (women as mothers) and fertility of the soil (women as cultivators)). Men, on the other hand, oversaw mixed husbandry, including responsibilities for all domestic mammals. They were also the main decision makers and custodians of land. Mazrui discusses how such stratification has persisted in modern Kenyan society, noting that in Kericho, a tea-growing area in Kenya, it is largely women who still pick tea leaves in times of harvest.[32]

These roles have led to two competing schools of thought. The first school of thought views these social roles as signifying that African men and women 'have different and complementary functions, and therefore equal and complementary power relations'.[33] This is then interpreted as meaning that patriarchy has less of a hold in the African setting, a view which critics see as a pretext for a particular kind of patriarchy. Indeed, the second school of thought posits that, even in instances where there is a level of 'female power', it 'has always been subject to male authority and highly circumscribed in terms of what it could accomplish in critical areas of social and cultural life'.[34] This second school of thought correctly captures the social and cultural context in Kenya whereby, as much as the roles given to women make them the backbone of society, they are less valued and do not amount to any real substantial power for women in the home and in society. Mazrui describes this as the *centring* and not the *empowerment* of women, as further discussed in the sub-section on gender equality below.[35]

The fifth function Mazrui espouses is culture as a means of communication, whereby it provides language 'rich in metaphors or poetry'.[36] The sixth function is culture as defining production and consumption and influencing them.[37] The seventh and last function is culture as a basis of identity, being 'crucial in defining the "we" and the "they" and marking the frontiers of solidarity'. For instance, Mazrui observes that among Kenyan African tribal communities 'what constitutes a Kikuyu or a Maasai … is [predominantly] a function of such cultural variables as lineage-systems, Kinship and language'.[38]

[30] ibid 155.
[31] ibid 155 and 202.
[32] ibid.
[33] Ousseina (n 6).
[34] ibid 5–6.
[35] Mazrui (n 5) 193, 202–03 and 331; text to nn 66–68.
[36] Mazrui (n 5) 155 and 158.
[37] ibid 156.
[38] ibid.

The seven functions of culture help us appreciate the importance of culture in Kenya, particularly in the formation of one's identity. The functions listed show how culture can be a positive force in influencing work ethic, enriching artistic expression through unique metaphors and poetry, cultural dances and dressing, approach to the environment, and world view. However, of great concern is the fourth function of culture as a basis of stratification, which has propagated the patriarchal tendency of considering women as being subordinate to men in all spheres of life, leading to gender inequality.

i. Right to Culture in the Kenyan Constitution

The right to culture in the 2010 Constitution is encapsulated in Article 11(1), which 'recognises culture as the foundation of the nation and as the cumulative civilization of the Kenyan people and nation'. It enjoins the State to 'promote all forms of national and cultural expression through literature, the arts, traditional celebrations, science, communication, information, mass media, publications, libraries and other cultural heritage'.[39] Article 44(1) further mandates that every person has the right to use their language of choice and to participate in the cultural life of their choosing. This right is to be exercised by persons individually or with other members of their cultural or linguistic community.[40] These provisions allude to the pluralistic nature of Kenyan society.[41]

The Constitution also recognises and regulates negative types of customary law. As can be recalled from the earlier discussion, customary law is an aspect of culture. Article 2(4) of the Constitution states that 'any law, including customary law that is inconsistent with the Constitution is void to the extent of the inconsistency, and any act or omission of the Constitution is invalid'. Article 44(3) further provides that a person shall not compel another to perform, observe or undergo any cultural practice or rite. In relation to children, Article 53(1)(d) mandates that every child has the right 'to be protected from abuse, neglect, harmful cultural practices, all forms of violence, inhuman treatment and punishment, and hazardous or exploitative labour'. With respect to young people, Article 55(d) obliges the State to ensure that the youth 'are protected from harmful cultural practices and exploitation'. This is also the case for land and property rights, with Article 60(1)(f) requiring the 'elimination of gender discrimination in law and practices related to land and property in land'.

The above provisions limiting the application of harmful cultural practices have been relied on in recent cases such as that of *Agnes Ombuna v Birisira Ombuna*.[42] In this case, a Court of Appeal three-judge bench (Otieno, Azangalala

[39] Constitution of Kenya 2010, Art 11(2)(a).

[40] ibid Art 44(2).

[41] YP Ghai, 'Ethnicity, Nationhood and Pluralism: The 2010 Kenya Constitution' in YP Ghai and J Ghai (eds), *Ethnicity, Nationhood and Pluralism: Kenyan Perspectives* (Nairobi, Katiba Institute, 2013) 95; text to nn 76–108.

[42] *Agnes Ombuna v Birisira Ombuna* [2014] eKLR.

and Kantai JJA) rendered unconstitutional the practice of woman-to-woman marriage under Gusii customary law. This type of marriage occurs where a wife is barren or unable to give birth to sons. Upon the death of her husband, or in agreement with her husband, she is required to marry another woman to bear children (sons) with another man, normally of the wife's choosing. The children of the new wife would then be considered children of the (deceased) husband of the first wife for purposes of continuing the family name. The learned judges stated that, whereas both parties acknowledged that the practice was in existence, given that the respondent had daughters only, under the 2010 Kenyan Constitution,

> it would appear that any woman need not go through such a marriage in order to perpetuate her lineage … The practice is evidence of discriminatory practices in favour of male children who in most traditional African societies were the only ones entitled to inherit real estate … That changed with the coming into force of the Law of Succession Act – Cap 160, Laws of Kenya, which does not make a distinction between sons and daughters of a deceased intestate.
>
> The position was crystallized by the Constitution of Kenya 2010 which, in Article 60(1), provides as follows:
>
> '60(1) **Land in Kenya shall be held, used and managed in a manner that is equitable, efficient, productive and sustainable, and in accordance with the following principles -**
>
> …
>
> (f) **elimination of gender discrimination in law and practices related to land and property in land.**'[43]

This case emphasises the fact that the right to culture is not absolute, particularly in the context of harmful practices.

Kenya has ratified and acceded to several international and regional instruments that provide for both narrow and broad rights to culture. These are binding upon the State and are part of Kenyan law by virtue of Article 2(6) of the Constitution, which mandates that treaties and conventions ratified by the State shall form part of Kenyan law. These instruments include the International Covenant on Civil and Political Rights (ICCPR), the International Covenant on Economic, Social and Cultural Rights (ICESCR) and the African Charter. Article 27 of the ICCPR sets out the right of ethnic, religious and linguistic minorities in a State Party to enjoy their culture, profess and practise their religion, and use their own language. Article 15 of the ICESCR goes a step further in providing, inter alia, that everyone in a State Party should have the right to take part in cultural life and the protection of their cultural intellectual property. Notably, the ICCPR provision is a minority protection whereas the right to culture in the ICESCR applies to everyone.

A more comprehensive protection of the right to culture is found in the African Charter. Article 17(2) provides for the right of every person to freely take part in

[43] ibid 5. Highlighted in bold in the judgment.

the cultural life of their community. It continues that 'The promotion and protection of morals and traditional values recognized by the community shall be the duty of the State' (Article 17(3)). The African Commission on Human and Peoples' Rights has stated that this right to culture only protects 'positive African values consistent with human rights standards, and implies an obligation on the State to ensure the eradication of harmful practices that negatively affect human rights'.[44]

However, largely because the provision does not have a claw-back clause limiting its application, the provision has been interpreted variously and has been the subject of scholarly debates. For instance, the African Charter's requirement for States to promote and preserve culture has been faulted for not appreciating the fluidity and flexibility of culture as social mores change, especially in the context of regressive cultural practices. On the matter, Mutua argues for a holistic and harmonious interpretation of the African Charter, which would require those applying the provision on culture to reconcile it with the one on the elimination of discrimination to balance competing interests.[45] This is more so because of the risk in the broad wording of the right to culture in the Charter, which not only requires non-interference by the State in an individual's enjoyment and manifestation of their culture, but also mandates the State to promote and preserve culture. This includes both cultural activities and cultural institutions, as well as artistic freedom.[46] The chapter takes a similar approach on the need for clarity when it comes to grossly invidious and oppressive cultural practices.

B. Religion

i. Right to Religion in the Kenyan Constitution

The Kenyan Court of Appeal has, in a recent judgment, referred to religion as a belief in the supernatural and the holding of religious convictions that may not necessarily make sense to others, but such beliefs, nevertheless, deserve respect and space from others for them to flourish.[47]

Article 8 of the Constitution declares that 'There shall be no State religion'. This provision has been the subject of much debate as to its meaning. Ghai posits that the provision essentially makes Kenya a secular rather than an atheist State, which would presumably mean that all religions should be treated equally by being given

[44] African Commission on Human and Peoples' Rights, *Principles and Guidelines on the Implementation of Economic, Social, Political and Cultural Rights in the African Charter on Human and Peoples' Rights* (2010) 38.

[45] M Mutua, 'The African Human Rights System: A Critical Evaluation' (2000) *Human Development Occasional Papers (1992–2007)* 1, 10.

[46] African Commission (n 44).

[47] *Mohamed Fugicha v Methodist Church in Kenya (suing through its registered trustees) & 3 Others* [2016] eKLR (*Fugicha*) 22; *Regina (Williamson) v Secretary of State for Education and Employment* [2005] UKHL 15 [23].

ample freedom of worship.[48] However, this description is unclear as to whether, aside from allowing the practice of all religions in private, which is essential to the freedom of religion, the State has a duty to promote or facilitate all religions equally. It is also silent as to whether the State favours religion as opposed to non-religion; and whether there is a prohibition on religion engaging in the affairs of State, or the State engaging in the affairs of religion.

Reference to American scholarship, which has for a long time interrogated the principle of separation of State and religion, is helpful in shedding more light on the matter. Cliteur's typology of the five models of the relationship between State and religion is particularly helpful.[49] The first model is political atheism, where there is 'an official state policy aiming to eradicate all sympathy for religious ideas' and which promotes atheist convictions among its citizens.[50] The second is the religiously neutral State model, whose main aim is political secularism in terms of not advocating for or against religion and putting a ban on the financing of churches and other religious institutions. Cliteur further explains that, under this model, 'All religions … may be represented in society, but none of them has a privileged position'.[51]

The third model, multiculturalism, aims to treat all religions equally and to help them equally. However, this model is said to exclude non-religious views.[52] The fourth model is that of a State Church. Cliteur argues that in this model, the 'state and [its official] church have an intimate connection in upholding the public order'. Nevertheless, he adds that the priority given to the official State religion because of its historical basis as, for instance, the first religion adopted in the State, does not lead to the oppression of other religions.[53] The fifth and last model is theocracy. This is where 'one religion is favoured above other religions, and other religions are suppressed – often by law and force'.[54]

Applying Cliteur's typology to the provision in Article 8 of the Kenyan Constitution that there shall be no State religion, this certainly gestures towards a high level of State neutrality. This then leads us to the conclusion that Kenya is a secular State as defined under Cliteur's second model. The fact that the Constitution does not require the State to finance any churches or religious institutions, although there is no specific prohibition on this, backs the view that Article 8 leans more towards requiring State neutrality. The Fourth Schedule of the Constitution merely places the function of dealing with anything related to the relationship between religion and State with the national government, as opposed to county governments. This is similar to the US Constitution's First Amendment

[48] Ghai (n 41) 94.

[49] P Cliteur, 'State and Religion against the Backdrop of Religious Radicalism' (2012) 10(1) *International Journal of Constitutional Law* 127, 128.

[50] ibid 128–29.

[51] ibid 131.

[52] ibid 132.

[53] ibid.

[54] ibid.

provision that 'Congress shall make no law respecting an establishment of religion' (the 'Free Establishment' clause), which has been interpreted as meaning that the US is a religiously neutral State.[55]

Kymlicka's rendition of the Rawlsian approach to the separation of State and religion aptly captures the type of State neutrality manifest in the Kenyan context. He describes the Rawlsian approach as one which

> protects each religious community by separating church from state. It removes religion from the public agenda, leaving adherents of the competing doctrines free to pursue their beliefs in private churches. In the group-rights model, on the other hand, church and state are closely linked. Each religious community is granted official status and a substantial measure of self-government.[56]

This account gives a broader and fitting explanation of what the constitutional requirement that there be no State religion under the State neutrality model should mean in Kenya. It should mean that religion is removed from the public agenda and citizens are left free to practise their different religions. Nevertheless, the Constitution does not really give religions a measure of self-governance except for Kadhis' courts (Islamic courts in Kenya). These courts are a kind of self-governing body in relation to the adjudication of personal law disputes (marriage, divorce and succession) between persons who profess the Islamic faith.[57] This is a salient exception to the State neutrality model as it allows religion onto the public agenda of dispute resolution.

A State neutrality model is essential in a pluralistic society like Kenya where people are diverse and value different ways of life influenced by either religion or non-religion. To respect and value pluralism, the State should accommodate different ways of life. The State neutrality model ensures that pluralism thrives and enables the State to show equal concern and respect for everyone in society. Therefore, if we conceive the separation between State and religion in this way, it should also mean that the State should not favour religion over non-religion.

The core provision on freedom of religion is encapsulated in Article 32 of the 2010 Constitution, which provides:

> (1) Every person has the right to freedom of conscience, religion, thought, belief and opinion.
> (2) Every person has the right, either individually or in community with others, in public or in private, to manifest any religion or belief of a day of worship.
> (3) A person may not be denied access to any institution, employment or facility, or the enjoyment of any right, because of the person's belief or religion.
> (4) A person shall not be compelled to act, or engage in any act, that is contrary to the person's belief or religion.

[55] ibid 144.

[56] W Kymlicka, 'Two Models of Pluralism and Tolerance' in D Heyd (ed), *Toleration: An Elusive Virtue* (Princeton, NJ, Princeton University Press, 1998) 82.

[57] See text to nn 82–99.

The Article 32 guarantee respects not only an individual's autonomy and right not to be forced to change their religious convictions or way of thinking but also their right to be able to practise and manifest their religion. The Court of Appeal in the *Fugicha* case affirmed that this provision, although framed by the claimant as a legitimate expectation, was a way of giving Muslim females a right to manifest their belief by donning the *hijab*.[58] In the case, the *hijab* consisted of a white headscarf and a pair of white trousers underneath the uniform skirts.[59] The three-judge bench (Waki, Nambuye and Kiage JJA) was satisfied that the wearing of the *hijab* is a belief that is genuinely held and of utmost or exceptional importance to Muslim girls. Respecting Muslim girls' freedom to hold and manifest their religion, the judges observed that 'Freedom of religion protects the subjective belief of the individual'.[60] Therefore, it was not up to them to 'judge on the basis of some "independent objective" criterion the correctness of the beliefs that give rise to Muslim girls' belief'.[61]

The judges added that people's 'religious convictions need not make sense to us in order for us to accord them the necessary respect and space for them to flourish'.[62] Indeed, as discussed below, respect for an individual's exercise of 'free and informed consent' to cultural and religious practices is an important aspect of accommodation and toleration. The judges thus concluded that refusing the claimant's 'daughters and other Muslim girls from donning the *hijab* did place them at a particular disadvantage or detriment because the *hijab* is genuinely considered to be an item of clothing constituting a practice or manifestation of religion'.[63]

In addition to the Article 32 guarantee, Kenya is a party to the ICCPR and African Charter, which also provide for the right to freedom of religion (Articles 18 and 8 respectively). The guarantee of this right in Article 18 of the ICCPR includes the right to have or adopt a religion and the freedom to manifest this religion in worship, observance, practice and teaching, either individually or in community with others.

It is important to respect people's individual and collective freedom of belief and right to manifest their religion. However, as with the right to culture, there is a need to limit this freedom under Article 24 of the Constitution when it is, inter alia, unreasonable, unjustifiable and does not respect human dignity and equality. The necessity of such limits when it comes to gender equality is discussed below.

[58] *Fugicha* case (n 47).
[59] ibid 15.
[60] ibid 22.
[61] ibid 21.
[62] ibid 22.
[63] ibid 21.

C. Gender Equality: Challenges Posed by Harmful Patriarchal Cultural and Religious Norms

Baraza correctly observes that the main challenge to gender equality in Kenya, particularly with regard to marriage and family matters, 'remains patriarchy grounded on deep rooted culture [and religion] that subordinates women to men'.[64] The definition of 'patriarchy' propounded by Ousseina is adopted. She refers to it as 'the system in which social life and societal institutions in a given society are structured in such a way as to give men relative control over critical aspects of women's lives'.[65] Most of the cultural norms of the more than 42 ethnic communities in Kenya consider women as being subordinate to men. This is also the case with many of the religions practised in the country (for instance Christianity, Islam and Hinduism), which require a woman to submit to her husband – given that only heterosexual marriages are currently legal.

The previous sections underscored the importance of culture and religion in the formation of a person's identity, and the need to accommodate and respect people's right to choose to be guided by cultural or religious edicts. But, even as we appreciate the crucial role that culture and religion play in a person's life, this section cautions against romanticising too much about the significance of these two rights. It emphasises the need to flag the harms some cultural and religious norms have caused, and continue to cause, specifically to women. Culture, particularly, has been a great impediment to women's access to their economic, social and political rights.

Women are considered the bedrock of society in African traditional culture, as well as in most of the religions practised in Kenya. Nevertheless, as Mazrui notes, women in Kenya are indeed *centred* – being the custodians of water, by ensuring its supply in the home; of earth, by cultivating the land and bearing children; and of fire, by overseeing the supply of rural fuel (firewood) – but not *empowered*.[66] He explains that the roles women have traditionally been allocated emphasise their importance in society but reduce their freedom to, for instance, own land and pursue formal education. Viewed from this perspective, in most cases, cultural and religious roles allocated to women place them at the *centre* of society 'but fall short of *empowering* them'.[67] This lack of emphasis on *empowering*, and not just *centring*, women in cultural and religious settings has meant that women's rights in such circumstances remain a challenge, as they fall prey to the exercise of unfair cultural and religious practices. Such practices include wife inheritance, widow cleansing, female genital mutilation, early/forced marriages and malignant polygamy.

[64] Baraza (n 13) 2.
[65] Ousseina (n 6) 5.
[66] Mazrui (n 5) 193, 202–03 and 331.
[67] ibid 193.

The emphasis on the role of women and girls being in the home also leads to their low levels of participation in socio-political fields and the low enrolment of girls in schools. Most customary laws exclude women from land ownership and inheritance, leading to their lack of access to land, which is also a root cause of other disadvantages.[68]

Kenya's 2010 Constitution is a major boost in guaranteeing women's equality rights. Numerous articles incorporate principles of gender equality and require the elimination of cultural and religious practices that are harmful to women. As highlighted in Chapter 3, Article 27(3) requires the equal treatment and granting of equal opportunities to women and men in all spheres of life. Article 45 goes on to require full and free consent of both parties to a marriage. This intends to curb the practice of forced marriage and provides for equal rights of both parties to a marriage, during the marriage and upon its dissolution. The fact that these progressive guarantees are encapsulated in the supreme law of the land is a powerful force in engendering respect for women's equal rights.

However, as discussed below, the de facto practice of harmful cultural and religious norms is still a major setback in Kenya. Tied to this, the law is largely silent on how to resolve the tensions between the right to culture and religious practices that are deeply patriarchal and women's right to equality. The goal of the chapter is, therefore, to find the right balance in the application of these two sets of rights. As the Constitution of Kenya Review Commission noted in its final report, as much as there is a need to ensure respect for ethnic and religious diversity, it is important to do away with beliefs and practices that 'constitute serious impediments to realising the objectives of national development', which include gender equality.[69] The next section further interrogates this point by unpacking key rationales of the right to culture and religion, analysed through the lens of harmful practices that violate gender equality.

II. Key Rationales for the Right to Culture and Religion Analysed Through the Lens of Harmful Practices that Violate Gender Equality

Having set out the definitions and legal underpinnings of the rights to culture, religion and gender equality, this section offers a critical analysis of key rationales for the right to culture and religion from the lens of harmful practices that violate gender equality. It interrogates the question of whether cultural and religious practices that discriminate against women should be recognised and accommodated,

[68] See Ch 2, text to nn 16–23.

[69] Constitution of Kenya Review Commission, *The Final Report of the Constitution of Kenya Review Commission. Approved for issue at the 95th Plenary Meeting held on 10 February 2005* (2005) 56.

thereby allowing cultural and religious equality to win over women's individual rights. The key rationales for accommodating the right to culture and religion include: (1) reasonable accommodation (2) pluralism and the plurality of the Kenyan legal system; and (3) the exercise of personal autonomy and free and informed consent.

A. Reasonable Accommodation

The principle of reasonable accommodation is one of the main justifications for the protection of cultural and religious equality. In the *Fugicha* case, the Kenyan Court of Appeal rightly observed that the principle of reasonable accommodation had not previously received judicial pronouncement or affirmation by Kenyan courts.[70] Nevertheless, it made a profound observation that captures what the principle should mean in the Kenyan context. Guided by one of the clauses in the Constitution's preamble, the Court stated that respecting the equal right of others to be different in their religious or, by extension, cultural persuasion is

> a call to broadmindedness and respect for others including those whose creeds and the manner of their manifestation may be unappealing or baffling. It is a duty to uphold the autonomy and dignity of those whose choices are discordant from ours and acknowledgement of heterodoxy … as opposed to a forced and unlawful artificial and superficial homogeneity that attempts to suppress difference and diversity. The people of Kenya in the Preamble to the Constitution proclaim that we are '*proud of our ethnic, cultural and religious diversity and determined to live in peace and unity as one indivisible sovereign nation.*' That is the ethos that it is incumbent upon all schools to teach to students from an early age.[71]

This statement aptly captures what the content of the principle of reasonable accommodation should be in a culturally and religiously diverse country like Kenya.

The Court of Appeal also cited with approval Langa CJ's delineation of the content of reasonable accommodation in the South African Constitutional Court decision in *MEC for Education: Kwazulu-Natal & Others v Pillay*.[72] The case concerned the wearing of a nose stud by an Indian Tamil Hindu female learner at Durban Girls' High School in South Africa, which the learner's mother stated was part of a religious ritual and long-standing family tradition upon reaching physical maturity.[73] As in the *Fugicha* case, where the school refused to allow Muslim students to wear the *hijab* as a supplementation of the school uniform, the school management in *Pillay* had refused to grant the learner an exemption to wear a

[70] *Fugicha* (n 47) 27–28.
[71] ibid 27.
[72] *MEC for Education: Kwazulu-Natal & Others v Pillay* 2008 (1) SA 474 (CC) (*Pillay*).
[73] ibid [7].

nose stud for cultural reasons. Giving content to what the principle of reasonable accommodation should mean in such a context, Langa CJ stated:

> At its core [reasonable accommodation] is the notion that sometimes the community, whether it is the State, an employer or a school, must take positive measures and possibly incur additional hardship or expense in order to allow all people to participate and enjoy all their rights equally. It ensures that we do not relegate people to the margins of society because they do not or cannot conform to certain social norms.

This statement resonates with the above-quoted statement by the Kenyan Court of Appeal in the *Fugicha* case. They both emphasise the importance of going beyond toleration and actively providing the space or necessary exemptions for those whose beliefs and practices are discordant from ours for them to flourish. As du Plessis rightly observes, 'such jurisprudence affirms and, indeed, celebrates the Other beyond the confines of mere tolerance or even magnanimous recognition and acceptance'.[74] This reflects the substantive notion of equality, extensively discussed in Chapter 3, that requires us to embrace and celebrate difference.[75] In this chapter, substantive equality particularly applies in situations where a seemingly neutral criterion would nevertheless disproportionately affect a certain cultural or religious group, without compelling justification, in a way that inhibits their full social participation.

Nonetheless, the need to balance conflicting fundamental rights makes it essential to limit the right to freedom of culture and religion in some scenarios. Limitations are especially necessary to curb the practice of harmful cultural and religious practices. Such limitations should, however, comply with Article 24 of the 2010 Constitution, the limitations clause.

B. Pluralism and the Plurality of the Kenyan Legal System

Tied to the rationale of reasonable accommodation is the idea of pluralism and the plurality of the Kenyan legal system. Yash and Jill Ghai give a narrow but fitting definition of pluralism as 'an ethic of respect that seeks to recognize and enable diversity as a common good … a move away from the hegemony of one ethnic group to the accommodation of all groups'.[76] According to Raz, a pluralist society is one which 'place[s] a high value on recognizing the existence of a plurality of valuable ways of life, and of the possibility of change and generation of novel valuable forms of life'.[77] This means that pluralism celebrates difference of the many

[74] L du Plessis, 'Religious Freedom and Equality as Celebration of Difference: A Significant Development in Recent South African Constitutional Case-Law' (2009) 12(4) *Potchefstroom Electronic Law Journal* 10, 26.

[75] Ch 3, text to nn 49–60.

[76] YP Ghai and JC Ghai (eds), *Ethnicity, Nationhood and Pluralism: Kenyan Perspectives* (Nairobi, Katiba Institute, 2013) 1–2.

[77] J Raz, 'Free Expression and Personal Identification' (1991) 11 *OJLS* 303, 311.

existing cultures and religions present in a polity, no matter how conflicting and incommensurable these beliefs may be in terms of what count as valuable ways of life. It requires tolerance, accommodation and inclusivity of ideals that clash with one's own, as long as they are sanctioned by law.[78] A key aspect of pluralism is the acknowledgement of the importance of culture and religion, alongside other social influences, to the formation of one's identity.[79]

The third paragraph of the 2010 Constitution's Preamble alludes to the pluralistic nature of Kenyan society. It underscores that the people of Kenya take pride in their 'ethnic, cultural and religious diversity' and are 'determined to live in peace and unity as one indivisible sovereign nation'. This statement mirrors the core understanding of pluralism, 'that cultural diversity and political unity can co-exist'.[80] As highlighted earlier, Kenya's Court of Appeal has interpreted this statement as requiring tolerance and accommodation 'of the autonomy and dignity of those whose choices are discordant with ours' in order to live in harmony in spite of diversity. It has also referred to it as a clarion call against attempts to suppress difference and diversity.[81]

Aside from the idea of pluralism – the accommodation of different ways of life – there is also a plural legal system in Kenya. Kamau points out that this plural legal system is manifest in the fact that customary, religious and State laws coexist within the same social context.[82] This practice is mostly predominant in former colonies in Africa and Asia, where secular colonial laws were seen as being superimposed on religious and customary laws of the indigenous populations who were the majority. The presence of plural legal systems in these States (eg Kenya, South Africa and India) upon the attainment of independence was thus regarded as imperative in preserving religious and customary laws that a significant number of the population identified with. However, a major question that this chapter interrogates is whether a plural legal system sufficiently attains the values of pluralism. For instance, in relation to religious norms or customary law, does a plural legal system respect internal pluralism, including equality between men and women, and the possibility of exit from religious and customary norms that are, prima facie, discriminatory? This point is discussed below.

The origins of the plural legal system in Kenya can be traced back to the colonial era, when the first official legislation to be enacted, the East African Order in Council of 1897, established a tripartite system of courts. The Native Tribunals for the indigenous African population applied African customary laws with the caveat that the laws could only be applied so long as they were not repugnant to justice and morality.[83] The national Supreme Court, with subordinate courts

[78] Ghai and Ghai (n 76) 16.

[79] ibid 3.

[80] ibid 12.

[81] See text to n 71; *Fugicha* (n 47) 27.

[82] W Kamau, 'Law, Pluralism and the Family in Kenya: Beyond Bifurcation of Formal Law and Custom' (2009) 23(2) *International Journal of Law, Policy and the Family* 133, 135.

[83] Baraza (n 13) 3.

below it, applied English law and common law in cases involving non-Africans or Christians in general.[84] The Muslim system at the Kenyan coastal strip applied Islamic law (on personal law matters including marriage, divorce, inheritance and succession) for all those who professed the Muslim faith.[85] The national Supreme Court with its subordinate courts nevertheless had supervisory powers over the other court systems. Notably also, Islamic courts did not have criminal jurisdiction over Muslims, which was instead vested in the English court system.[86] Hindus in Kenya were subject to some of the personal laws passed by the British in India. These included the Indian Divorce Act, which was later replaced with the Hindu Marriage and Divorce Act.[87]

As colonialism drew to a close, the African population in Kenya pressed for an integrated system. This was because, as Ghai and McAuslain note, 'Africans increasingly regarded their own system as an overt indication of the second class justice meted out to them by the colonial authorities, and the English system available to the immigrant as another unjustified privilege for the immigrants'.[88] Munoru adds that 'while [Africans] could be subjected to other system of courts and law, the other races could not be subjected to customary law'.[89] Moreover, it is argued that 'elites within the country became adept at negotiating the common law or civilian structures and, as a result, had a vested interest in seeing them continue'.[90] All these reasons contributed to the integration of the legal system and, as Munoru highlights, 'Elimination of racial undertones in the court system and in the application of the laws to the citizens'.[91]

The effect of the integration was to give primacy to the formal national legal system. However, customary and Islamic law were still applicable. Kadhis' courts, a court system in Kenya where the adjudicators, referred to as Kadhis, apply Muslim personal law where all parties are Muslims, were retained, with the possibility of appeal to the High Court. Upon appeal, the High Court is to sit with a Chief Kadhi or two other Kadhis as assessor(s) but is not bound to apply Islamic law.[92] The plural legal system has therefore been maintained, save for the fact that customary laws are now enforced by national courts instead of the colonially established Native Tribunals.

[84] ibid.

[85] GGS Munoru, 'The Development of the Kenyan Legal System, Legal Education and Legal Profession' (1973) 9 *East African Law Journal* 1, 1.

[86] ibid.

[87] Baraza (n 13) 4; Hindu Marriage and Divorce Act, Ch 157, Laws of Kenya (repealed).

[88] YP Ghai and P McAuslan, *Public Law and Political Change in Kenya: A Study of the Legal Framework of Government from Colonial times to the Present* (Nairobi, Oxford University Press, 1970) 164. See also East African Order-in-Council, 1902, *5.20*.

[89] Munoru (n 85) 2.

[90] S Joireman, 'Inherited Legal Systems and Effective Rule of Law: Africa and the Colonial Legacy' (2001) 39(4) *Journal of Modern African Studies* 571, 577.

[91] Munoru (n 85) 2.

[92] ibid 4; Kadhis' Courts Act Cap. 11, Laws of Kenya.

However, Kamau argues that the type of plural legal system currently exercised is of the weak kind. Reflecting Griffiths' definition, she describes a 'weak form plural legal system' as one where 'parallel legal regimes co-exist but depend for their legitimacy on the "recognition" or accommodation accorded to them by the dominant state legal order'.[93] Griffiths expounds that, in this pluralistic legal system, the parallel legal regimes are dependent on the controlling formal State legal system.[94] Indeed, as stated earlier, under Article 2(4) of the 2010 Constitution, 'Any law, including customary law, that is inconsistent with [the] Constitution is void to the extent of the inconsistency, and any act or omission in contravention of [the] Constitution is invalid'. This provision represents what Griffiths had in mind – for other legal regimes like customary law to be checked by the formal legal system with the top-most guiding instrument being the Constitution. Additionally, in section 3(2) of Kenya's Judicature Act, the application of African customary law in civil cases is said to only be applicable in so far as it is 'not repugnant to justice and morality or inconsistent with any written law' (the 'repugnancy clause').[95]

Nevertheless, as discussed below, there is an exemption from the automatic application of the constitutional equality provisions given to Islamic personal law, as applied by Kadhis' Courts. This exemption mirrors a kind of 'strong plural legal system' defined as 'a situation in which not all law is State law nor administered by a single set of State legal institutions, and which law is therefore neither systematic nor uniform'.[96] This is evidenced by the fact that the exemption ideally means that some Islamic personal laws, which are nevertheless a violation of formal gender equality laws, will pass constitutional muster. As will be argued, this exemption is problematic as it creates internal incoherence in the Constitution, aside from the fact that it is aimed at respecting the right to religion.

However, on appeal to secular courts, we revert to a 'weak form plural legal system' as Islamic law need not be applied, even if a Kadhi or Chief Kadhi is to sit as an assessor in such cases to advise on matters of Islamic law.[97] This is further expounded on in section 5 of Kenya's Judicature Act, which states that the jurisdiction of Kadhis' courts shall not 'limit the jurisdiction of the High Court or of any subordinate court in any proceeding which comes before it'. The Court of Appeal in its 2015 decision in *RMM v BAM* affirmed this position and stated that it had concurrent jurisdiction in personal law cases between Muslims.[98] It proceeded to hold that *Essa v Essa* is still good law, where it was held that the equitable

[93] Kamau (n 82) 135; J Griffiths, 'What Is Legal Pluralism?' (1986) 18(24) *Journal of Legal Pluralism and Unofficial Law* 1, 5.

[94] Griffiths (n 93).

[95] Judicature Act Cap. 8, Laws of Kenya, s 3(2).

[96] Griffiths (n 93) 5.

[97] The Civil Procedure Act Cap. 21, Laws of Kenya, s 65(1)(b) provides that, on appeals to the High Court, the Chief Kadhi or two Kadhis are to sit in as assessor or assessors.

[98] *RMM v BAM* [2015] eKLR (CA) [33] (Waki, G.B.M. Kariuki, Mwilu, M'inoti and Murgor JJA).

distribution of matrimonial property between spouses applies to Muslims and non-Muslims alike.[99]

Importantly, as much as the various personal laws applied in the plural legal system are perceived as bifurcated and distinct from each other, Kamau rightly stresses that 'in reality, these "systems" do not operate independently but interact in various mutually constitutive ways'.[100] Indeed, using the example of practice in relation to marriage, she correctly observes that many current marriages in Kenya 'do not conform to either the traditional or [w]estern concepts of marriage'. For instance, many Christian couples today choose to have a pre-wedding celebration observing some customary rites, such as slaughtering a goat (*ngurario* among the Kikuyu) and negotiating bride wealth (a cultural practice in almost all tribes in Kenya).

Kamau also notes that some Kenyan couples 'tend to engage in long periods of cohabitation and procreation before they have a church wedding, if ever, and bridewealth is normally paid over a period', making marriage 'a process rather than a single event'.[101] Another similar practice is that of 'outside wifeship', which is 'where a married man will take up other women whom he supports and with whom he has children, without going through formal marriage, either customary or statutory'.[102]

However, the Marriage Act of 2014 discourages these two practices as couples in long cohabitation are not protected upon the breakdown of the relationship or in relation to succession when one of them is deceased. This is because the Act requires all types of marriages, including polygamous ones, recognised under the Act to be registered, and does not acknowledge cohabitation.[103] The types of marriages recognised under section 6 of the Act include Christian, civil, customary, Hindu and Islamic marriages. Section 52 further allows ministers of any other faith to apply to the Registrar of Marriages to be appointed marriage officers for purposes of the Act and section 93 tasks the Cabinet Secretary, under whose docket the Marriage Act falls, with the duty to make rules for the celebration of other marriages. Notable, also, in *Mary Wanjuhi Muigai v Attorney General & Another*, Ngugi J, reading into provisions of the Act, clarified that section 6 is intended to apply to all faiths recognised in the country, aligning it with the 2010 Constitution's Article 27 equality guarantee and freedom of religion in Article 32.[104]

Nevertheless, as much as the non-recognition of presumption of marriage by cohabitation in the 2014 Marriage Act may curb such practices, in instances where they are still practised, children from these relationships, including 'outside wifeship', can still inherit from either parent and are entitled to maintenance.

[99] ibid; *Essa v Essa* (1996) EA 53.
[100] Kamau (n 82) 138–39.
[101] ibid.
[102] ibid 139.
[103] See Marriage Act No. 4 of 2014, Laws of Kenya.
[104] *Mary Wanjuhi Muigai v Attorney General & Another* [2015] eKLR [65].

This is by virtue of Article 53(e) of the 2010 Constitution, which grants equal parental responsibility to the mother and father of a child, whether they are married or not.

On matters of inheritance, it is observed that the predominant cultural belief that women should not inherit land or own property often interferes with the application of Islamic law's rule that daughters and widows should inherit (though sons and widowers get double the amount daughters and widows get).[105]

The intermingling of the various 'systems' in Kenya is important for the analysis in the chapter as it means that culture and religion have a great influence on the lives of many Kenyans, especially outside the watchful eye of the formal legal system.

Going back to the appreciation of pluralism in Kenya, its recognition does not mean that we should ignore cultural and religious intra-group oppressive tendencies, disadvantaging individuals within the group who may need formal law's protection. If cultural and religious groups are given unregulated freedom of self-government, 'there may be little or no scope for individual dissent within each religious [and cultural] community, or little or no freedom to change one's faith [or customs]'.[106] Tied to this point, it has been observed that historically, cultural and religious intolerance has mostly been internal as against dissenters rather than from external forces and groups.[107]

Indeed, there are some deeply patriarchal and oppressive cultural and religious practices that greatly violate the gender equality of women within such groupings. A balance should therefore be struck between a group's collective freedom to practise their customs and beliefs, and the interests of individuals within the group (eg women whose culture it is too) who may be affected by some of these customs and beliefs.[108] Based on this context, a pragmatic approach needs to be taken in dissecting the relationship between culture, religion and gender equality.

C. Personal Autonomy and Free and Informed Consent

Personal autonomy is one, if not the most important, rationale behind the exercise by individuals or groups of their freedom of culture and religion. Chapter 4, invoking Raz, defined personal autonomy as a principle which 'views an autonomous person as being part author of their life, having a degree of control over their destiny, having freedom to choose between valuable options on how to fashion their life'.[109] It was, however, pointed out that the exercise of personal autonomy

[105] J Walsh, *Double Standards: Women's Property Rights Violations in Kenya* (Human Rights Watch Vol. 15(5)(A), March 2003) 40.

[106] Kymlicka (n 56) 82.

[107] ibid 85.

[108] See *Sandra Lovelace v Canada*, Communication No. 24/1977: Canada 30/07/81, UN Doc CCPR/C/13/D/24/1997 (1981).

[109] Ch 4, text to nn 71–73; J Raz, *Morality of Freedom* (Oxford, Clarendon Press, 1986) 370–71.

is subject to certain preconditions. Three helpful preconditions for the exercise of autonomy, as set out by Raz, include 'appropriate mental abilities [necessary to comprehend what choices available mean, free from coercion and manipulation], an adequate range of options, and independence'.[110] It is this principle that is behind the idea that individuals should have the right to exercise free and informed consent to participation in cultural and religious practices.

Reinforcing this argument, various commentators in the field of moral philosophy contend that free and informed consent springs from 'the right which each of us possesses to be treated as a person, and in the duty which all of us have, to have respect for persons, to treat a person as such, and not as an object'.[111] In the context of free and informed consent to cultural and religious practices, the South African Constitutional Court in the *Pillay* case aptly stated:

> A necessary element of freedom and of dignity of any individual is an 'entitlement to respect for the unique set of ends that the individual pursues.' One of those ends is the voluntary religious and cultural practices in which we participate. That we choose voluntarily rather than through a feeling of obligation only enhances the significance of a practice to our autonomy, our identity and our dignity.[112]

It therefore follows that, where genuine free and informed consent is given, we should respect the choice of the acceptor. Raday adds that such choice is valid even where it may disadvantage the acceptor.[113] She observes that this would effectively mean that, in the context of gender-discriminatory cultural norms, 'in situations of genuine consent, there will be no complaint emanating from women disadvantaged by the patriarchal community nor much opportunity to intervene'.[114] However, this prompts the question of whether the law should intervene or not in situations where women give free and informed consent to harmful cultural and religious practices. Raday rightly observes that 'Consent cannot be recognized as effective when inegalitarian norms are so oppressive they undermine, at the outset, the capacity of members of the oppressed group to exercise an autonomous choice to dissent'. She contends that in such instances, consent should not be taken as being genuine.[115]

Certainly, in the exercise of personal autonomy, establishing what amounts to genuine 'free and informed consent', by members of a community, to cultural and religious practices that discriminate against them and are deeply oppressive, is a difficult task. This is particularly so when giving consent means that a person also forfeits essential individual rights, such as the right to life, health and personal security.

[110] Raz (n 109) 370, 372 and 373.

[111] See B Freedman, 'A Moral Theory of Informed Consent' (1975) 5(4) *The Hastings Center Report* 32, 32; R Faden and T Beauchamp, *A History and Theory of Informed Consent* (New York, NY, Oxford University Press, 1986) 4.

[112] *Pillay* (n 72) [64].

[113] Raday (n 14) 701.

[114] ibid 702.

[115] ibid.

An empirical study done by Human Rights Watch on how the practice of wife inheritance and ritual cleansing in Kenya affects women's property rights and, by extension, their right to health and personal security, unearths core demerits of personal autonomy.[116] Wife inheritance refers to the practice whereby a widow is married off to a brother or other male relative of her deceased husband so that she and her children, if any, can continue to occupy the matrimonial home and access any resources of her late husband.

Ritual cleansing is 'a short-term or one-time sexual encounter with a man paid to have sex with the widow' for it is believed that 'widows are contaminated with evil spirits when their husbands die'.[117] These customs are mainly practised by the Luo and Luhya ethnic communities in Kenya. The man chosen for the ritual cleansing is not meant to wear a condom. There are no similar requirements for widowers when their wives die.[118] A widow can refuse to be inherited or cleansed. However, such refusal comes at the risk of forfeiting any claims to the matrimonial property (unless one has sons), excommunication by her community, and being chased away from her matrimonial home.

As one woman interviewed in the study recounted, 'I consented to being inherited in that I wanted to be taken care of … I feared that if I refused to be inherited, people would be brought in by force to inherit me'.[119] The report gives chilling accounts of the disadvantages that befell both the women who refused to be inherited and cleansed, and those who consented. Most of those who refused ended up either moving back to their parents' homes or living in dire poverty in slum areas, especially women from rural areas whose economic base was agriculture.[120] For those who accepted to be inherited and cleansed, this came at the risk of them contracting HIV/AIDS as the man chosen for the ritual cleansing is not usually meant to wear a condom, and women's belittled status makes it hard for them to negotiate safe sex, most especially when they are inherited by the brother of their deceased husband. Many women therefore consent to such harmful practices to keep their property and stay in their communities.[121]

As highlighted earlier, Article 60(1)(f) of the 2010 Constitution prohibits gender discrimination in laws and practices touching on land and property rights. However, despite positive laws such as this one, the de facto practice of gender-discriminatory customs and beliefs continues outside the watchful eye of the law, especially in rural areas. For instance, one of the elders interviewed by Human Rights Watch in its study on the violation of women's property rights stated that 'he knows the Law of Succession Act [stipulating that women and men should get equal inheritance] applies in his village, but in practice, only sons inherit'.[122]

[116] Walsh (n 105).
[117] ibid 12.
[118] ibid.
[119] ibid 20–21.
[120] ibid 16.
[121] ibid 12.
[122] ibid 34.

Hence, because of the hardships many women are bound to face when they choose to 'opt out' of cultural and religious practices, many of them decide to 'opt in'. This makes the notion of 'free and informed consent' questionable in situations like those depicted above as there are so many set outcomes that dictate one's decision. This example exposes the negative side of culture and religion, and why we should not romanticise so much about whole-hearted tolerance of the two, as this may come at a grave cost for the most vulnerable within ethnic and religious groups, most especially women and girls.

In such situations of 'extreme oppression' and 'coercive patriarchal' norms, it is hard not to agree with Raday that consent should be invalidated. She rightly asserts that 'where individuals are compelled by socioeconomic necessity to accept an inferior status, their consent cannot be freely given'.[123] We see this type of reasoning in the Kenyan High Court's decision in the *Ombuna* case, discussed earlier, which rendered unconstitutional the practice of woman-to-woman marriage by the Kisii community. As will be recalled, the practice was said to discriminate against daughters by requiring a widow without sons or a barren woman to marry another wife who would bear children (sons) with another man to perpetuate the deceased husband's name and lineage. In the case, the woman who was obligated to enter such a marriage had daughters and the practice hence discriminated against them.

Raz expounds on the idea that independence to exercise genuine free and informed choice may be flawed. He concedes that what amounts to adequate exercise of control in choosing from a range of options can be problematic, even if the person is said to be free from coercion or manipulation. He rightly observes that people's choices can still be heavily influenced by circumstances which they are forced into, or by their own ignorance or weakness.[124] Nussbaum refers to this as 'adaptive preferences' or 'entrenched satisfactions', whereby 'habit, fear, low expectations, and unjust background conditions deform people's choices and even their wishes for their own lives'.[125]

There are examples of flawed choices or adaptive preferences in the Kenyan context in the statements of women recounted in various reports. In a World Bank report on *Gender and Economic Growth in Kenya*, one woman stated that 'Women having equal rights to inherit land will interfere with our culture, in which the natural order is that a woman comes after the man'.[126] Another woman in the Human Rights Watch report on the violation of women's land and property rights is reported as having stated: 'If we give land to a woman … she will be arrogant and

[123] Raday (n 14) 702–03.
[124] Raz (n 109) 373.
[125] M Nussbaum, *Women and Human Development: The Capabilities Approach* (Cambridge, Cambridge University Press, 2000) 114.
[126] A Ellis, J Cutura, N Dione, I Gillson, C Manuel and J Thongori, *Gender and Economic Growth in Kenya: Unleashing the Power of Women* (Washington, DC, The World Bank, 2007) 22, Box 3.1.

won't serve her man'.[127] Seeing the havoc the failure to recognise women's right to inherit has wreaked in the country, as highlighted in multiple reports and cases, such viewpoints by women can be flagged as a possible case of one's own ignorance or adaptive preference, having internalised women's inferior status in most, if not all, cultures in Kenya. Such attitudes have been said to be a result of socialisation. One statement that aptly summarises this puts it thus:

> Very few women have property registered in their name. Why? Patriarchy. The message is always reinforced that women can't own property. Even some women believe this. Women are socialized in many ways to think that this is the domain of men … Even well educated women fall in the same trap.[128]

Of course, we could say, as Raz does, that to the extent a woman's choice is influenced by her circumstances, she does not really live an autonomous life because of the lack of an adequate range of options to choose from. However, realistically, even if there may be a range of options a person can choose from, issues like lack of knowledge about the existence of other choices may largely affect choice. Take, for instance, a rural uneducated married woman living in a patriarchal society with no property or wealth to her name. She may want to get out of a violent marriage but, even though there may be alternatives available to her, such as equal division of matrimonial property by a court upon divorce, she may not be aware of this. Alternatively, even if she is aware of it, she may not have resources to pay for legal fees unless legal aid is accessible. The fact that cases in Kenya take more than a year, at the very least, to be concluded would also affect the woman in question's choice if she does not have anywhere else to turn to for shelter for herself and, as is usually the case, her children as well.

It is for reasons such as the ones discussed here that Raz adds another precondition for the exercise of autonomy. He argues that 'Autonomy is valuable only if exercised in pursuit of the good' and that 'it requires only the availability of morally acceptable options'.[129] Such an approach is indeed desirable in identifying what genuine free and informed consent that should be accommodated entails. This additional precondition helps unpack what Raday terms 'lesser infringements' to women's right to equality that should be allowed, which will be further discussed in the ensuing section.[130]

From this analysis, we can conclude that individual autonomy of women to participate in cultural and religious practices should be respected only to the extent that such practices can be categorised as 'lesser infringements' of their right to equality. This means that harmful cultural and religious practices such as wife inheritance, widow cleansing, female genital mutilation and forced/early marriage should not be tolerated, regardless of choice. Noting both the importance of the

[127] Walsh (n 105) 35.
[128] ibid.
[129] Raz (n 109) 381.
[130] Raday (n 14) 710.

right to religion and culture, and the need to limit patriarchal cultural and religious practices that are extremely oppressive, I now move on to a discussion of proposed approaches to balancing the two sets of rights.

III. Proposed Approaches to Balancing between Gender Equality and Accommodating the Right to Culture and Religion

The search for the correct balance between the right to gender equality and cultural and religious equality is prompted by the need for a holistic understanding of human rights that considers their universality, indivisibility, interdependence and interrelatedness. The 1993 Vienna Declaration and Programme of Action emphasises that this requires all human rights to be treated 'in a fair and equal manner, on the same footing, and with the same emphasis'.[131] Ghanea argues that if indeed freedom of religion or belief and gender equality are to be enjoyed alongside each other, we need to embrace an approach to resolving the tensions between them by reading them together.[132] She argues that if we are to view rights in this way, we can then appreciate the fact that 'no right can be used as the basis for extinguishing other rights, nor denying rights and freedoms to others'. This would mean that freedom of religion and culture would need 'to be cognizant of non-discrimination on the basis of sex, and women's rights need to be vigilant of non-discrimination on the basis of religion [or culture]'.[133]

Indeed, even though most of the fundamental rights in the 2010 Constitution are not absolute, the limitations clause (Article 24 of the Constitution) stresses that a limitation to a right should not lead to a derogation from its core or essential content.[134] This echoes the fact that a limitation should not lead to the complete obliteration of another right. It is, therefore, argued that there should not be a conflation of harmful cultural and religious practices with the concepts of culture and religion, in and of themselves, as has often been the case.[135] This is particularly so in relation to sweeping statements that culture and religion are generally the main root cause of violation of women's rights, without being careful to state that what is actually meant is harmful cultural and religious practices. As Ghanea importantly points out, appreciation of the synergies between gender equality and freedom of religion and culture enables us to have 'a holistic understanding

[131] UN General Assembly, Vienna Declaration and Programme of Action, 12 July 1993, A/CONF.157/23, [5].

[132] N Ghanea, *Women and Religious Freedom: Synergies and Opportunities* (Washington, DC, United States Commission on International Religious Freedom, 2017) 5.

[133] ibid.

[134] The Constitution of Kenya, 2010, Art 24(2)(c).

[135] Ghanea (n 132) 6; SE Merry, 'Gender Justice and CEDAW: The Convention on the Elimination of All Forms of Discrimination Against Women' (2011) 9(1) *Journal of Women in the Middle East and the Islamic World* 49, 54–56.

of alleged victims' multiple identities, rather than essentialist understandings of sex/gender'.[136] This is in recognising that the identity of a woman may be defined by both her gender and her religion or culture. Hence, she may require protection of both her identities and may not want to entirely lose one to safeguard the other.

Therefore, instead of faulting culture and religion in their entirety, which would violate cultural and religious equality, this section highlights the need to eliminate harmful practices in religion and culture to relieve the tensions between such practices and gender equality.

From this background and previous discussions in the chapter, this section proposes several methods for balancing between gender-discriminatory, or potentially gender-discriminatory, cultural and religious norms and the right to gender equality. These include: (1) application of the limitations clause; (2) accommodating 'lesser infringements'; and (3) the right of exit.

A. Application of the Limitations Clause

Fundamental rights such as the right to culture, religion and equality are not absolute and may be subject to certain limitations if compelling reasons for doing so are adduced. Indeed, as Ghai argues, 'Accommodating widely divergent concepts of morality, gender relations, cultural practices etc. requires negotiated concessions, give and take, that would be impossible if each person's right were absolute'.[137] As will be recalled, the criteria for limiting fundamental rights are encapsulated in Article 24 of the Constitution, which stipulates:

> (1) A right or fundamental freedom in the Bill of Rights shall not be limited except by law, and then only to the extent that the limitation is reasonable and justifiable in an open and democratic society based on human dignity, equality and freedom, taking into account all relevant factors, including—
> (a) the nature of the right or fundamental freedom;
> (b) the importance of the purpose of the limitation;
> (c) the nature and extent of the limitation;
> (d) the need to ensure that the enjoyment of rights and fundamental freedoms by any individual does not prejudice the rights and fundamental freedoms of others; and
> (e) the relation between the limitation and its purpose and whether there are less restrictive means to achieve the purpose.
> …
> (2) …
> (c) shall not limit the right or fundamental freedom so far as to derogate from its core or essential content.

[136] Ghanea (n 132) 5; S Cusack and L Pusey, 'CEDAW and the Rights to Non-Discrimination and Equality' (2013) 14(1) *Melbourne Journal of International Law* 1, 38.
[137] Ghai (n 41) 146–47.

These factors to be considered when deciding whether a limitation to a fundamental right is justifiable are similar to the elements considered in conducting a proportionality test as applied across jurisdictions.[138] The evidentiary burden of proving that a right to culture or religion should be limited, in relation to practices that violate gender equality, lies with the person seeking such a limitation. The same onus applies to a person claiming that gender equality should be limited to allow for the exercise of a cultural or religious practice.

In illustrating how the limitations clause can be applied to limit the rights to freedom of culture and religion when it comes to cultural and religious practices that violate gender equality, I will use the example of female genital mutilation (FGM). According to the 2014 Kenya Demographic and Health Survey, the practice persists, with 21 per cent of Kenyan women aged between 15 and 49 reported as having undergone FGM.[139] The survey also records that 11 per cent of women and men believe the practice is required by their community or religion, or that the practice should continue.[140] In Kenya, the practice is most prevalent in rural areas and among the Kisii, Somali, Maasai, Samburu and Kuria ethnic groups, which record an over 90 per cent prevalence rate, despite legal sanctions.[141]

The first part of the limitations clause, Article 24(1), states that any limitation should be *imposed by law* and, even then, it should be shown that the limitation is *reasonable and justifiable in an open democratic society based on human dignity, equality and freedom*. As will be recalled, harmful cultural and religious practices such as FGM are proscribed by the Constitution in Articles 53(1)(d) and 55(d), which require the protection of children and the youth from harmful practices. Article 44(3) further protects all persons from being compelled to perform, observe or undergo any cultural practice or rite. Supplementing these constitutional provisions, the State has enacted several laws seeking to curb the practice of FGM, the most essential being the Prohibition of Female Genital Mutilation Act.[142]

On whether the limitation is *reasonable and justifiable in an open democratic society based on human dignity, equality and freedom*, the second part of the limitations clause (Article 24(1)(a)–(e)) sets out five factors to be considered in establishing this. The first factor is 'the nature of the fundamental right or freedom'. On the nature of the rights to freedom of culture and religion, Sections I and II outlined their importance in the formation of one's identity and the need to respect a person's autonomy to exercise their customs and beliefs, even those that may be

[138] eg in Canada, as illustrated by the approach taken in *Vriend v Alberta* [1998] 1 SCR 493 [107]. See also Ch 5, text to nn 158–67.

[139] See Kenya National Bureau of Statistics, *2014 Kenya Demographic and Health Survey* (2014) xxiv and 331; Kenya National Bureau of Statistics, *2003 Kenya Demographic Health Survey* (2003).

[140] ibid.

[141] Federation of Women Lawyers (FIDA-Kenya), *Protection Against Female Genital Mutilation: A Review of the Implementation of the Children's Act* (Nairobi, FIDA-Kenya, 2009) 2; E Kiragu, M Wachira and E Kangatta-Lan, *Status of Women and Girls in Kenya: Urgent Need to Uphold Human Rights* (Nairobi, Centre for Rights Education and Awareness, 2007) 13.

[142] Prohibition of Female Genital Mutilation Act No. 32 of 2011, Laws of Kenya, ss 19, 20 and 21.

discordant with one's own. FGM is both a cultural and religious practice which involves partial or total removal of the external female genitalia or other injury to female genital organs as a rite of passage into adolescence or for other cultural and religious reasons.[143] It is said to be conducted to ensure a girl's virginity, increase her likelihood of good marriage prospects, and is generally 'motivated by beliefs of what is considered proper sexual behavior for women and what is necessary to prepare them for marriage'.[144]

Having set out the nature of the freedom of culture and religion and that of FGM, we now move to the second factor, 'the importance of the purpose of the limitation'. There are different types of FGM, ranging from the removal of the small piece of skin that covers the clitoris to a more severe process where all or part of the external genital organs are removed, and the vaginal opening is closed with stitches.[145] As expected, the practice causes severe pain and has several immediate and long-term health consequences for women who undergo 'the cut'. The effects include physical and psychological trauma, difficulties in childbirth, HIV infection, maternal mortality, chronic pain, infertility, tetanus, decreased sexual enjoyment and infections.[146] The purpose of limiting FGM is therefore to protect women's right to life, health and personal security, because of the negative harmful physical and psychological consequences of the practice. And, also, because the reasons behind the practice, as highlighted earlier, are intended to control a woman's sexuality, which violates their human dignity.

The third factor requires us to consider 'the nature and extent of the limitation'. The Prohibition of Female Genital Mutilation Act outlaws FGM for all women and makes it illegal to practise or procure it or take somebody abroad to undergo it.[147] Importantly, section 19(6) of the Act provides that 'it is no defence to a charge under this section that the person on whom the act involving female genital mutilation was performed consented to that act, or that the person charged believed that such consent was given'. This supports the standpoint taken earlier that there cannot be genuine free and informed consent to harmful cultural and religious practices. The Act also prohibits derogatory remarks about women who have not undergone FGM and offenders may be jailed for six months or fined Ksh 50,000 (US$500) or both.[148] These provisions will be further discussed in the fifth factor to be considered.

The fourth factor is 'the need to ensure that the enjoyment of rights and fundamental freedoms by any individual does not prejudice the rights and fundamental freedom of others'. In relation to this factor, the interest of communities that practise FGM as part of their right to freedom of culture and religion effectively

[143] Kenya National Bureau of Statistics, *2014 Kenya Demographic and Health Survey* (n 139) 331.
[144] ibid; Kiragu, Wachira and Kangatta-Lan (n 141) 13.
[145] See Kiragu, Wachira and Kangatta-Lan (n 141); FIDA-Kenya, *The Prohibition of Female Genital Mutilation Act 2010, Abridged Version* (Nairobi, FIDA-Kenya, 2014) 4.
[146] FIDA-Kenya, *Protection Against Female Genital Mutilation* (n 141) 2.
[147] Prohibition of Female Genital Mutilation Act (n 142).
[148] ibid s 25.

prejudices the rights of individual women to gender equality, life, health and personal security.

The fifth factor is 'the relation between the limitation and its purpose and whether there are less restrictive means to achieve the purpose'. This closely relates to the third factor, which sets out the specific provisions prohibiting the practice of FGM and the ridiculing of those who have not undergone 'the cut'. As was stated, the purpose of the limitation is clear, to protect women and girls from the physical and psychological negative consequences of FGM which infringe on their right to life, health and personal security. The prohibition also safeguards women's human dignity due to the invasive nature of the practice and reasons behind it, as previously articulated. There are indeed less restrictive means that can be applied instead of FGM. For instance, it has been suggested that FGM can be replaced with the 'introduction of "alternative rites of passage", which replace the practice with rituals that retain cultural significance of a coming-of-age ceremony without physically harming the young women involved'.[149] The option of having non-oppressive alternative rites of passage also means that the limitation as required by Article 24(2)(c) is narrowly tailored, in such a way that it does not derogate from the core or essential content of cultural and religious freedoms to put in place coming-of-age ceremonies.

Based on the analysis, we can conclude that the prohibition of FGM, even if it is a prima facie breach of the right to culture and religion, is *reasonable and justifiable in a democratic society based on human dignity, equality and freedom*. Such an analysis is particularly applicable to harmful practices. The next two proposed approaches are largely tied to the limitations analysis, and the arguments made thereunder can be applied to make a case for whether a cultural or religious practice should be limited.

B. Accommodating 'Lesser Infringements'

It was argued earlier that respecting the principle of personal autonomy means that we should respect women's autonomy to live under patriarchal cultural and religious norms if such choice is free from coercion or manipulation. However, citing Raz, it was observed that, at times, 'people's choices can still be heavily influenced by circumstances which they are forced into, one's own ignorance or one's weakness'.[150] This is particularly so when it comes to 'extremely oppressive' and 'coercive patriarchal' norms.[151] For this reason, I agreed with Nussbaum that there is something wrong with some 'adaptive preferences' influenced by dire conditions or low expectations such as putting up with domestic violence.[152] But how

[149] Kiragu, Wachira and Kangatta-Lan (n 141) 14.
[150] See text to n 124.
[151] See text to nn 124–28.
[152] See text to nn 124–26.

can we sieve out personal choices that should be respected, even if they amount to 'adaptive preferences', and those, like putting up with abuse, that should not be tolerated in the context of culture and religion? Raday argues that respect for women's choices to live under patriarchal norms should only be for what she terms 'lesser infringements' to women's right to equality.[153] This is one way of determining personal choices that should or should not be respected. Nevertheless, Raday does not discuss what such 'lesser infringements' include. On the matter, she simply recommends that constitutional authorities should put in place 'a spectrum of measures to create an educational and economic infrastructure that will augment women's autonomy'.[154]

We are therefore left with the question: What counts as a 'lesser infringement'? Taking a controversial example, could polygamy amount to a 'lesser infringement' of a woman's right to equality? The widespread cultural acceptance of polygamy in Kenya is seen in the fact that, even if Kenya is a party to CEDAW,[155] which requires that practices like polygamy should be done away with, polygamy is still recognised under Kenyan law for customary and Islamic law marriages. For instance, section 6(1)(c) of the Marriage Act of 2014 includes customary law marriage, which may be polygamous or potentially polygamous, as one of the recognised marriages in Kenya that should be registered.[156] Notably also, the Matrimonial Property Act of 2013 covers the distribution of matrimonial property in a polygamous marriage divorce.[157]

The 2015 High Court decision in *Mary Wanjuhi Muigai v Attorney General & Another* sheds light on the matter.[158] Ngugi J stated that, because a woman does not have the same right as a man to marry a second spouse, 'it must be accepted that polygamy precludes equality between men and women'.[159] However, she noted that polygamous marriages are accepted in many cultures in Kenya. Therefore, its registration 'was necessary to bring some degree of certainty to a system of marriage practiced by many, yet was outside the reach of the law'. This was in acknowledgement of the challenge, in previous succession cases, faced by women who claimed to be married under customary law but had to adduce evidence to prove that they were indeed wives, and therefore entitled to inherit upon the demise of their husbands.[160]

Nevertheless, Ngugi J held that '*the practice of polygamy and registration of polygamous marriages without consent of the previous wife or wives is inconsistent*

[153] Raday (n 14) 710.
[154] ibid.
[155] See CEDAW, *Concluding observations of the Committee on the Elimination of Discrimination against Women – Kenya*, 5 April 2011, CEDAW/C/KEN/CO/7, [18], [45] and [46]. Here, the CEDAW Committee urges Kenya to 'Bring all marriage laws under the prohibition of polygamy'.
[156] Marriage Act 2014 (n 103).
[157] Matrimonial Property Act No 49 of 2013, Laws of Kenya, s 8.
[158] *Muigai v Attorney General* (n 104).
[159] ibid [70].
[160] ibid [71].

with the equality provisions of the Constitution'.[161] This is by virtue of Article 45(3) of the Constitution, which provides for the equal rights of parties to a marriage, before, during and after the marriage.

In striking a difficult balance between polygamy's violation of gender equality and the necessity of granting legal protection to the many women who choose to enter polygamous marriages, even though such choices may be adaptive preferences or influenced by circumstances women are forced into, Ngugi J stated:

> While this Court accepts that permitting polygamous marriages without the consent of a previous wife or wives is not consistent with the Constitution, and that indeed the practice of polygamy is in itself not consistent with the equality principles in the Constitution, it also recognizes that there are situations and practices that it cannot regulate, and that must be left to the wishes and dictates of the people, through their duly elected representatives, as well as to the individual choices of those adults contracting marriages, and who willingly enter into polygamous marriages.[162]

The above statement by Ngugi J, and her holding that the practice of polygamy and registration of marriages should only be done with the consent of a previous wife or wives, alludes to two elements that can make polygamy a 'lesser infringement'. First, her statement above shows that polygamy can only amount to a 'lesser infringement' if a woman gives her consent to such a marriage. In accordance with Article 45(3) of the Constitution, as interpreted by Ngugi J, this should be both consent to be married under customary law, which allows polygamy, and to the marriage of an additional wife or wives.

The second element relates to the widespread de facto practice of polygamy necessitating legal recognition and protection. According to various reports on the reform of marriage laws before the enactment of the 2014 Marriage Act, as highlighted by Ngugi J, the logic behind the recognition of polygamous marriages was a practical one. Despite polygamy being discriminatory against women, its recognition was viewed as a 'lesser evil' meant to guarantee protection for the numerous women married under polygamous customary marriages who would otherwise lose protection if no legal recognition existed.[163] These two elements are best reflected in Ngugi J's statement that 'there are situations and practices that [the Constitution] cannot regulate, and that must be left to the wishes and dictates of the people'.[164] Nevertheless, this should not act as a blanket protection of such cultural practices. Social programmes to educate women about their rights should be undertaken to facilitate their making of informed choices. However, even if this happens, there is still the recurring question of whether women truly have a range of valuable options available to them if the circumstances in which they live make them select a choice that largely disadvantages them.

[161] ibid [78] (emphasis added in the case).
[162] ibid [77].
[163] ibid [71] and [75].
[164] ibid [77].

Another helpful approach to determine what constitutes 'lesser infringements' would be to sieve out harmful cultural and religious practices that essentially amount to grossly oppressive practices that should not be tolerated. What amounts to harmful cultural and religious practices is discussed in the 2014 joint General Comment No. 31 of the Committee on the Elimination of Discrimination against Women (CEDAW Committee) and Committee on the Rights of the Child (CRC Committee), which sets out comprehensive criteria of what harmful cultural and religious practices that violate gender equality would entail.[165] This General Comment is of persuasive nature to Kenyan courts and other State organs since the country has ratified CEDAW and the Convention on the Rights of the Child (CRC).[166] Setting out the criteria for identifying harmful practices, it states:

a. They constitute a denial of the dignity and/or integrity of the individual and a violation of human rights and fundamental freedoms enshrined in the two Conventions;
b. They constitute discrimination against women or children and are harmful insofar as they result in negative consequences for them as individuals or groups, including physical, psychological, economic and social harm and/or violence and limitations on their capacity to participate fully in society or develop and reach their full potential;
c. They are traditional, re-emerging or emerging practices that are prescribed and/or kept in place by social norms that perpetuate male dominance and inequality of women and children, based on sex, gender, age and other intersecting factors; [and/or]
d. They are imposed on women and children by family, community members, or society at large, regardless of whether the victim provides, or is able to provide, full, free and informed consent.[167]

Applying the criteria, the report flags some of the most prevalent cultural and religious practices that amount to harmful practices. These include 'female genital mutilation, child and/or forced marriage, polygamy, crimes committed in the name of so-called honour and dowry related violence'.[168] However, as stated earlier, the practice of polygamy in the Kenyan context has been a difficult one to flag as a harmful practice in the law, more so because of de facto polygamy such as the 'outside wifeship' practice, which was discussed earlier.

The criteria set out by the CEDAW and CRC Committees comprehensively capture the invidious nature of practices such as FGM, which explains why they

[165] UN Committee on the Elimination of Discrimination against Women and Committee on the Rights of the Child, *Joint general recommendation/general comment No. 31 of the Committee on the Elimination of Discrimination against Women and No. 18 of the Committee on the Rights of the Child on harmful practices*, 4 November 2014, CEDAW/C/GC/31-CRC/C/GC/18.

[166] See indicators.ohchr.org. Kenya acceded to CEDAW in 1984 without reservations and ratified the CRC in 1990.

[167] UN Committee on the Elimination of Discrimination against Women and Committee on the Rights of the Child (n 165) [15].

[168] ibid [6].

should be made illegal. Moreover, Raday argues that 'If discrimination results in the infringement of women's human dignity, in violence, or in economic injury, intervention is justified'.[169] Ideally, the notion of 'lesser infringements' presupposes that cultural and religious practices that are not flagged as harmful practices, though they may not guarantee equal rights between men and women, should be considered 'lesser infringements' and accommodated. However, this is a complex category with much room for disagreement. This is illustrated in the summary of what Kenyans wanted in the road to adoption of the 2010 Constitution, as noted in the Constitution of Kenya Review Commission's final report. They wanted culture and religion to 'be respected, recognised, promoted, preserved and protected so long as they are not harmful, oppressive and discriminatory and or [*sic*] forced on an individual'.[170] In this statement, 'discriminatory' can be argued to include 'lesser infringements'. Therefore, whether practices like polygamy amount to 'lesser infringements' or not should be determined on a case-by-case basis to see whether the balance should be drawn in favour of accommodation.

C. Right of Exit

Another important approach that helps allay the tensions between culture/religion and gender equality is the 'right of exit', or right to withdraw consent to a system that is discriminatory on the basis of gender. On the 'right of exit', Raday argues that in situations where lack of genuine consent to oppressive patriarchal cultural and religious norms is transparent, 'the right to equality entails the provision of a parallel system to which women may turn'. She uses polygamy as an example and argues that 'where the culture or the religion allows polygamy, women must have the legal option of nonpolygamous marriage', such as the option of entering a civil marriage which provides a 'non-patriarchal' alternative.[171]

The 'right of exit' is present in the Kenyan legal system through the presence of formal laws governing all spheres of life that are bereft of gender inequality and offer an alternative to patriarchal cultural and religious norms. For instance, as was pointed out earlier, the 2014 Marriage Act grants individuals the right to contract marriage in either civil form or according to the rites of a specified custom or faith.[172] This includes customary and Islamic marriages, which are presumed to be polygamous or potentially polygamous.[173] To establish a 'right of exit' from a polygamous or potentially polygamous marriage, section 8 provides for the right to convert a polygamous marriage to a monogamous one, as long as the husband only has one wife at the time of conversion. Generally, persons professing all faiths or non-religion may opt to enter a civil marriage.

[169] Raday (n 14) 704–05.
[170] Constitution of Kenya Review Commission (n 69) 94.
[171] Raday (n 14) 705.
[172] Marriage Act 2014 (n 103).
[173] ibid s 6(3).

Also, in terms of matrimonial property, section 14 of the Matrimonial Property Act sets a rebuttable presumption that matrimonial property acquired during marriage, but registered in the name of one spouse, is held in trust for the other spouse.[174] It continues to provide that matrimonial property jointly registered means that both spouses have equal beneficial interests to it. These formal legal requirements could be invoked by a woman seeking to exit patriarchal cultural and religious norms that deny women the right to own property or inheritance upon divorce or the death of their husbands.

However, seeing that in most cases a woman would have to move the court to ensure that her rights to matrimonial property upon divorce or inheritance upon the demise of her husband are respected, access to justice may be a great impediment to the 'right of exit'. This is because of the costly nature of litigation and the length of time it takes for a case to be concluded, as extensively discussed in Chapter 8.[175] Another obstacle to the 'right of exit' is some women's lack of awareness about their legal rights enabling them to exit from the application of patriarchal, cultural and religious norms.[176] This problem is especially acute for women residing in rural areas. This has prompted recommendations for the government to conduct more civic education on matters such as women's property rights.[177]

Therefore, for the 'right of exit' to be a practical and available option for women, as it should be, the State needs to work on issues such as providing legal aid and civic education on alternatives to gender-discriminatory cultural and religious practices. The State should also require the judiciary to provide frequent reports on timelines for the handling and disposal of cases, and on what the judiciary is doing to reduce case backlog.

IV. Exemption of Islamic Personal Law from the Automatic Application of Equality Provisions in the Bill of Rights and What this Means for Gender Equality

The previous sections have analysed and critiqued the key rationales for the right to freedom of culture and religion through the lens of cultural and religious practices that violate gender equality. Having discussed the limits of rationales like reasonable accommodation, pluralism and personal autonomy in the context of intra-group dissent to harmful cultural and religious practices, the explicit exemption of Islamic law from automatic application of equality provisions in the Bill

[174] Matrimonial Property Act (n 157).
[175] Ch 8, text to nn 2–6.
[176] Walsh (n 105) 41.
[177] ibid 37.

of Rights raises many questions. This exemption is found in Article 24(4) of the Constitution which provides:

> The provisions of this Chapter on equality shall be qualified to the extent *strictly necessary* for the application of Muslim law before the Kadhis' courts, to persons who profess the Muslim religion, in matters relating to personal status, marriage, divorce and inheritance (emphasis added).

The provision thus exempts Islamic law from the automatic application of equality provisions in the Bill of Rights. Article 170 of the Constitution endorses the application of Islamic law by Kadhis' courts. The jurisdiction of the Court is however limited to 'the determination of questions of Muslim law relating to personal status, marriage, divorce or inheritance in proceedings in which all the parties profess the Muslim religion and submit to the jurisdiction of the Kadhis' courts'.[178] The High Court has further held that Kadhis' courts do not have jurisdiction over issues of custody and maintenance of children, further narrowing the range of issues that can be adjudicated by a Kadhi.[179] However, the presence of Kadhis' courts does not oust the jurisdiction of secular courts to hear and determine matters of personal law between Muslims. As stated earlier, this is highlighted in section 5 of the Kadhis' Courts Act, which states that the presence of Kadhis' courts does not 'limit the jurisdiction of the High Court or any other subordinate court in any proceeding which comes before it'.[180] The jurisdiction of Kadhis' courts therefore runs concomitantly with that of secular courts, and appeals from decisions of Kadhis' courts can be made to the High Court and Court of Appeal. An essential point to be noted here, as highlighted earlier, is that a Kadhi or Chief Kadhi usually sits in an appeal to secular national courts as an assessor to advise on matters of Islamic law.[181]

This section examines the legitimacy of this exemption. An analysis of the legitimacy of Article 24(4) is essential to this chapter as the exemption given to Islamic law affects the transformative nature of the equality guarantee and its harmonious interpretation. The exemption is vague since there is no guidance in the Constitution on what is implied by Islamic laws that make it *strictly necessary* to limit equality provisions in the Bill of Rights. The Constitution's silence on this issue makes the provision susceptible to misinterpretation and creates internal incoherence. This is particularly so in relation to Islamic law norms that are discriminatory against women and thus a limitation to the strong emphasis on the equal rights of men and women in Article 27(3). For this reason, the main aim of this section is to address the question: How can Article 24(4) be construed to make sure that the right to religion by Muslim minorities is freely enjoyed, while at the

[178] Constitution of Kenya 2010, Art 170(5).
[179] *SMH v SAA* [2013] eKLR (HC); *GSA v ASA* [2014] eKLR (HC); *ZHZ v SDS* Civil Appeal No 45 of 2013 (HC); *HMM v KJD* [2014] eKLR (HC).
[180] Kadhis' Courts Act, Cap. 11, Laws of Kenya.
[181] See n 97.

same time respecting gender equality? It also tests whether the proposals offered in the preceding section, for dealing with different types of cultural and religious norms that clash with gender equality, can be applied to Islamic personal laws that may violate women's right to equality.

A. Background of the Contention between Islamic Personal Law Norms and Gender Equality

As stated in the introduction, approximately 10.9 per cent of Kenyans are Muslim. Islam is also the dominant religion in the Coastal, North Eastern and Upper Eastern regions of the country.[182] This means that Islam plays a significant role in the lives of many Kenyans. Notably, Islam is one of the oldest religions in Kenya, having been spread eons ago by Arab and Indian traders in Kenya's coastal region.[183] This is evidenced by the 1330 report by the Moroccan explorer, Abu Abdallah ibn Batuta, who documented that the people living in the Kenyan coast of Mombasa at the time were *Shāfi ʿī* Muslims with a justice system administered by *qadis* (or Khadi as referred to in Kenya).[184] As mentioned above, the 2010 Constitution limits the applicability of Islamic law to issues of personal law (marriage, divorce and inheritance), excluding those on child custody. Hence, the most contentious Islamic laws in Kenya are those touching on women's rights, as men and women rarely have equal rights in Islamic personal law.[185] The practice is the same as in many other religious and cultural groups in Kenya as discussed in Section I.

The inclusion of Islamic law in Kenya's legal system can be traced to the compromises that were made at the time of independence for Kenya to retain its 10-mile coastal strip, which was originally the dominion of the Sultan of Zanzibar. One of the agreements signed between the Kenyan government and the Sultan in October 1963 was that Kadhis' courts should be preserved and their jurisdiction retained in Islamic law matters relating to personal status in cases where all parties professed the Muslim religion.[186]

This agreement was the main basis for the retention of Kadhis' courts in Kenya post independence. Nevertheless, the inclusion of Kadhis' courts in the 2010 Constitution was a highly divisive issue.[187] Opponents of their inclusion – who

[182] C Salvadori, 'Twelve Mosques: The History of Islam in Kenya' (2009) 38(1) *Kenya Past and Present* 33.
[183] ibid 34.
[184] J Chesworth, 'Kadhi's Courts in Kenya: Reactions and Responses' in A Tayob (ed), *Constitutional Review in Kenya and Kadhis Courts: Selected Papers Presented at the Workshop* (Cape Town, St. Paul's University's Department of Religious Studies and Centre for Contemporary Islam of the University of Cape Town, 2010) 3.
[185] Modirzadeh (n 16) 207.
[186] S Kimeu, 'Historical and Legal Foundations of the Kadhi's Courts in Kenya' in A Tayob (ed), *Constitutional Review in Kenya and Kadhis Courts: Selected Papers Presented at the Workshop* (Cape Town, St. Paul's University's Department of Religious Studies and Centre for Contemporary Islam of the University of Cape Town, 2010) 20–21; Chesworth (n 184) 5.
[187] Chesworth (n 184) 9.

mostly comprised Christian religious leaders – argued that 'Kenya is a secular state with a secular Constitution. It therefore provides no room for religious institutions within the state structure'.[188] It was also argued that the inclusion of Kadhis' courts favoured one religion over others and was thus a violation of equal treatment of all religions.[189]

Nevertheless, arguments by most opponents made no mention of the history surrounding the inclusion of Kadhis' courts, the need for tolerance and reasonable accommodation. The attacks thus 'left Muslims feeling marginalised'.[190] At the other end of the spectrum, proponents of Kadhis' courts argued that they were harmless to non-Muslims as they only applied in marriage, divorce and inheritance matters where both parties professed the Islamic faith and consented to the court's jurisdiction.[191] Furthermore, it was contended that 'since the Kenyan Constitution is based on Christian values, similar recognition should be had to Islamic personal law'.[192] Resolving the stand-off on the matter, the Committee of Experts tasked with drafting the Constitution gave reasons for its decision to include Kadhis' courts in the final draft of the Constitution as follows:

> The obvious danger [of not including Kadhis' courts in the Constitution] would be that the Coast, along with a sea belt of an exclusive economic zone of 200 miles enjoyed by the country in terms of resources and access to the sea … would separate from Kenya as the terms on which the Coast was integrated would have been breached. In other words, provision for the existence of the [Kadhis'] Courts in the Constitution is part of the constitutional and territorial foundation of Kenya as well as the basis for the protection of the diversity of Muslims and their belonging within Kenya. All this had to be preserved for the peace, stability, integrity, and economic good of the country.[193]

The chairperson of the Committee, Nzamba Kitonga, added that the decision not to view Kadhis' courts as a contentious issue was informed by more than 12,000 written memoranda received from Kenyans. Very few of these submissions considered the courts a contentious issue, as did only a small section of evangelical Christians.[194] This background clarifies what is indisputable and what is in issue. What is indisputable is the legitimacy of Kadhis' courts, whose inclusion is part of the 'constitutional and territorial foundation of Kenya'. The problem is with the vague exemption for Islamic law in Article 24(4).

[188] Kimeu (n 186) 26.
[189] ibid.
[190] Chesworth (n 184) 9.
[191] Kimeu (n 186) 27.
[192] ibid.
[193] Committee of Experts on Constitutional Review, *Final Report of the Committee of Experts on Constitutional Review* (2011) 60.
[194] See M Mraja, 'Current Debates on the Harmonized Draft Constitution of Kenya' in A Tayob (ed), *Constitutional Review in Kenya and Kadhis Courts: Selected Papers Presented at the Workshop* (Cape Town, St. Paul's University's Department of Religious Studies and Centre for Contemporary Islam of the University of Cape Town, 2010) 33.

B. Practice under the Previous Constitution on Islamic Personal Law and Gender Equality

Section 82(4) of the previous Constitution, which was wider than the exemption in Article 24(4), exempted all personal laws from the application of the prohibition of gender discrimination. This provision left Kenyan women open to discrimination in matters relating to personal law (marriage, divorce and inheritance) in both religion and culture, areas where women are most vulnerable.[195] The provision led to several judicial decisions and provisions in legislation denying women equal rights on account of religious or customary laws. For instance, in *Mwanthi v Mwanthi & Another*, the Court of Appeal, applying Kikuyu customary law, held that married daughters could not inherit the estate of their deceased Kikuyu father.[196] On laws that are detrimental to women's equal rights, sections 32 and 33 of the Law of Succession Act allow the application of customary laws, even those that deny women the right to inherit, to listed regions where land is held communally.[197] The plight of women resulting from the previous exclusion of personal law from application of the prohibition of gender discrimination was one of the main reasons for the inclusion of Article 27(3) of the 2010 Constitution, emphasising the equal rights of men and women in all spheres of life. Therefore, viewed from this context, the exemption given to Islamic personal law becomes suspect as it fails to consider the milestones made in moving away from regressive jurisprudence under the previous Constitution.

However, an ethnographic assessment of 129 cases before the Malindi Kadhis' courts by Susan Hirsch, under the previous Constitution, shows that the application of Islamic law had key benefits for Muslim women.[198] She notes that one-quarter of all cases in these courts pertained to requests for divorce and maintenance, and were mostly filed by women. She adds that almost all these women received judgments in their favour.[199] Moreover, Hirsch argues that Swahili Muslim men are, in fact, quite critical of Kadhis' courts, 'which are seen as disempowering men and allowing women to air shameful stories in public'.[200] As Hirsch stresses, intricate accounts of marriage disputes are considered by Swahili Muslims, particularly men, as being 'shameful, dangerous, and best left untold'. Women who tell such narratives in public or to courts 'are considered unable to persevere'.[201] Thus, considering Hirsch's ethnographic assessment, Islamic personal law as administered by Kadhis' courts can be viewed as a place for women to challenge their oppression.

[195] Kenya Land Alliance, *A Case for Women's Land Rights in the Proposed New Constitution* (2006) 5.

[196] *Mwanthi v Mwanthi & Another* (1995–98) 1 EA 229 (CA).

[197] Law of Succession Act, Cap. 160, Laws of Kenya.

[198] SF Hirsch, *Pronouncing and Persevering: Gender and the Discourses of Disputing in an African Islamic Court* (Chicago, IL, University of Chicago Press, 1998) 129.

[199] ibid 4.

[200] ibid 10.

[201] ibid 8.

The majority of cases reviewed in Hirsch's study reveal that, pre 2010, there was positive jurisprudence by the Kadhis' courts on issues of marriage, divorce and maintenance upon divorce. This fact is significant to my analysis as it proves that at one end of the continuum it is important to acknowledge the positive aspects of Kadhis' courts in providing an avenue where Muslim women can challenge oppression in matters of Islamic personal law.

Moreover, the fact that women can petition for a divorce in Islamic courts challenges the right of unilateral divorce through the *talaq* law, which is enjoyed by Muslim men.[202] *Talaq* provides that only a man may divorce his wife, even if he is required to provide for her. However, Hirsch's assessment does not consider other areas of personal law (inheritance and succession) where Kadhis' courts have jurisdiction.

As much as positive jurisprudence in the Kadhis' courts on marriage and divorce can be identified under the previous Constitution, there are other Islamic law norms on personal law that are said to be irreconcilable with gender equality. For example, Ghai argues that some of the gender equality concerns as to the application of Islamic law include 'the difference in inheritance by women and men under Muslim law'.[203] Other Islamic personal laws regarded as discriminatory against women include the provision that 'a man may beat his wife, even if lightly, [and that] the evidence of two women, is equal to evidence of one man'.[204] However, Muslim commentators have noted that the law of evidence in Islamic law where the evidence of one man is said to be equivalent to that of two women is not applicable in Kenya's Kadhis' courts. On matters of evidence, section 6 of the Kadhis' Courts Act unequivocally mandates that 'all witnesses called shall be heard without discrimination on grounds of religion, sex or otherwise'. This procedural requirement has been said to mean that the evidence of a woman has the same weight as that of a man and, in this sense, 'the *Shari'a* as followed in Kenya [has] in fact already developed for Kenyan Muslims'.[205]

In addition to the examples put forward about how some Islamic personal law practices violate gender equality, Fitzgerald comments that 'concerns remain over coercion of women to submit to these courts [Kadhis' courts]'.[206] It is therefore important to embark on an analysis of the views of Muslim women as to why they supported the inclusion of Kadhis' courts and to the application of Islamic law so far under the 2010 Constitution, to determine whether the trend is still the same.

[202] See N Abiad, *Sharia, Muslim States and International Human Rights Treaty Obligations: A Comparative Study* (London, British Institute of International and Comparative Law, 2008) 29.

[203] Ghai (n 41) 55.

[204] See *Jesse Kamau & 25 Others v Attorney General* [2010] eKLR (HC); Surah 2:228–232, Surah 65:1–7 and Surah 2:282 of the Quran.

[205] A Tayob, 'Muslim Responses to Kadhis Courts as part of Kenya's Constitutional Review' in A Tayob (ed), *Constitutional Review in Kenya and Kadhis Courts: Selected Papers Presented at the Workshop* (Cape Town, St. Paul's University's Department of Religious Studies and Centre for Contemporary Islam of the University of Cape Town, 2010) 60.

[206] J Fitzgerald, 'The Road to Equality? The Right to Equality in Kenya's New Constitution' (2010) 5 *The Equal Rights Review* 55, 65.

C. Views of Muslim Women on Islamic Personal Law as Administered by Kadhis' Courts and Gender Equality

The Constitution of Kenya Review Commission's final report highlights the fact that Muslim women supported the inclusion of Kadhis' courts in the Constitution to handle matters related to Islamic personal law among Muslims. The report observes that 'Through these courts, Muslim women have succeeded in fighting protection and enforcement of their rights as guaranteed under Islamic law and to challenge negative cultural practices and customs of Muslim communities that tend to undermine these rights'.[207] This statement suggests that Muslim women wanted to preserve Islamic law as applied by Kadhis' courts because they see it as an avenue to dismantle patriarchy. Abdi adds that in Kadhis' courts, 'the rights of women to inherit property and to be treated with respect within marriage is assured'.[208] Nevertheless, she notes the calls for reforms to Kadhis' courts so that they can better address women's needs. In this regard, one Muslim woman stated: 'we also want to be allowed to have lawyers who understand Islamic law to help us in the cases instead of having to argue cases out of court without the proper knowledge'.[209]

Ousseina's interviews with Muslim women leaders, activists, educationalists and reformers in Kenya is particularly enlightening on the views of Muslim women regarding the relationship between the application of Islamic personal law by Kadhis' courts and gender equality.[210] One of the people interviewed by Ousseina was Judge Abida Ali-Aroni, who was at one point chairperson of the Constitution of Kenya Review Commission and is now a High Court judge in Kenya. She raises several concerns about Kadhis. First, she points out that many Kadhis (pre 2010 Constitution) were not properly trained in Islamic jurisprudence and often performed multiple roles: as *imams* preaching in mosques on Fridays, political and social spokespersons for the Muslim community, and finally as judicial officers in Kadhis' courts.[211] She states that this was a challenge because

> when you have a [K]adhi that may have knowledge of the Qur'an but has not been properly trained into the adjudication of such matters and sits as [K]adhi, sits as an African man, sits as a Muslim man and you are there as a woman, he will not see your point of view.[212]

This has, however, improved as the 2010 Constitution requires persons to be appointed as Kadhis to have knowledge of Islamic law, although there are still calls

[207] Constitution of Kenya Review Commission (n 69) 206–07.

[208] D Abdi, 'Real Gains for Muslim Women', *Kenyan Woman* (Nairobi, Issue Number 01, January 2010).

[209] ibid.

[210] Ousseina (n 6).

[211] ibid 131.

[212] ibid 133.

to ensure that Kadhis are also trained lawyers, aside from being knowledgeable in Islamic law.[213]

Ali-Aroni J also observes that, before the 2010 Constitution, Kadhis applied patriarchal gender ideologies 'often rooted within traditional conservatism', the result of which mainly affected women and children. Tied to the danger of Kadhis applying patriarchal gender ideologies is the lack of religious literacy among Muslim women in Kenya.[214] On this matter, Ali-Aroni J notes, as recounted by Ousseina, that having Muslim women engage in critical Islamic literacy 'would assist them in fighting against the violation of their human rights'.[215] She additionally cites the fact that, in some instances, Islamic law provides more rights for women than secular law does. Therefore, she concludes that Islamic law does not marginalise women but the negative practices of certain people.[216] Overall, Ousseina records that Ali-Aroni J advocates for the retention of Kadhis' courts for Muslim personal law as long as there is 'high judicial accountability on the part of Kadhis, similar to what judges within the secular framework have to answer to'.[217] Ousseina also concludes by stating that, of all the interviews she conducted with Muslim women, as much as they hold different ideologies, 'all concur in their support for [K]adhi courts and about the urgent need for educated Muslim women to intervene in Islamic education and transform patriarchal Islamic institutions and practices'.[218]

These accounts reveal that many Muslim women support the application of Islamic personal law and truly see it as a place for their empowerment, if it is free from the incorrect application of Islamic law, and if the demand for high judicial accountability for Kadhis' courts, similar to secular courts, is heeded.

D. Practice under the 2010 Constitution on Islamic Personal Law and Gender Equality

From my analysis of more than 20 cases before the Kadhis' courts, and subsequent appeals to the High Court and Court of Appeal, various conclusions can be drawn. Six relevant cases were picked out to act as examples of the issues arising. First, most of the cases before these courts relate to divorce and are mostly brought by women.[219] Second, the judgments are generally in favour of women and are usually upheld by the High Court on appeal.[220] However, there are cases before the

[213] ibid 133–35.
[214] ibid 131–32.
[215] ibid 140 and 143.
[216] ibid 143.
[217] ibid 178.
[218] ibid.
[219] eg *AAAN v MJK a.k.a. SJK* [2015] eKLR; *NHA v MMMSA* [2015] eKLR (KC).
[220] See *UAH v MOM* [2011] eKLR (HC); *UMM v IMM* [2014] eKLR (HC); *Republic v Chief Kadhi & Another, Interested Parties Ibrahim Juma Salim & Another* [2012] eKLR (HC).

Kadhis' courts that show prima facie discrimination against women. For example, in *In the matter of the Estate of Salim Ibrahim Juma*, the Principal Kadhi approved the distribution of the deceased's estate according to Islamic law requirements, that the widow of the deceased should receive one-quarter of the estate if she did not have any children and an eighth if she bore children.[221] If the case related to a widowed husband, he would have received one-quarter of the wife's estate, if she left behind a child, and one-half if there were no surviving children. For the children, each son is entitled to twice the share of a daughter. These divisions, while considered fair under Islamic law, are undeniably discriminatory on the basis of gender.

The position in post-2010 cases is quite similar to that in pre-2010 cases on marriage and divorce before Kadhis' courts. Nonetheless, the continued application of prima facie discriminatory practices in matters of inheritance and succession, as well as the concerns raised by Muslim women, noted above, about Kadhis' courts, demonstrate why clarity is necessary on the way Article 24(4) is construed. The section below makes various recommendations on how to confront the lack of clarity and its impact on gender equality.

E. Applying Proposed Approaches to Balancing between Culture/Religion and Gender Equality to the Exemption Given to Islamic Law in Article 24(4)

As the analysis above shows, there are many positive norms under Islamic law and, therefore, it would not be prudent to declare that the whole of Islamic law is against equality. Such a generalisation was made in the case of *Jesse Kamau* under the previous Constitution, where the Court held that Muslim law generally regards women as being less than men in matters of both marriage and divorce.[222] An informed approach to reconciling Islamic law norms that come into conflict with gender equality is thus required. I apply here the approaches proposed earlier, which include: (i) innovative interpretation of the exemption in the limitations clause; (ii) recognising personal autonomy/free and informed consent and the 'right of exit'; and (iii) only respecting consent for 'lesser infringements'.

i. Innovative Interpretation of the Exemption in the Limitations Clause

The first proposal relates to the innovative interpretation of Article 24(4) in a way that is consistent with the Constitution's transformative nature and does not

[221] *In the Matter of the Estate of Salim Ibrahim Juma* Succession Case No 186 of 2011 (KC).
[222] *Jesse Kamau* (n 204) 41.

negate the right to equality. This relates to the interpretation of the term 'strictly necessary' as proposed by Murray. She argues that

> [i]ts [Article 24(4)] insistence that qualifications be 'strictly necessary' might be read to permit no greater invasion of the right to equality than is in any event permitted by clause (1) [Article 24(1)] which allows reasonable limitations that are proportionate to their goals ...[223]

The fact that the exemption is included in the limitations clause, and not as an explicit exception in the equality clause, may be interpreted to inhibit the provision from being applied in a way that suggests Islamic laws automatically trump equality. An exception would remove the issue from the equality guarantee in all cases, but a limitation allows balancing and requires proportionality. Hence, a proportionality analysis may be helpful in determining Islamic law norms that are considered *strictly necessary* in limiting the right to equality. However, the provision is still vague and requires clarity through judicial interpretation or by statute; more so because it is still unclear who should decide which Islamic law norms can limit the right to equality. It is hard to tell if Kadhis will approach the interpretation of Article 24(4) in this way. This echoes the aphorism that 'liberty finds no refuge in a jurisprudence of doubt'.

This proposal borrows a leaf from the decision of the Botswana Court of Appeal in the case of *Ramantele v Mmusi & Others*.[224] The case challenged a customary law rule, which provided that women could not inherit because of their gender. Section 15(4) of the Botswana Constitution, like Article 24(4) of the Kenyan Constitution, exempted personal law from application of the equality clause (section 3 in the Botswana Constitution). In a unanimous decision written by Lesetedi J, the Court of Appeal stated that the equality clause in section 3 of the Constitution was an umbrella provision under which the section 15 exemption was subordinate. Therefore, any limitation, like that in section 15(4), would be limited by the equality provisions in section 3. Accordingly, it was stated that

> the derogations contained in Section 15(4) of the Constitution are not unchecked. They must be rational and justifiable either as being intended to ensure that the rights and freedoms of any individual do not prejudice the rights and freedoms of others *or* as being in the public interest.[225]

It was also stated that a customary rule should not be 'inconsistent with the values of or principles of natural justice ... unconscionable either of itself or in its effect ... inhuman ... [and should be] applied ... with the object of achieving justice and equity between the disputants'.[226]

[223] C Murray, 'Kenya's 2010 Constitution' (2013) 61 *Neue Folge Band Jahrbuch des öffentlichen Rechts* 747, 761–62.
[224] *Ramantele v Mmusi and Others* [2013] BWCA 1 (CA).
[225] ibid [72] (emphasis in the judgment).
[226] ibid [49].

Applying this test, Lesetedi J held that applying the rule that women cannot inherit to the respondents, four sisters who had used their own money to develop part of the homestead and taken care of their mother, in favour of a child (the son of their deceased half-brother) who had provided no assistance and did not live on the homestead, would go 'against any notion of fairness, equity and good conscience'.[227] It was therefore held that the four sisters were entitled to inherit the family home. Similar arguments can be made on a case-by-case basis in challenging discriminatory Islamic personal laws in Kenya.

ii. Recognising Personal Autonomy/Free and Informed Consent and the 'Right of Exit'

As highlighted earlier, Muslim women championed the application of Islamic personal law as administered by Kadhis' courts. Based on that discussion, we can conclude that there should be respect for women's autonomy to consent to the application of Islamic personal laws, which may not guarantee gender equality, when they choose to settle their claims in Kadhis' courts. This is only if proper safeguards are put in place to ensure that other steps like opting out of these laws are genuinely feasible for women. Since Article 170 of the Constitution allows for the application of Islamic law by Kadhis' courts only when both parties profess the Muslim religion and consent to the jurisdiction of the court, this essentially provides for the 'right of exit'.[228]

Moreover, the fact that the jurisdiction of Kadhis' courts runs concurrently with that of secular courts, and that persons who profess the Muslim faith can also file personal law cases in secular courts, further cements the 'right of exit'. This position was affirmed in *Ahmed Swaleh & 3 Others v Abdulgader Swaleh & 3 Others*.[229] The case related to the distribution of the estate of a deceased person. The issue before the Court related to an application to transfer the case from the Kadhis' court to the High Court as one set of beneficiaries (the applicants) did not want the estate to be determined by the Kadhis' court. Odero J noted that Article 170(5) of the Constitution only allowed Kadhis' courts to listen to matters where all parties submit to its jurisdiction. Therefore, considering the applicants' dissent to such jurisdiction, the Court allowed the matter to be transferred to the High Court and refused the respondents' request that the High Court judge sit with a Kadhi and the estate be distributed in accordance with Islamic law. Giving reasons for rejecting the request, Odero J stated that the law to be applied in the High Court would be the law of succession, which has no provision for a judge to sit with a Kadhi in determining the estate of a deceased Muslim. The judge also

[227] ibid [50].
[228] Constitution of Kenya 2010, Art 170(5).
[229] *Ahmed Swaleh & 3 Others v Abdulgader Swaleh & 3 Others* [2014] eKLR (HC).

noted that the request, if granted, would go against the desire of the applicants not to submit to the jurisdiction of a Kadhis' court. Hence, women who feel aggrieved by practices that violate gender equality, such as the unequal shares in inheritance, may seek redress in secular courts which are to apply equality guarantees.

Nevertheless, the question whether the 'right to exit' is a feasible choice still looms large. This is especially because of the perceived higher status of cultural and religious edicts, as compared to secular law. As recommended earlier, social programmes to educate women on their rights and the options available to them, in relation to exiting from discriminatory religious or cultural practices, should be actively carried out by the relevant State organs and civil society. These safeguards can also include the suggested reforms to ensure high judicial accountability by Kadhis and the provision of Islamic law education for women, so that they know what their rights are and detect improper patriarchal interpretations of Islamic law. In addition, the former Chief Justice, Willy Mutunga, publicly endorsed the need to appoint female Kadhis, which, if implemented, will be a positive development in ensuring gender equality within Kadhis' courts.[230]

iii. Accommodation of 'Lesser Infringements'

As much as free and informed consent should be respected and allowed, this should only be for 'lesser infringements' as judged on a case-by-case basis depending on context and subject to appeal. This should only be an option if provisions are put in place to ensure that such consent is genuine and that there are feasible opt-out options for women. These exclude extremely oppressive patriarchal norms and harmful practices such as early/forced marriage, FGM and other forms of violence.

Based on the above analysis, I now come back to the question: what is the appropriate construction of Article 24(4)? It is submitted that the exemption is vague and can be susceptible to misinterpretation, either in a way that leads to an unacceptable violation of gender equality or in a way that does not consider the autonomy to give genuine free and informed consent to religious practices. Apart from the interpretive and practical recommendations given on the various ways of approaching the conceptualisation of Article 24(4), the provision still needs to be clarified through a statute or a constitutional amendment. It will also be interesting to see how higher courts (the Court of Appeal and Supreme Court) interpret Article 24(4) in trying to reconcile secular national laws with Islamic law. There are no clear-cut answers to this challenging issue. However, the analysis and proposals given here may be helpful in finding a fitting balance between respecting the right to freedom of religion and gender equality.

[230] Ousseina (n 6) 135.

V. Conclusion

Concluding the discussion of competing conceptions of equality, this chapter has explored the tense relationship that exists between cultural and religious accommodation and gender equality. It has been observed that, to reconcile the two conceptions of equality, we should appreciate the importance of respect for freedom of culture and religion, which are particularly justified by personal autonomy to exercise free and informed consent. However, in the same vein, the significance of gender equality has also been considered and scenarios unique to the Kenyan context highlighted, which led to the conclusion that, in order to balance the two sets of equality claims, the exercise of extremely oppressive and harmful cultural and religious practices should be prohibited. In such instances, the capacity to give free and informed consent should be considered as suspect, and such consent negated by application of the limitations clause. This was distinguished from 'lesser infringements', which were said to include cultural and religious norms that, though they may be considered as violating gender equality, do not amount to harmful practices according to the definition given in the joint General Comment No. 31 of the CEDAW Committee and CRC Committee.

Importantly also, the chapter has argued that there should always be laws put in place for the 'right of exit' for women who consent to a gender-discriminatory cultural or religious practice, but later decide to opt out. These proposals on how to find a balance between respect for culture/religious equality and gender equality in the context of patriarchal norms informed the analysis of the constitutional exemption of Islamic personal law from the automatic application of the equality guarantees in the Bill of Rights. The approaches helped to unpack how to ensure women's rights are guaranteed in the context of patriarchal Islamic personal law norms. Overall, the chapter has shown how a holistic approach to constitutional interpretation can help in balancing competing equality rights in the Constitution.

7

The Interrelationship between Socio-economic Rights and Status-based Equality

The previous 1963 Kenyan Constitution was conspicuously silent on socio-economic rights (SERs). However, the growing gap between the rich and the poor, deplorable living conditions, and lack of access to quality education, food, health-care services, security and housing for the poor meant that the importance of SERs could no longer be ignored.[1] The deplorable state of SERs in the country was also criticised by the United Nations Committee on Economic, Social and Cultural Rights (CESCR), referring to the situation as a 'socio-economic crisis' and calling on the government to increase the steps it was taking to resolve this state of affairs.[2] Thus, the entrenchment of SERs in the 2010 Constitution was seen as imperative to help solve the multiple socio-economic problems facing the country, particularly the vicious cycle of poverty affecting more than 40 per cent of the population.[3]

Poverty in Kenya disproportionately affects those discriminated against because of their status (eg women and persons with disabilities). This chapter argues, therefore, that efforts to realise SERs should consider the interrelationship between SERs and status-based equality, more so because status-based discrimination is a major cause and consequence of socio-economic deprivation.[4] The chapter particularly examines the relationship between status-based equality and redistributive equality. 'Status-based equality' is used to denote non-discrimination on grounds of a person's status such as sex and disability. Redistributive equality is arguably furthered by SERs through their goal of providing the bare minimum to all in terms of resources and services.

[1] Constitution of Kenya Review Commission, *The Final Report of the Constitution of Kenya Review Commission. Approved for issue at the 95th Plenary Meeting held on 10 February 2005* (2005) 52–55.

[2] See CESCR, *Report on the Fortieth and Forty-First Sessions* (28 April–16 May 2008, 3–21 November 2008) paras 354–97.

[3] Kenya National Bureau of Statistics, *Basic Report on Well-Being in Kenya: Based on the 2015/2016 Kenya Integrated Household Budget Survey (KIHBS)* (2018) 44–45; J Cilliers, B Hughes and S Turner, *Reducing Poverty in Africa: Realistic Targets for the Post-2015 MDGs and Agenda 2063* (African Futures Paper 10, 2014) 1.

[4] See United Nations Office of the High Commissioner (OHCHR), *Guiding Principles on Extreme Poverty and Human Rights*, adopted by the Human Rights Council by consensus on 27 September 2012, in resolution 21/11, 3.

An analysis of the relationship between SERs and status-based equality in the Kenyan context is necessary for two main reasons. First, the discussion is crucial and relevant because the 2010 Kenyan Constitution is unique in its explicit recognition of the relationship between the two. It specifically mandates that in fulfilling SERs, the State should prioritise the needs of vulnerable individuals and groups whose socio-economic disadvantage is usually caused or reinforced by status-based discrimination.[5] Hence, the chapter contends that there is a textual mandate to consider status-based inequality in realising SERs. This argument is backed by the Constitution's drafting history. The Constitution of Kenya Review Commission (CKRC), noting the country's peculiar social and economic realities, stated that the inclusion of SERs in the Constitution was essential to facilitate the eradication of both poverty and inequality in the country.[6] The chapter therefore asserts that this awareness needs to be carried forward in current jurisprudence and initiatives to realise SERs.

Second, the relationship between the two is essential because poverty[7] and inequality in Kenya overlap as 'the pattern of who is poor is entrenched and reflects long-standing discrimination in the society'.[8] Accordingly, those vulnerable to discrimination on the basis of different aspects of their identity, such as gender, disability or HIV status, tend to have poorer access to social goods and services.[9] Therefore, a normative argument has been made that advancing redistributive equality measures through SERs, without bearing in mind their implications for status-based inequality, can be harmful and detrimental.[10] For example, constructing healthcare facilities and educational institutions in realising SERs will deny physically disabled persons using wheelchairs equal enjoyment of such social services, if ramps are not included to reasonably accommodate their special needs. The relationship between SERs and status-based equality thus raises compound and important questions on the significance of an equality-sensitive approach to the interpretation and application of SERs in Kenya.

This chapter examines the textual basis in Kenya's 2010 Constitution that makes an analysis of the interrelationship between SERs and status-based equality in the Kenyan context essential. It also examines how the interrelationship between the two arises, and its importance and application. An 'equality-sensitive' approach to be applied in the implementation and adjudication of SERs is then recommended.

[5] Explicit reference to this point can be found in Arts 20(5)(b), 21(3) and 53–57 of the 2010 Kenyan Constitution.

[6] Constitution of Kenya Review Commission (n 1) 118–19.

[7] Used interchangeably in this chapter with the words 'socio-economic deprivation' and 'socio-economic disadvantage'.

[8] See G Brodsky and S Day, 'Denial of the Means of Subsistence as an Equality Violation' (2005) *Acta Juridica* 149, 163–64.

[9] See Equal Rights Trust and Kenya Human Rights Commission, *In the Spirit of Harambee: Addressing Discrimination and Inequality in Kenya* (London, Prontaprint Bayswater, 2012) 5.

[10] See S Fredman, 'Redistribution and Recognition: Reconciling Inequalities' (2007) 23 *South African Journal of Human Rights* 214, 215.

This approach will form the basis for the analysis in Chapter 8 on the extent to which Kenyan courts have and can consider the interrelationship between SERs and status-based equality when adjudicating SERs claims that have a bearing on equality.

I. Interrelationship between Socio-economic Rights and Status-based Equality in the Kenyan Constitution

This section shows that the need for an analysis of the interrelationship between SERs and status-based equality in Kenya is not just a normative argument but is supported by several constitutional mandates. Kenya's 2010 Constitution is unique because it explicitly recognises the interrelationship between SERs and status-based equality. This is in appreciation of the peculiar social and economic realities in the country, characterised by widespread poverty and gross inequalities.

Article 43 is the main constitutional provision guaranteeing SERs. It provides:

> (1) *Every person* has the right—
> (a) to the highest attainable standard of health, which includes the right to health care services, including reproductive health care;
> (b) to accessible and adequate housing, and to reasonable standards of sanitation;
> (c) to be free from hunger, and to have adequate food of acceptable quality;
> (d) to clean and safe water in adequate quantities;
> (e) to social security; and
> (f) to education.
> (2) A person shall not be denied emergency medical treatment.
> (3) The State shall provide appropriate social security to persons who are unable to support themselves and their dependants (emphasis added).

The use of the term 'every person' in stipulating who should benefit from SERs brings in an equality element to the way these rights should be provided. This means the State should extend these rights to those who are unjustly excluded, where they are provided to some and not others who are similarly situated. It also obliges the State to make reasonable accommodation, say in provision of health-care and education, to ensure that all persons, including those with disabilities, have equitable access to such rights.

However, SERs are not absolute and their provision is subject to limitations. One of these limitations can be found in Article 21(2) of the Constitution, which provides that 'The State shall take legislative, policy and other measures, including the setting of standards, to achieve the *progressive realisation* of the rights guaranteed under Article 43' (emphasis added). This standard of progressive realisation is relatively new to Kenyan jurisprudence. Hence, attempts to give it meaning and develop it further have mostly referred to the understandings of it given by the CESCR, in relation to the similarly worded but non-identical provisions in Article 2(1) of the International Covenant on Economic, Social and Cultural

Rights (ICESCR). This requires each State Party to the Covenant to take steps 'to the *maximum of its available resources, with a view to achieving progressively the full realisation of the rights* recognised in the … Covenant' (emphasis added).

The ICESCR along with various other international and regional human rights instruments ratified by Kenya complement provisions entrenched in the Constitution. Hence, because entrenched SERs are new in Kenyan legal discourse, international human rights instruments ratified by Kenya have been and continue to be instrumental in fleshing out the content of these rights, as will be seen when discussing some of the current SERs cases in Chapter 8. The Supreme Court has affirmed reference to international human rights instruments ratified by Kenya in interpretation of the 2010 Constitution, which, it notes, generously adopts the language of these instruments.[11] Other courts adjudicating on SERs claims have also made a similar affirmation.[12]

Relating to the inclusion of progressive realisation in Article 2(1) of the ICESCR, the CESCR explains that this standard was adopted in recognition of the fact that full realisation of SERs cannot be achieved within a short period of time due to resource constraints in many states that are parties to the Covenant.[13] Nevertheless, the CESCR has noted that the standard of progressive realisation does not leave a socio-economic right devoid of any meaningful content.[14] As such, the whole obligation is not postponed. First, the State has the immediate obligation to take deliberate, concrete and targeted steps towards the realisation of SERs and not to take any retrogressive measures.[15] This duty requires the development of policies, strategies and programmes to implement SERs and hence has no great resource implications. Thus, such an excuse by a State for not swiftly coming up with the requisite laws and policies for implementing SERs would be unjustified. Second, there is an immediate obligation of non-discrimination, meaning that the provision of SERs should not be done in a discriminatory manner.[16]

Third, the CESCR has stated that, within the standard of progressive realisation, there is a minimum core obligation placed upon every State Party 'to ensure the satisfaction of, at the very least, minimum essential levels of each of the rights' in the ICESCR. It further recognises the essential nature of this obligation by

[11] *In the Matter of the Principle of Gender Representation in the National Assembly and the Senate* Advisory Opinion No 2 of 2012 (SC) [52].

[12] See *John Kabui Mwai & 3 Others v Kenya National Examination Council & 2 Others* [2011] eKLR (HC) [6]; *Mitu-Bell Welfare Society v Attorney General & 2 Others* [2013] eKLR (HC) [15].

[13] CESCR, *General Comment No. 3: The Nature of States Parties' Obligations (art. 2, para. 1, of the Covenant)*, 14 December 1990, E/1991/23, [1] and [9].

[14] ibid [9].

[15] ibid [2].

[16] eg CESCR, General Comment No. 20: *Non-discrimination in economic, social and cultural rights (art. 2, para. 2, of the International Covenant on Economic, Social and Cultural Rights)*, 2 July 2009, E/C.12/GC/20, [7] provides that 'Non-discrimination is an immediate and cross-cutting obligation in the Covenant'.

stating that 'If the Covenant were to be read in such a way as not to establish such a minimum core obligation, it would be largely deprived of its raison d'être'.[17]

These three points flowing from the standard of progressive realisation under Article 2(1) of the ICESCR can be said to also apply to the progressive realisation standard for the implementation of SERs in Article 21(2) of the Kenyan Constitution.

The ICESCR's Article 2(1) 'maximum available resources' requirement acknowledges that resources may be limited at various stages of implementing SERs, and hence more reason why these rights should be progressively realised. In close relation to this requirement, the Kenyan Constitution similarly recognises that resources for implementing SERs may be limited. However, it goes further than the ICESCR in providing express guidelines that the State should follow in supporting a claim that it has limited resources to implement a socio-economic right at a given point. These guidelines are encapsulated in Article 20(5). It is this provision that can be said to explicitly include a status-based equality element to how SERs are implemented. Article 20(5) requires that

> [i]n applying any right under Article 43, if the State claims that it does not have the resources to implement the right, a court, tribunal or other authority shall be guided by the following principles—
>
> (a) it is the responsibility of the State to show that the resources are not available;
> (b) *in allocating resources, the State shall give priority to ensuring the widest possible enjoyment of the right or fundamental freedom having regard to prevailing circumstances, including the vulnerability of particular groups or individuals*; and
> (c) the court, tribunal or other authority may not interfere with a decision by a State organ concerning the allocation of available resources, solely on the basis that it would have reached a different conclusion (emphasis added).

By requiring the State to give priority to vulnerable groups and individuals, Article 20(5)(b) adds a status-based equality component to the implementation of SERs. This point is also emphasised in Article 21(3) of the Constitution providing that all State organs and public officers have a duty to address the needs of vulnerable groups.[18] It lists vulnerable groups in Kenya as including, but not limited to, 'women, older members of society, persons with disabilities, children, youth, members of minority or marginalised communities, and members of particular ethnic, religious or cultural communities'. The word 'vulnerable' is understood here to stand for the effects of discrimination and the resultant disadvantage occasioned to a group because of possession of a particular status.

Arguably, prioritisation of the socio-economic needs of vulnerable groups in Article 20(5)(b) coincides with the minimum core obligation which the CESCR

[17] CESCR, *General Comment No. 3* (n 13) [10].

[18] This is in relation to the application of all rights and fundamental freedoms in the Bill of Rights and not just SERs.

has argued is attached to the standard of progressive realisation. This is particularly evident when we consider the understanding of the minimum core obligation as requiring reasonable priority setting in the provision of basic essential levels of each socio-economic right to those most vulnerable and in desperate need.[19]

What amounts to a minimum core obligation for various SERs is a contentious issue that remains unresolved. Nevertheless, by explicitly requiring the prioritisation of vulnerable individuals and groups in the implementation of SERs, it is clear that the State is to be held to account for failing to cater for the urgent needs of the most disadvantaged. The Kenyan Constitution thus extinguishes the need to dwell on a discussion of the contentious nature of a minimum core obligation. This is because a tangible provision already exists which performs the essential task of requiring priority setting for those in urgent need – the key point from the minimum core obligation discussion this chapter and the one that follows aim to highlight.

The relationship between SERs and status-based equality is also illustrated by the specific SERs to be guaranteed to the most disadvantaged groups in Kenya, as stipulated in Articles 53–57. These provisions set out specific SERs to be provided to children, women, persons with disabilities, the youth, members of minority or marginalised communities, and the elderly. During the constitutional drafting process, the Parliamentary Select Committee (PSC) had deleted Articles 53–57, noting that they did not provide any additional right not granted in Article 27 on the right to equality.[20] However, the constitutional drafting Committee of Experts retained this part, noting the demand by Kenyans throughout the constitutional review process for an expanded Bill of Rights guaranteeing specific SERs to women, children, the youth, the elderly and persons with disabilities.[21] Hence, Articles 53–57 additionally show the recognition in the Constitution of the interrelationship between status-based inequalities and socio-economic deprivation in the country.

Furthermore, the drafting history reveals that the drafters of the Constitution envisaged a strong link between SERs and status-based equality. Inclusion of Article 43 and other provisions like Articles 53–57 seeking to address the social and economic plight of specific disadvantaged groups 'was informed by a history of social exclusion and marginalisation' in the country.[22] During the constitutional drafting process, the CKRC stated that SERs were a necessary inclusion in

[19] D Bilchitz, *Poverty and Fundamental Rights: The Justification and Enforcement of Socio-Economic Rights* (Oxford, Oxford University Press, 2007) 208.

[20] Kenya National Assembly, *Report of the Parliamentary Select Committee on the Review of the Constitution on the Reviewed Harmonized Draft Constitution* (2010) 7.

[21] Committee of Experts on Constitutional Review, *Final Report of the Committee of Experts on Constitutional Review* (2011) 109.

[22] J Biegon, 'The Inclusion of Socio-Economic Rights in the 2010 Constitution: Conceptual and Practical Issues' in J Biegon and G Musila (eds), *Judicial Enforcement of Socio-Economic Rights under the New Constitution: Challenges and Opportunities for Kenya* (Nairobi, Kenya Section of the International Commission of Jurists, 2012) 34.

the Constitution in liberating a majority of Kenyans from the chains of poverty, largely caused by inequalities and bad governance.[23] This was based on the major concerns raised by Kenyans in their submissions to the CKRC, which related to problems of access to basic social amenities and inequalities.[24] The CKRC specifically stated that 'Meeting social and economic rights also requires us to address the enormous disparities of wealth and access to resources by a certain class and some regions that is obvious in Kenya'.[25] Therefore, the drafters of the Constitution acknowledged that Kenyans desired inclusive socio-economic development strategies 'to protect the socially disadvantaged and vulnerable', aside from the general goal of improving the livelihoods of all Kenyans and resolving other distributive socio-economic problems.[26]

The importance of acknowledging equality in the implementation of SERs is also emphasised in the Bill of Rights' main limitations clause in Article 24. As stated earlier, SERs are not absolute. Aside from the limitation created by Article 21(2) on the standard of progressive realisation and the related availability of resources limitation in Article 20(5) of the Constitution that are specific to SERs, Article 24, applying to all rights in the Bill of Rights, including SERs, provides:

> (1) A right or fundamental freedom in the Bill of Rights shall not be limited except by law, and then only to the extent that the limitation is reasonable and justifiable in an open and democratic society based on human dignity, *equality* and freedom, taking into account all relevant factors, including—
>
> (a) the nature of the right or fundamental freedom;
> (b) the importance of the purpose of the limitation;
> (c) the nature and extent of the limitation;
> (d) the need to ensure that the enjoyment of rights and fundamental freedoms by any individual does not prejudice the rights and fundamental freedoms of others; and
> (e) the relation between the limitation and its purpose and whether there are less restrictive means to achieve the purpose … (emphasis added).

Arguably, because Article 24(1) states that rights should only be limited 'to the extent that the limitation is reasonable and justifiable in an open and democratic society based on … equality', SERs should not be limited in a way that impedes equality. This would require the redistributive consequences of SERs to be read with status-based equality in mind. It also obliges the State to show how its SERs laws, policies and programmatic frameworks avoid reinforcing status-based inequality.

Additionally, the provision in Article 24(2)(c) requiring that a limitation of a right or fundamental freedom 'shall not limit the right or fundamental freedom so far as to derogate from its core or essential content' can be said to

[23] Constitution of Kenya Review Commission (n 1) 65.
[24] ibid 118–19.
[25] ibid 44.
[26] ibid 159.

require the prioritisation of those in desperate need, similar to the provision in Article 20(5)(b). This is in ensuring that a socio-economic right is not deprived of any meaningful content or, at worst, rendered nugatory.

These constitutional provisions, explicitly and implicitly highlighting the interrelationship between SERs and status-based equality, require us to investigate further how the relationship between the two arises, why it is important and how it is to be applied. It is worth noting that the interrelationship between the two is underdeveloped in Kenyan jurisprudence, and no work or commentary has yet considered how such a relationship can be effectively applied in the Kenyan context to address the mutually reinforcing problems of status-based and redistributive inequality.

II. Establishing the Analytical Framework for Linking Socio-economic Rights (Redistributive) and Status-based Equality

As discussed above, an evaluation of how the interrelationship between SERs and status-based equality arises, and its importance and application to the Kenyan context, is essential for addressing the mutually reinforcing harms of poverty and inequality in the country. To first explain how the interrelationship between the two arises, this section mainly draws on Fraser's and Fredman's analysis for understanding the link between the redistributive equality goal of SERs and status-based inequality.

A. What Does Status-based Inequality Mean?

As stated in the introduction, the term status-based inequality is used to denote discrimination based on a person's status such as sex or disability. The status aspect prohibits discrimination, whether direct or indirect, against individuals with a 'protected characteristic'. Article 27(4) of the Kenyan Constitution lists grounds for non-discrimination based on a person's status. However, as was noted in Chapters 3 and 4, this list is non-exhaustive and other new grounds can be added.[27] The term 'status-based inequality' has been used in reference to inequalities occasioned to an individual or group because of statuses such as those listed in Article 27(4).[28] The list of statuses that need special protection are usually based on a country's particular history and experience with discrimination, which creates what

[27] Ch 3, text to nn 75–76; Ch 4, text to nn 20–22.
[28] See Fredman, 'Redistribution and Recognition' (n 10) 214.

Loenen refers to as 'sensitive' groups that need stronger protection because of the 'suspectedness' of classifications based on their status.[29]

The conceptual underpinning behind the term is derived from philosophical perspectives on *recognition*, as developed by Fraser and Honneth among others.[30] Fraser explains that recognition comes from the Hegelian philosophy whereby 'one becomes an individual subject only in virtue of recognizing, and being recognized by, another subject'.[31] In the process of this reciprocal recognition some identities have become unjustly devalued, mostly due to social and cultural distinctions on who is lesser and who should be held in higher esteem. This in turn has led to discrimination and identity struggles based on a person's status such as race, gender, nationality, ethnicity or sexuality – what is referred to here as status-based inequality.[32] To remedy this situation, recognition seeks to revalue 'disrespected identities' of affected groups with the goal of achieving a 'difference-friendly world, where assimilation to majority or dominant cultural norms is no longer the price of equal respect'.[33]

Fredman further expounds on the meaning of recognition, which was briefly discussed in Chapters 3 and 5, as one of the four dimensions of substantive equality.[34] She explains that the recognition dimension 'aims to promote respect for dignity and worth, thereby redressing stigma, stereotyping, humiliation and violence because of membership of an identity group'.[35] Therefore, the term status-based equality is used here to stand for the recognition dimension of substantive equality, insisting on both the revaluing of devalued groups in society and the acknowledgement and celebration of their difference.

B. Redistributive Equality: Socio-economic Rights as a Floor

SERs are usually seen as aiming to achieve a myriad of socio-economic goals, ranging from the broad aim of improving the general livelihoods of all people to narrow redistributive goals that seek a more egalitarian distribution of resources and services.[36] This chapter focuses on the latter goal, also referred to as redistributive equality, which aims to oversee the redistribution of resources and wealth 'to correct the cycle of disadvantage experienced because of status or other protected characteristic'.[37]

[29] T Loenen, 'The Equality Clause in the South African Constitution: Some Remarks from a Comparative Perspective' (1997) 13 *South African Journal of Human Rights* 401, 407–08.

[30] See N Fraser and A Honneth, *Redistribution or Recognition? A Political-Philosophical Exchange* (London, Verso, 2003); S Fredman, *Discrimination Law* (2nd edn, Oxford, Oxford University Press, 2011).

[31] Fraser and Honneth (n 30) 10.

[32] ibid 11.

[33] ibid 7 and 13.

[34] Ch 3, text to nn 69–74; Ch 5, text to nn 53–54.

[35] Fredman, *Discrimination Law* (n 30) 25.

[36] Fraser and Honneth (n 30) 7.

[37] Fredman, *Discrimination Law* (n 30) 26.

Redistributive equality is asymmetrical because 'instead of aiming to treat everyone alike, regardless of status … [it] focuses on the group which has suffered disadvantage'.[38] In terms of their redistributive equality dimension, SERs in their simplest form act as a floor requiring the provision of a minimum threshold level of these rights essential to a person's survival, beneath which a person is said to be denied truly human functioning.[39] The basic essentials of the SERs encapsulated in the Kenyan Constitution – such as the right to food, health, housing and education – constitute such general conditions necessary to all persons for their survival. As Bilchitz rightly observes, 'Being in a state of health, for instance, will be of importance to anyone wishing to fulfil any purpose whatsoever and, similarly, having an adequate amount of food will be of great importance to any purposive human being'.[40]

The provision of basic essential minimums of SERs furthers redistributive equality because it largely targets the poor, vulnerable and marginalised, who are the most disadvantaged in the country. It is this redistributive goal of SERs that intersects with status-based equality, as these disadvantaged groups are also disproportionately affected by status-based discrimination. It is this link that the section below expounds on.

C. Conceptual Background of the Crucial Intersection between Socio-economic Rights and Status-based Equality

Having looked at what is meant by status-based inequality and SERs' redistributive equality goal, this section draws the two discussions together and expounds more broadly on the conceptual underpinnings of the interrelationship between the two and their importance. This can be said to arise in four ways. First, recognition of the relationship between the two is linked to the principle of interdependence, interconnectedness and indivisibility of human rights.[41] Fraser observes that, on the one hand, the redistributive aspect of equality that implicates SERs has traditionally been equated with 'class politics'. On the other hand, the concept of recognition that underlies status-based equality has been equated to 'identity politics', in relation to misrecognition of a person's status such as gender and nationality. Discussions of the two – class politics and identity politics – have often been dissociated from each other and have developed on different trajectories.[42] However, Fraser argues that class politics, by not considering the

[38] ibid.

[39] M Nussbaum, *Women and Human Development: The Capabilities Approach* (Vol 3, Cambridge, Cambridge University Press, 2001) 6.

[40] See Bilchitz (n 19) 41.

[41] This principle has been acknowledged in various UN documents and General Comments in relation to SERs by the CESCR. Eg CESCR, *General Comment No. 3* (n 13) [8].

[42] Fraser and Honneth (n 30) 8 and 12.

underlying identity politics that create and reinforce disadvantage, miss out on the 'gender-specific, "race"-specific, and sex-specific forms of economic injustice'.[43] She thus refers to the attempt to view the two as mutually exclusive in ongoing debates on inequality as a 'false antithesis', arguing that the two in many ways interconnect and hence are two-dimensional.[44]

To illustrate the interdependent nature of the redistributive and recognition aspects of equality, Fraser uses gender as an ideal type, showing injustices traceable to both maldistribution and misrecognition.[45] She argues that, on the one hand, gender maldistribution relates to the economic structure of society where women are assigned primary responsibility for unpaid domestic labour, and are also employed in 'lower-paid, female-dominated "pink collar" and domestic service occupations'. This then results in 'gender-specific forms of distributive injustice'.[46] On the other hand, Fraser argues that such undervaluation of women's work is also a recognition issue because of the fact that it is a person's gender that leads to 'status differentiation' deeply rooted in cultural values that privilege 'traits associated with masculinity, while devaluing everything coded as "feminine"'.[47] Thus, she surmises that gender is a hybrid category that is rooted in both the economic structure and status order of society, in such a way that 'Understanding and redressing gender injustice … requires attending to both distribution and recognition'.[48]

Tied to this perspective, it has been argued that at one end of the spectrum, constructing socio-economic redistributive equality measures without bearing in mind their implications for status-based equality can be harmful and detrimental.[49] This is because, without taking into account impact on status-based equality, well-meaning socio-economic programmes furthering redistributive equality 'can end up stigmatising and perpetuating discriminatory value judgments based on grounds such as race, gender and sexual orientation'.[50] For example, a socio-economic redistributive equality measure that guarantees social welfare for single mothers only can be beneficial but may entrench stereotypical gender roles that view women as having primary responsibility for childcare. This happened in the South African case of *President of the Republic of South Africa & Another v Hugo*, where the issue in contention was a presidential pardon given to prisoners who were single mothers, because of their special role in caring for young children, and not to single fathers, thus entrenching stereotypes on parenting roles.[51]

[43] ibid 8.
[44] ibid 11–16.
[45] ibid 19.
[46] ibid 20.
[47] ibid 21.
[48] ibid 19.
[49] See Fredman, 'Redistribution and Recognition' (n 10) 215.
[50] S Liebenberg and B Goldblatt, 'The Interrelationship between Equality and Socio-Economic Rights under South Africa's Transformative Constitution' (2007) 23 *South African Journal of Human Rights* 335, 351.
[51] *President of the Republic of South Africa & Another v Hugo* 1997 (4) SA 1 (CC).

At the other end of the spectrum, 'status-based measures are limited in their inability to mobilise the redistributive measures necessary to make real equality of opportunity and genuine choice possible'.[52] According to Fredman, this is because 'Anti-discrimination law acts either to prevent prejudiced action or to require the removal of unjustifiable practices … which disproportionately exclude members of disadvantaged status groups. [It does not] address status inequalities which require resources to correct them'.[53] Wesson further explains that constitutional entrenchment of SERs is essential as 'they *authorise* the extension of principles of substantive equality to areas where they would not otherwise apply'.[54] Substantive equality and, by extension, status-based equality, cannot solely be invoked in making a claim for the provision of social goods – this is the job of entrenched SERs. Justiciable SERs give the basis for making a claim for the provision of minimum basic resources that are necessary to allow individuals to be free from threats to their survival. Equality can then follow up by insisting that such rights should not be applied in a discriminatory manner in such a way that, where rights are provided to some, they should equally be extended to others who are similarly situated.

Hence, the importance of SERs cannot be gainsaid as, where they are not guaranteed, there is nothing for status-based equality to latch on to in emphasising that the distribution of such rights should be done in a way that respects equality. Thus, SERs, when viewed in the redistributive sense, and a status-based conception of equality are mutually reinforcing. Each of these rights makes up for the areas where the other falls short.

The interdependence between SERs and status-based equality has been linked to the definition of equality as requiring 'the full and equal enjoyment of all rights and freedoms', present in Article 27(2) of the Kenyan Constitution.[55] The provision implicates the need to accommodate disadvantaged groups and take special positive measures to make sure that they equally enjoy and benefit from the provision of all rights including SERs. This would mean, for instance, that in constructing healthcare facilities and other social infrastructure, special needs of the physically disabled should be considered to make sure that they fully and equally enjoy the provision of such SERs. Therefore, ramps for physically disabled persons using wheelchairs should be constructed, as failure to do so may reinforce the exclusion and disadvantage they already face.[56] Full and equal enjoyment therefore requires

[52] Fredman, 'Redistribution and Recognition' (n 10) 215.

[53] ibid 221.

[54] M Wesson, 'Equality and Social Rights: An Exploration in Light of the South African Constitution' (2007) *PL* 748, 749.

[55] See S Liebenberg, *Socio-Economic Rights: Adjudication Under a Transformative Constitution* (Cape Town, JUTA, 2010) 207.

[56] See Liebenberg and Goldblatt (n 50) 339.

that SERs should be implemented in such a way that their provision does not lead to an unequal impact.

Second, the relationship between SERs and status-based equality can be said to be significant in enabling prioritisation of the needs of vulnerable groups in the redistribution of socio-economic goods and services. It helps us recognise that 'there are some [in society] who are more vulnerable than others, some whose very survival is threatened by the conditions in which they live and by their lack of access to such goods as food and water'.[57] This is particularly essential where such disadvantage is caused or reinforced by pre-existing status-based inequality.

As stated earlier, it is this need to prioritise the eradication of the dire living conditions of the most disadvantaged that relates to the understanding of the minimum core obligation as 'a means of specifying priorities'.[58] Consequently, as Bilchitz states, if a government programme does not, as a matter of priority, cater for such urgent needs, it denies those affected the protection of their minimal and fundamental interests.[59] An appreciation of how status-based inequality has a hand to play in making certain individuals and groups worse off, both socially and economically, helps in making a case for the prioritisation of the needs of these groups.

Third, it is argued that since the right to equality is not subject to progressive realisation, a status-based equality approach can be fused with the demand for the immediate delivery of SERs, where these rights are already provided to some but not extended to similarly situated individuals.

Fourth and last, the relationship between SERs and status-based equality is tied to the overarching nature of equality as a constitutional principle through the lens of which other human rights can be viewed.[60] This is particularly in relation to the wording of rights and clauses in the Constitution, which read that they must be enjoyed by all, using phrases such as 'everyone', 'all' or 'nobody'. The inclusion of SERs in the 2010 Constitution, which are to be guaranteed to 'everyone' or 'every person', automatically brings in an equality dimension to how these rights should be distributed. Such provisions therefore demand that any socio-economic benefits provided to some should be equally extended to similarly situated persons excluded from such benefits.

From this conceptual basis, I interrogate below how poverty best brings out the interrelationship between the redistributive equality goal of SERs and status-based equality.

[57] Bilchitz (n 19) 208.
[58] ibid; text to nn 18–26.
[59] ibid.
[60] See J Clifford, 'Equality' in D Shelton (ed), *The Oxford Handbook on International Human Rights Law* (Oxford, Oxford University Press, 2013) 7; S Baer, 'Equality' in M Rosenfeld and A Sajó (eds), *The Oxford Handbook of Comparative Constitutional Law* (Oxford, Oxford University Press, 2012) 3.

D. Poverty as Bringing Out the Crucial Intersection between the Redistributive Equality Goal of Socio-economic Rights and Status-based Equality

Essentially, poverty is synonymous with socio-economic deprivation and disadvantage.[61] An interrogation of poverty and how it affects people's access to socio-economic goods provides the contextual basis for identifying the interests to be safeguarded and advanced by SERs.[62] The link between poverty and SERs can be summarised as follows: a deprivation of SERs and means of achieving them leads to poverty, and it is the manifestations of poverty that are used to identify conditions to be addressed through the application of SERs and their redistributive equality goal. Relating this to status-based inequality, status-based discrimination is one of the main causes of deprivation of socio-economic goods that leads to poverty. Indeed, manifestations of poverty, such as poor living conditions, lack of adequate housing and lack of access to education and health-care, disproportionately affect women, persons with disabilities and persons living with HIV/AIDS, whose vulnerability is largely because of status-based discrimination.

Poverty is also a cause of discrimination because of the stigma, powerlessness and humiliation that is often attached to being poor. This is, for instance, because of the inability of the poor to afford the necessities that a society considers indispensable for participation. The classic example, as espoused by Adam Smith, is the linen shirt. He observes that 'in the present times … a creditable day-labourer would be ashamed to appear in public without a linen shirt, the want of which would be supposed to denote that disgraceful degree of poverty which, it is presumed, nobody can well fall into without extreme bad conduct'.[63]

Poverty is therefore the issue that needs to be looked at here as it highlights the crucial link between the redistributive goal of SERs and status-based inequality. To quote the Equal Rights Trust's report on inequality in Kenya, 'poverty is the unavoidable backdrop to any discussion of discrimination and inequality in Kenya'.[64]

This discussion suggests that poverty is much more than income inequality but also affects people's dignity, access to power, and equality of participation. Hence the need to have a much broader understanding of poverty as being multidimensional. This is discussed below.

[61] This is the justification for poverty being used interchangeably with socio-economic deprivation and disadvantage.

[62] S Wilson and J Dugard, 'Taking Poverty Seriously: The South African Constitutional Court and Socio-Economic Rights' (2001) 22 *Stellenbosch Law Review* 664, 665–67.

[63] A Smith, *An Enquiry into the Nature and Causes of the Wealth of Nations* (E Cannan ed, vol 1, London, Methuen, 1776) 691.

[64] Equal Rights Trust and Kenya Human Rights Commission (n 9) 45.

i. *Poverty as Being Much More Than Income Inequality*

The definition of poverty and how it is measured has been highly debated and contested. Traditionally, the term has been associated with a person's low income and subsequent low living standards because of insufficient resources.[65] In the recent past, poverty has mostly been identified using income- and consumption-based poverty measures.[66] However, the discussion in the earlier section on how poverty brings out the crucial link between the redistributive equality goal of SERs and status-based inequality requires a richer understanding of poverty, which is not only income based. This is because solely concentrating on income to produce identifiers of poverty ignores recognition issues and lack of participation. Kakwani and Silber note that the application of income as the sole measure of poverty limits the incorporation of other important dimensions of poverty such as 'life expectancy (longevity), literacy, the provision of public goods, freedom and security'.[67] Thus, a focus on income alone is not enough to capture people's diverse lived experiences of poverty, as it masks other inequalities of recognition and power. The inextricable link between socio-economic disadvantage and status-based inequality therefore requires an idea of poverty that goes beyond income, one that appreciates the multidimensional nature of poverty and looks further at inequality of capabilities and inequalities of power.

There is now a growing appreciation of the fact that poverty is multidimensional. Besides their low income or lack of resources, the poor are also affected by a lack of proper access to shelter, food, education and healthcare, as well as insecurity, powerlessness, exposure to discrimination, social exclusion and stigmatisation because of living on the margins of society.[68] As such, besides monetary deprivation, poverty also constitutes a denial of human rights and human dignity.[69]

In recognition of this fact, the United Nations Development Programme (UNDP) Human Development Index (HDI) has been developed as a better approach to measure poverty, which considers its multidimensional nature. The HDI is said to be a combination of both the Basic Needs Approach (BNA) and Amartya Sen's capabilities approach.[70]

On the one hand, the BNA identifies a basket of certain minimum requirements in terms of goods and services that are viewed as being essential for people to

[65] See R Lister, *Poverty* (Cambridge, Blackwell/Polity Press, 2004) 14 and 21; Oxford Poverty & Human Development Initiative (OPHI), 'Multidimensional Poverty' www.ophi.org.uk/research/multidimensional-poverty/.

[66] See N Kakwani and J Silber (eds), *The Many Dimensions of Poverty* (New York, NY, Palgrave Macmillan, 2007) xi.

[67] ibid xv.

[68] See OPHI (n 65); OHCHR (n 4) 2; United Nations Children's Fund (UNICEF), *Poverty Reduction Begins with Children* (New York, NY, UNICEF, 2000) 39.

[69] See UNICEF (n 68).

[70] S Fukuda-Parr, 'The Human Development Paradigm: Operationalizing Sen's Ideas on Capabilities' (2003) 9(2–3) *Feminist Economics* 301.

lead decent lives. These include food, shelter, clothing, education, health services, proper sanitation and safe drinking water, which have been aggregated to come up with the three spheres of human development (health, education and living standard) focused on in the HDI.[71] Those who do not have access to such minimum requirements are considered poor and their situation must be improved. However, the claim of universal applicability of the approach has been criticised for its arbitrariness since it assumes that all people have the same needs, yet these may vary depending on a person's context, culture or unique individual needs.[72]

On the other hand, the capabilities approach provides the conceptual framework for the HDI.[73] Fukuda-Parr notes that Sen's capabilities approach has played a key role in developing tools for measuring human development and poverty other than the traditional focus on income.[74] Sen's capabilities approach perceives human life as consisting of a set of 'doings and beings', which he refers to as *functionings*.[75] He explains that a functioning is 'an achievement of a person: what he or she manages to do or be', using resources and facilities that are available to a person.[76] Such functionings range from simple achievements, like the opportunity to be well nourished, literate, undertake usual movements, have shelter or be safe, to quite complex achievements, such as achieving self-respect or 'waging a political campaign for election'.[77] Functionings also depend on a range of personal and social factors, such as gender, health, metabolic rates, pregnancy, age or education.[78] A person's capability is then a derived notion reflecting 'the various combinations of functionings (doings and beings) he or she can achieve'.[79] Thus, Sen argues that a person's *capability* 'to do and be' depends on 'the *opportunity* to be able to have combinations of functionings' and on a person's freedom to make use of this opportunity or not, in choosing to lead one type of life or another.[80]

Therefore, in terms of redistributive status-based inequality, 'if groups differ systematically in the level of achieved functionings, then one may conclude that the members of those groups did not have access to the same capabilities, unless there are plausible reasons why they would systematically choose differently'.[81]

[71] See International Labour Office (ILO), *Employment, Growth and Basic Needs: A One-World Problem* (Geneva, ILO, 1976) 32; Kakwani and Silber (n 66) xiv.

[72] ILO (n 71) 33.

[73] Fukuda-Parr (n 70) 301.

[74] ibid.

[75] See A Sen, *Development as Freedom* (Oxford, Oxford University Press, 1999) ch 3.

[76] A Sen, 'Development as Capabilities Expansion' (1989) 19 *Journal of Development Planning* 41, 43–44.

[77] See Sen, 'Development as Capabilities Expansion' (n 76) 44; A Sen, 'Human Rights and Capabilities' (2005) 6(2) *Journal of Human Development* 151, 154; S Alkire, 'Capability Approach and Well-Being Measurement for Public Policy' (2015) 94 *OPHI Working Paper* 1, 3.

[78] Sen, 'Development as Capabilities Expansion' (n 76) 47.

[79] ibid 44.

[80] Sen, 'Human Rights and Capabilities' (n 77) 154.

[81] I Robeyns and RJ van der Veen, *Sustainable Quality of Life: Conceptual Analysis for a Policy-relevant Empirical Specification* (AH Bilthoven, Netherlands Environmental Assessment Agency, 2007) 46.

Sen's capabilities approach is expressed in the meaning of human development set out in Human Development Reports as 'an expansion of the real freedoms of people to pursue lives that they value and have reason to value' – an expansion of human capabilities.[82]

Other than creating the conceptual framework for the HDI country measurements, the capabilities approach has been used to come up with various other averages. One example is the Gender Inequality Index (GII). This reflects gender-based inequalities in reproductive health (measured by maternal mortality and adolescent birth rates), empowerment (measured by the share of parliamentary seats held by women and attainment in secondary and higher education by each gender), and economic activity (measured by the labour market participation rate for women and men).[83] In terms of calculations, a value of 0 shows a low level of gender inequality, and 1 the highest level. This average helps in giving statistical evidential proof that poverty and inequality almost always go together, as illustrated in the ensuing section using Kenya's figures, hence buttressing the argument that 'measures to alleviate poverty should be coordinated with measures to combat discrimination, in pursuit of full and effective equality'.[84]

Nevertheless, income and consumption-based measurements of poverty are not completely done away with in identifying redistributive inequality, as it is argued that poor levels of health, education and living standards can all be traced back to lack of income.[85] Moreover, a lot of statistics on poverty and inequality, such as the Gini coefficient, use income distribution within a country to measure socio-economic inequality. Noting the importance of recognising the multidimensional nature of poverty and the fact that most of the statistics on socio-economic inequality use income distribution as their guide, both perspectives are vital to identifying redistributive inequality. However, it is argued that income-based measures should be applied with the caveat that the reliance on income alone may be misleading.

Inequalities of power and of participation also contribute to and reinforce poverty. Young fittingly notes that redressing harms that are a direct result of status-based discrimination could be effectively done through the withdrawal of action or policies that have a negative impact on affected groups.[86] Policies and legislation could also be effective in making provisions to redress the socio-economic disadvantage experienced by vulnerable groups because of their status.

[82] See United Nations Development Programme (UNDP), *Human Development Report 2010: The Real Wealth of Nations – Pathways to Human Development* (New York, NY, Palgrave Macmillan, 2010) 85; Fukuda-Parr (n 70) 303.

[83] UNDP, *Kenya Human Development Report 2015, Work for Human Development: Briefing Notes for Countries on the 2015 Human Development Report* (2015) 5.

[84] Equal Rights Trust, *Economic and Social Rights in the Courtroom: A Litigator's Guide to Using Equality and Non-Discrimination to Advance Economic and Social Rights* (London, Equal Rights Trust, 2014) 136.

[85] See Lister (n 65) 14–20.

[86] IM Young, 'Equality of Whom? Social Groups and Judgments of Injustice' (2001) 9 *Journal of Political Philosophy* 1, 4.

This suggests that access to power and political participation are crucial aspects in condemning some to poverty and can also be a key tool in redressing disadvantage. Nevertheless, Young notes that most non-professionals and disadvantaged groups rarely 'participate in making decisions that affect the conditions of their lives and actions, and in this sense most people lack significant power'.[87] This results in a state of powerlessness whereby power is exercised over these groups of people without their exercising it.[88] Thus, the point of view of the poor and disadvantaged, based on their lived experiences of poverty, rarely makes it to the policy decision-making level, since those with power are mostly professionals or people of a higher social class, whose ways of life differ greatly from theirs.

In Kenya such inequalities of participation have mostly been visited upon minority and marginalised communities, persons with disabilities, women and the youth, which has led to their getting the short end of the stick in the provision of socio-economic goods and services. Powerlessness caused by inequalities of participation allows us to recognise that political participation by disadvantaged groups, with participation being a key dimension of substantive equality, is an integral part of addressing poverty, and a lack of political voice can reinforce it.

III. Applying the Analytical Framework to Kenya

The historical and current social context in Kenya demonstrates the importance of recognising the interrelationship between SERs and status-based equality. This is best brought out by an analysis of statistics on poverty in the country which show that 'the pattern of who is poor is entrenched and reflects long-standing discrimination in the society'.[89] Accordingly, Kenya's GII value for 2014 was 0.552 and the country was ranked 126 out of 155 states globally in gender inequality.[90] The high GII value indicates that women in Kenya are most affected by poverty, due to poorer access to healthcare, education, political participation and formal employment, which were focused on when measuring the GII. This state of affairs is mostly a result of cultural norms and social stereotypes that discriminate against women. Also, the 2016 government of Kenya report to the UN Committee on the Elimination of Discrimination Against Women flags issues relating to the feminisation of poverty in the country.[91] This is particularly so in relation to the fact that only 29 per cent of women work in formal wage employment, yet nearly 40 per cent of households in the country are run solely by women, resulting in nearly all such households being affected by poverty.[92]

[87] IM Young, *Justice and the Politics of Difference* (Princeton, NJ, Princeton University Press, 1990) 56.
[88] ibid.
[89] Brodsky and Day (n 8).
[90] UNDP (n 83) 6.
[91] CEDAW, *Consideration of reports submitted by States parties under article 18 of the Convention, Eighth periodic report of States parties due in 2015: Kenya* (2016) CEDAW/C/KEN/8, [78] and [141].
[92] ibid [141].

Recent national statistics show that Kenya's overall poverty rate was 36.1 per cent in 2015–16.[93] In addition to this, a 2014 report by the Institute of Security Studies (ISS) recorded that 18.4 million Kenyans (40 per cent of the country's population of 46.3 million at the time) lived in extreme poverty.[94] This is based on the standard applied by ISS that anybody earning or spending less than US$1.25 a day is extremely poor.[95] The ISS report applied the Gini coefficient to measure inequality of income distribution within a country, with 0 representing complete equality and 1 absolute inequality.[96] Kenya's national Gini coefficient was estimated at 0.445, signalling huge inequalities in wealth and income between the rich and the poor.[97]

The poor in Kenya face various denials of their dignity and equality. These include: poor access to adequate healthcare, because of its prohibitive cost; lack of nutritious food; unsafe housing, with the poor in urban areas mostly living in slums;[98] unequal access to justice; and a poor learning environment because of classroom congestion and a shortage of learning materials.[99] In terms of lack of housing, it is reported that issues such as landlessness and the presence of many squatters in the country are 'linked to the failure of the post-independence governments to implement a comprehensive resettlement programme'.[100] Also, in many instances, the poor are excluded from decision making because participation requires travel to central areas out of their reach. Hence, decisions affecting them largely fail to 'reflect the reality under which they live … [and] the constraints and privations which they suffer'.[101]

In addition to the statistics set out here on the general extent of poverty in Kenya, there is also the problem of ethno-regional variations in well-being as a result of political inequalities of participation, as highlighted in Chapter 3.[102] These facts and figures show that in order to deal with socio-economic disadvantage in the country, a complete contextual picture of deprivation needs to be drawn, which reveals a close relationship between socio-economic deprivation and status-based inequality. Furthering this argument, a 2013 World Bank Kenya report highlights that 'For each percentage point that inequality falls, the poverty rate falls by an additional 1.7 percentage points for Kenya's observed trajectory

[93] Kenya National Bureau of Statistics (n 3) 44–45.

[94] Cilliers, Hughes and Turner (n 3) 1.

[95] ibid.

[96] ibid 3.

[97] See also KS Njonjo, *Exploring Kenya's Inequality: Pulling Apart or Pooling Together?* (Nairobi, Society for International Development, 2013).

[98] Sixty per cent of the population in Kenya's capital of Nairobi live in slums. See United Nations Human Settlements Programme (UN-HABITAT), *Nairobi Urban Sector Profile* (Nairobi, UN-HABITAT, 2006) 4.

[99] G Musila, *Framework Briefing Paper on How the New Constitution Addresses Social Exclusion and Marginalization of Women, Ethnic Minorities/Indigenous Groups and the Poor* (Nairobi, Report for Oxfam GB, November 2011) 30–31.

[100] ibid 15.

[101] ibid 13.

[102] Ch 3, text to nn 7–13.

for income growth'.[103] Therefore, the report argues that 'poverty reduction can be achieved through two complimentary [*sic*] channels: growth and redistribution in favour of the poor (reduction of inequality)'.[104] Consequently, to achieve the Constitution's transformative goal of social justice, social context needs to be combined with the constitutional provisions discussed earlier, which recognise the need to guarantee equality and prioritise the socio-economic needs of the most disadvantaged when implementing SERs.

IV. Pulling it All Together

The textual, conceptual and contextual analysis in this chapter leads to the conclusion that the implementation and adjudication of SERs that have a bearing on status-based equality need to be done in an *equality-sensitive* manner. I use the term 'equality-sensitive' to mean that the enforcement of SERs needs to pay attention to four issues, as discussed in various parts of the chapter. First, attention should be paid to the recognition dimension of substantive equality on the extent to which enforcement pays attention to stigma, stereotypes and other forms of recognition harms that have contributed to some groups being worse off, socially and economically, than benchmark populations (discussed in Sections II and III). Second, implementation of SERs should consider historical and social context revealing status-based redistributive inequalities (the redistributive dimension) that need to be addressed when implementing SERs (discussed in Section III). Three, regard should be had to the participative dimension on the extent to which some vulnerable groups have been affected by political inequalities and exclusion from decision making on SERs issues that affect them (discussed in Sections II and III). Lastly, implementation should consider how the enforcement of SERs can lead to structural change (the transformative dimension), through prioritising the needs of vulnerable groups and the accommodation of difference – say for persons with disabilities and minority cultures – as the Constitution envisions (discussed in Sections I and II). These four points are inspired by Fredman's four-dimensional view of the goals of substantive equality as were first set out in Chapter 3.[105]

V. Conclusion

This chapter has cast light on the fact that poverty or socio-economic deprivation mostly affects those who face status-based discrimination. Therefore, efforts

[103] J Randa and P Gubbins, *Kenya Economic Update: Time to Shift Gears – Accelerating Growth and Poverty Reduction in the New Kenya* (Washington, DC, World Bank Group, 2013) 40.
[104] ibid 52.
[105] Ch 3, text to nn 69–74; Fredman, *Discrimination Law* (n 30) 25–33.

to realise SERs need to adopt new tools of enforcement to address the interconnected harms of socio-economic deprivation and status-based inequality. More so, it has been shown that the need to recognise the inextricable link between SERs and status-based equality is not just a normative argument, but accords with the constitutional mandate requiring the State and its organs to prioritise the needs of vulnerable groups when implementing SERs.

The chapter has also argued that an acknowledgement of the relationship between SERs and status-based equality through the application of an equality-sensitive approach can enhance responsiveness of the State, courts and other stakeholders to the mutually reinforcing patterns of poverty and status-based inequality in the country. Thus, as the case-law analysis in Chapter 8 will further reveal, the failure to forge new tools in the implementation of SERs that embrace an equality-sensitive approach to address the twin harms of poverty and inequality in Kenya, runs the risk of reinforcing status-based disadvantage.

8

Interrelationship between Socio-economic Rights and Status-based Equality in Current Kenyan Jurisprudence

It was argued in Chapter 7 that the implementation and adjudication of socio-economic rights (SERs) should be done in an equality-sensitive manner in order to reach the most vulnerable and root out inequality in the country, as required by various constitutional mandates. To do this, attention needs to be paid to four issues arising out of the interrelationship between SERs and status-based equality. These include: (1) recognition harms, such as social stereotypes, prejudice and stigma; (2) pre-existing redistributive inequalities; (3) inequalities of participation; and (4) the ways in which SERs can lead to overall structural change. Applying this analytical framework, the chapter examines the extent to which Kenyan courts have considered the interrelationship between SERs and status-based equality when adjudicating SERs claims. This will be through an analysis of whether there has been a recognition of the four issues to be considered, in order to apply an equality-sensitive approach in SERs cases that touch on the poor and vulnerable in the country. The chapter also shows how a failure to apply an equality-sensitive approach, in such cases, runs the risk of reinforcing disadvantage. It then makes recommendations on how this can be avoided by applying the equality-sensitive analytical framework mentioned above.

It is important to note that SERs jurisprudence in Kenya under the 2010 Constitution is relatively new, but there are a growing number of cases on the rights to health, housing and education that will be discussed in the chapter, specifically where the relationship between SERs and status-based equality arises. Almost all the current SERs cases have been heard in the High Court and, in particular, the Constitutional and Human Rights Division, which is part of the High Court hierarchically.[1] No SERs cases have as yet gone to the Supreme Court, which is the

[1] See P Mukaindo, 'A Case of Mistaken Identity? Demystifying the "Constitutional Court" in Kenya' *Kenya Law* (Nairobi, 2 May 2013). The Constitutional and Human Rights Division is part of the High Court hierarchically and plays a leading but not exclusive role in constitutional interpretation. Any High Court 'wields power to determine and interpret a constitutional question arising from any matter properly before it'.

highest court in Kenya. Hence, all cases looked at will be from the High Court, in addition to one recent right-to-housing decision by the Court of Appeal, the second-highest court in Kenya hierarchically.

I. Access-to-justice Challenges that Warrant an Equality-sensitive Approach to Socio-economic Rights Adjudication

Article 165 of the Kenyan Constitution empowers the High Court to enforce the Bill of Rights. Subsequent appeals can be made to the Court of Appeal and lastly to the Supreme Court. This means that all guarantees in the Bill of Rights, including SERs, are made justiciable and are capable of being invoked before the courts as to whether they have been denied, violated, infringed or threatened.[2] However, justiciable SERs could have inequitable results due to access-to-justice challenges that mainly affect the poor and disadvantaged. Accordingly, there is a risk that individual SERs claims are likely to worsen inequalities since access to courts is mostly available to people who are relatively well off.

Access-to-justice challenges therefore affect all four issues to be considered for SERs adjudication to be done in an equality-sensitive manner. First, by mostly benefiting the relatively well-off individual claimants able to access the court, SERs adjudication can reinforce recognition harms by leaving out the poor and most disadvantaged, who disproportionately face status-based discrimination. Second, the individual nature of SERs litigation threatens to exacerbate redistributive inequality by mostly benefiting those able to afford litigation. Third, access-to-justice challenges are a participation concern as inability to access the courts inhibits one from participating in judicial enforcement of SERs, which also further marginalises these groups in their ability to enjoy their SERs. Fourth, the individualised nature of SERs claims affects the achievement of overall structural change, by only focusing on the socio-economic needs of the particular litigants in a case.

Hence, in order to take an equality-sensitive approach to the adjudication of SERs, a key first step would be for courts not to just look at the individual pleadings in a particular case. In individual claims that have a bearing on vulnerable groups not before the court, judges should also consider the greater social context surrounding the socio-economic right in question and the overall impact the

[2] See J Biegon, 'The Inclusion of Socio-Economic Rights in the 2010 Constitution: Conceptual and Practical Issues' in J Biegon and G Musila (eds), *Judicial Enforcement of Socio-Economic Rights under the New Constitution: Challenges and Opportunities for Kenya* (Nairobi, Kenya Section of the International Commission of Jurists, 2012) 14.

judgment will have. As Fuller and Winston rightly point out, an adjudicative determination does not only affect the lives and future relations of individual litigants before a tribunal, it also impacts upon 'the future relations of other parties who see themselves as possible litigants before the same tribunal'.[3]

To this extent, the first sub-section looks at the argument that because of access-to-justice challenges, the individualised nature of SERs claims is likely to reinforce *beneficiary and policy area inequality*.[4] It is then contended that a factoring in of an equality-sensitive approach in SERs cases would require courts to take a holistic contextual approach to SERs adjudication. This would mean that a court, in reaching a decision on such cases, should consider different factors at play in relation to the socio-economic right at issue. Factors to be considered include, but are not limited to, how the cases are framed, who the litigants are and, most importantly, the social context within which the need for the right in question arises. This last factor will be the focus of this section because of its great capacity to mitigate and balance out the access-to-justice challenges associated with the justiciability of SERs.

The second sub-section considers the limits of adjudication. It argues that the task of examining the social context in which SERs claims arise, and how the crafting of the court's decision or relief granted may affect social ordering in general and not just the lives of individual litigants in a case, is not a job for the courts alone. This is because the court, in most instances, may not have the required capacity or wealth of information to determine the extended social implications of its judgment, and the effects of its decision on groups not before it. Because of this concern, it is contended that determination of social context should be a collaborative process. It thus necessitates the involvement of amici curiae, fact-finding commissions and other interlocutors whose work is essential in aiding the court to be aware of and obtain the necessary information on social context and the likely social implications of its judgment. Through such collaborative investigation of the effects of judicial intervention, 'the adjudicator can be better informed of complex repercussions and, so, can properly demarcate and give effect to rights in a more-polycentric setting'.[5] The court may also employ an inquisitorial procedure to seek such information from parties before it or, in some instances, as has happened in some of the current SERs cases in Kenya, conduct its own factual and statistical inquiry.[6] I now delve deeper into these two challenges below.

[3] L Fuller and K Winston, 'The Forms and Limits of Adjudication' (1978) 92 *Harvard Law Review* 353, 357.

[4] V Gauri and D Brinks, *Courting Social Justice: Judicial Enforcement of Social and Economic Rights in the Developing World* (New York, NY, Cambridge University Press, 2008) 335.

[5] JWF Allison, 'Fuller's Analysis of Polycentric Disputes and the Limits of Adjudication' (1994) 53 *CLJ* 367, 382.

[6] See text to nn 52–61.

A. Individual versus Systemic Change

i. The Individualised Nature of Socio-economic Rights Adjudication

As much as SERs in Kenya are now justiciable and any person who feels that his or her right is violated is free to approach the court, there are access-to-justice challenges, such as the high cost of litigation, that inhibit the most disadvantaged from making SERs claims. As such, a major concern about the adjudication of SERs cases is whether the legal process ends up favouring relatively well-off individual claimants who can afford litigation and who consequently benefit from adequate reparation in terms of delivery of the right sought. This concern has led some commentators to argue that the individual nature of rights litigation can indeed exacerbate inequalities.[7] Gauri and Brinks' account of how the nature of litigation and some methods of presenting claims before courts may actually reinforce inequality in the provision of SERs is helpful in articulating the arguments made here.[8] They use Brazil, South Africa, India, Indonesia and Nigeria as their case studies, but their conclusions are also relevant to the Kenyan context, as will be shown using an analysis of current Kenyan case law on the right to health.

Gauri and Brinks argue that the judicial enforcement of SERs can have retrogressive effects on the equal distribution of public social goods by reinforcing *beneficiary inequality* and *policy area inequality*.[9] First, in relation to reinforcing beneficiary inequality, they argue that, if the reality is indeed that it is the relatively well off who can in most cases afford to litigate their SERs claims, then only those who have direct access to courts 'will directly benefit from judicial allocations'. Thus, 'the courts would be acting as a rationing device for services that are nominally available to all but in practice available only to those who can afford lawyers and litigation'.[10] Beneficiary inequality therefore reinforces redistributive inequality, which predominantly affects the poor, who largely consist of vulnerable groups that face status-based discrimination.[11]

Second, they argue that in instances where it is mostly the relatively well off who can afford access to courts, this may lead to policy area inequality, whereby 'the wealthy use the courts as a mechanism to focus the government's attention on issues that are important to the wealthy and to block the government's efforts to focus on issues that are important to the poor majority'. As a result, policy-making may end up favouring policy that 'disproportionately benefits "legally enfranchised" elites'.[12] This is so even if such cases are brought as collective claims

[7] See C Flood and A Gross, 'Litigating the Right to Health: What Can We Learn from a Comparative Law and Health Care Systems Approach?' (2014) 16 *Health and Human Rights* 62, 63.

[8] Gauri and Brinks (n 4).

[9] ibid 335.

[10] ibid.

[11] See Ch 7, text to nn 61–64.

[12] Gauri and Brinks (n 4) 335.

that are said to be a matter of public interest. Thus, as much as collective claims and public interest litigation have been argued to be the best approach to avoid reinforcing beneficiary inequality, this too may have its problems. This is particularly in terms of SERs-related collective claims highlighting issues that mostly affect the relatively well off at the expense of the most disadvantaged.

Nevertheless, as Gauri and Brinks note, individual claims can have indirect collective systemic effects. They can also aid in overcoming 'political blockages, channel important information to political and bureaucratic actors, create spaces for deliberation and compromise between competing interests, and hold states accountable for incomplete commitments'.[13] They give the example of the Brazilian HIV/AIDS treatment litigation, where cases brought by relatively well-off individual claimants and AIDS activists eventually led to public health officials extending treatment for all those who were HIV positive.[14] However, they note that in contrast with the AIDS litigation, 'later generations of health-rights plaintiffs in Brazil are primarily motivated by the individual effects they can capture for themselves'. Thus, they observe that indirect collective systemic effects of individual SERs litigation are difficult to predict.[15]

The potential of the individualised nature of SERs litigation to reinforce beneficiary inequality is demonstrated by the recent Kenyan case of *Mathew Okwanda v Minister of Health and Medical Services & 3 Others*.[16] The case concerned a petition brought by Mr Okwanda, a retired elderly man, who was suffering from diabetes mellitus and argued that he had no financial means to manage the disease due to its prohibitive costs. He thus sought a declaration that he was entitled to the highest attainable standard of health as per Article 43(1)(a) of the Constitution. He also argued that he was entitled to reasonable care and assistance as an elderly person, by virtue of Article 57 of the Constitution, and sought free medicines as well as free treatment at the State's prime hospitals.[17]

The case did not proceed because of a lack of sufficient evidence.[18] Nevertheless, in his obiter dicta statements, Majanja J stated that 'There has to be a holistic approach to providing socio-economic goods and services that [focuses] beyond the individual'.[19] This is an important observation which highlights the challenges created by SERs adjudication, where those able to access the courts demand expensive medication and treatment at the expense of those who have no such access. As was noted in the case, Mr Okwanda was a former Workers Union chairperson

[13] ibid 6.

[14] ibid 339; D Brinks and V Gauri, 'The Law's Majestic Equality? The Distributive Impact of Judicializing Social and Economic Rights' (2014) 12 *Perspectives on Politics* 375, 380 and 383.

[15] Brinks and Gauri (n 14).

[16] *Mathew Okwanda v Minister of Health and Medical Services & 3 Others* [2013] eKLR (HC) (*Okwanda*).

[17] ibid [3]–[6].

[18] ibid [21].

[19] ibid [16]. See also *John Kabui Mwai & 3 Others v Kenya National Examination Council & 2 Others* [2011] eKLR (HC) [6].

and influential figure in Kenya's fight for multi-party democracy.[20] This means that he can be considered as belonging to the relatively well-off category of Kenyans. If the claim had succeeded, this would have led to beneficiary inequality by moving Mr Okwanda, a relatively well-off Kenyan able to access the court, to the front of the queue in the provision of his right to the highest attainable standard of health.

Notably also, if Mr Okwanda had been granted the relatively costly medication and treatment he sought, this would have opened the floodgates for numerous similar individual claims for costly treatment and medication. As indicated earlier, even though Gauri and Brinks note that individual SERs litigation can lead to indirect collective systemic effects, they also state that this is unpredictable. Hence, this outcome cannot wholly be relied on. Settling such individual claims would deplete the already limited resources available for overall structural change to improve general access to healthcare and other SERs in the country, particularly for the poor.[21] As Majanja J further observed, it would not be practical 'if the overall health budget was substantially increased to fund all health care programmes [as] this would diminish the resources available for the State to meet other social needs'.[22]

Various commentators have raised similar apprehensions. For example, Ferraz argues that if individualised legal remedies include the entitlement of individuals to satisfaction of all their health needs, including advanced treatment and irrespective of cost, this will deplete scarce resources required to meet the health needs of the whole population.[23] Also, Flood and Gross point out that 'litigation that results in successful claims to access expensive new drug therapies may siphon limited public resources needed for preventative and primary care of greater benefit to poorer patients or communities'.[24]

Application of the four-pronged criteria for an equality-sensitive approach would therefore require the court to consider whether the decision it gives redresses disadvantage, and would also lead to structural change rather than entrenching privilege. To do so, a consideration of social context is an important tool in assessing SERs claims that can help mitigate the inequality-reinforcing effects of the individualised nature of SERs adjudication. Due regard is, however, given to the points made earlier that individual cases like *Okwanda* can have indirect collective systemic effects, help overcome political blockages and stimulate discussions by political actors on the best approaches to the enforcement of SERs.

[20] *Okwanda* (n 16) [1].

[21] This is what happened in Brazil. See O Ferraz, 'The Right to Health in the Courts of Brazil: Worsening Health Inequities?' (2009) 11 *Health and Human Rights* 33.

[22] *Okwanda* (n 16) [21]. See also *Soobramoney v Minister of Health (KwaZulu Natal)* 1997 (12) BCLR 1696 (CC) [31], where the South African Constitutional Court stated that owing to the need for the State to manage its limited resources in realising SERs, 'There will be times when this requires it to adopt a holistic approach to the larger needs of society rather than to focus on the specific needs of particular individuals within society'.

[23] Ferraz (n 21) 34.

[24] Flood and Gross (n 7) 65.

ii. *Context as Mitigating the Risks of Socio-economic Rights Justiciability*

An analysis of social context injects an equality-sensitive approach to the adjudication of SERs claims, particularly those that intersect with or may have an impact on status-based equality. This is because an evaluation of social context enables the court to trace the roots of structural inequalities connected to a right in question, which have led to the socio-economic needs of a particular vulnerable group being far beyond those required by the general population. By applying a contextual approach, the court is then able to consider the possible social implications its decision might have both on the claimant(s) and on other disadvantaged groups not before it. The court will thus be in a better position to arrive at a final judgment that avoids reinforcing status-based inequality. If there is no such appreciation of context and the judgment's possible social implications, SERs adjudication runs the risk of maintaining existing structural disadvantages.

At the same time, as much as an analysis of social context is important in highlighting patterns of structural disadvantage that bring out the link between socio-economic deprivation and status-based inequality, it also has its challenges. Notably, the key challenge of this approach is its potential to deny immediate relief to individual claimants who are in urgent need, as this section will continue to show.

The decision of the Kenyan High Court in *PAO & 2 Others v Attorney General* is the best example of how context can be used to mitigate the risks associated with the individualised nature of SERs adjudication.[25] This case raised pertinent issues relating to the constitutional right of persons living with HIV/AIDS to the highest attainable standard of health. The case is particularly noteworthy as Ngugi J explicitly considered social context, which enabled the Court to avoid reinforcing both beneficiary and policy area inequality. This was done through an analysis of information provided by the claimants, interested party, amicus curiae as well as the judge's own statistical inquiry of government reports on the prevalence of HIV/AIDS in Kenya.[26]

The petition was filed by three independent petitioners and was supported by the Aids Law Project and the United Nations Special Rapporteur for Health, Anand Grover, as interested party and amicus curiae respectively. It challenged the constitutionality of sections 2, 32 and 34 of the Anti-Counterfeit Act 2008. The main argument raised by the petitioners was that, in adopting a broad definition of counterfeit goods which encompassed generic medication, the Act was likely to substantially increase the costs of essential drugs, especially HIV/AIDS medication, making them unaffordable to poor, vulnerable and marginalised individuals who rely on cheap generic medication, including many persons

[25] *PAO & 2 Others v Attorney General* [2012] eKLR (HC) (*PAO*).
[26] ibid [44]–[56].

living with HIV/AIDS. The petitioners argued that in severely limiting access to affordable essential drugs and medicines, the impugned sections of the Anti-Counterfeit Act infringed on their right to life, human dignity and health, contrary to Articles 26(1), 28 and 43(1)(a) of the Constitution, respectively.[27]

Moreover, the petitioners argued that the restriction of access to generic medication would disproportionately limit their rights contrary to Article 24(2)(c) of the Constitution.[28] This provides that limitations of rights should not derogate from the core or essential content of the rights.

In giving her decision, Ngugi J considered the economic and social context of the HIV/AIDS pandemic in Kenya, which constituted a serious threat to life and health of many Kenyans and is a major challenge to socio-economic development. Using statistical data, the Court estimated that the number of people living with HIV/AIDS in Kenya was between 1.3 and 1.6 million, with a general prevalence rate in the country of 7.4 per cent. It further estimated the cumulative number of children living with HIV/AIDS to be around 184,052, as of 2009, though efforts were being made by the government to reduce mother-to-child transmission of HIV.[29] The Court also noted that most of those living with HIV/AIDS in Kenya were poor and financially incapable of accessing branded antiretroviral (ARV) medication. They thus relied on generic medication, which was cheaper and more accessible to them. Therefore, the Court stated that the socio-economic context had to be considered in reviewing the constitutionality of the impugned provisions of the Anti-Counterfeit Act. It was acknowledged that should the implementation of the provisions have the effect of limiting access to generic ARV medication, this would *ipso facto* threaten the health and lives of the petitioners and other similarly placed disadvantaged individuals, in violation of their constitutional rights.[30]

Importantly, too, the Court referred to the UN Committee on Economic, Social and Cultural Rights (CESCR) General Comment No. 14 on the Right to Health,[31] which is applicable to Kenya by virtue of Article 2(6) of the Constitution, as discussed in Chapters 6 and 7.[32] Quoting the General Comment's stipulation that the right to health also requires the promotion of conditions in which people can lead healthy lives, the Court held that such conditions include making sure that 'people have access to the medication they require to remain healthy'.[33] The Court further relied on comparative jurisprudence from the South African Constitutional Court, which held in *Minister of Health & Others v Treatment Action Campaign & Others* that access to medicines was an essential component

[27] ibid [1]–[6].
[28] ibid [19]–[20].
[29] ibid [46]–[48].
[30] ibid [49]–[52].
[31] CESCR, *General Comment No. 14: The Right to the Highest Attainable Standard of Health (Art. 12 of the Covenant)*, 11 August 2000, E/C.12/2000/4.
[32] Ch 6, text to nn 19–20; Ch 7, text to nn 11–12.
[33] CESCR, *General Comment No. 14* (n 31) [4]; *PAO* (n 25) [61]–[64].

of the right to health, and failure of the State to ensure such access was a violation of the constitutional right to health.[34] Ngugi J, invoking both the negative and positive State obligations that flow from the constitutionally entrenched right to health, concluded that

> [t]he State's obligation with regard to the right to health therefore encompasses not only the positive duty to ensure that its citizens have access to health care services and medication but must also encompass the negative duty not to do anything that would in any way affect access to such health care services and essential medicines. Any legislation that would render the cost of essential drugs unaffordable to citizens would thus be in violation of the State's obligations under the Constitution.[35]

The Court held that the definition of counterfeit, as contained in section 2 of the Anti-Counterfeit Act, was likely to be read to include generic medication. Hence, it was likely to adversely affect the manufacture, sale and distribution of generic equivalents of patented drugs. This would affect the availability of generic drugs in Kenya, with adverse consequences to the right to health, dignity and life of the petitioners and similarly placed individuals.[36] The Court thus directed that it was incumbent on the State to make the necessary amendments to the Act, considering its constitutional obligation to ensure access to the highest attainable standard of physical and mental health for its citizens.[37]

Three key observations can be made from the judgment. First, the Court's careful analysis of social context was equality sensitive by not just considering whether the right was available, but whether applying it would redress disadvantage. This distinguishes *PAO* from *Okwanda*, which is also about access to medication. The analysis then led to a finding that interfering with provision of cheap generic ARV medication would have an adverse effect on those living with HIV/AIDS. This was because, according to the analysed statistics, those affected by the HIV/AIDS pandemic disproportionately consist of the most economically disadvantaged and vulnerable groups in the country. To this effect, the Court explicitly cited the disparate effects of HIV/AIDS on women and children, as well as the consequent low economic circumstances that result from living with and treating opportunistic diseases that come with being HIV/AIDS positive.[38] These observations on social context revealed the overall economic disadvantage faced by persons living with HIV/AIDS because of their status. Such observation then helped declare unconstitutional any legislation that had the potential to increase payments to access essential ARV medication.[39]

Second, even though three individual claimants lodged the claim, the decision of the Court had a positive impact on all persons living with HIV/AIDS,

[34] *PAO* (n 25) [61]–[65]; *Minister of Health v Treatment Action Campaign* (2002) 5 SA 721 (CC).
[35] *PAO* (n 25) [66].
[36] ibid [78].
[37] ibid [88].
[38] ibid [45]–[52].
[39] ibid [49]–[52].

particularly the indigent who can only afford cheap generic ARV medication. In this sense, by considering the effects of the Act on not only the claimants, but also similarly situated persons living with HIV/AIDS, the Court's decision avoided reinforcing beneficiary inequality.

Third, by highlighting the potential of the broad definition of counterfeit in the Act to adversely affect access to essential ARV medication by economically disadvantaged persons living with HIV/AIDS, the decision avoids reinforcing policy area inequality. This is because the legislation in question affects everyone who is HIV positive, and not just an elite group or privileged minority. The Court arguably also avoided reinforcing policy area inequality by recognising that the expensive nature of patented drugs (of benefit to rich pharmaceutical companies) would have a negative impact on persons infected with HIV/AIDS, many of whom are poor.[40] The approach and holding of the Court in *PAO* thus coincides with the observation made by Gauri and Brinks that courts can ensure litigation benefits the most indigent by making sure, as was done in the case, that legislation or programmatic frameworks do not overlook interests that need to be protected.[41] Again, the need for structural change was considered.

Nevertheless, even when taking a contextual approach, there is also the relative difficulty of enforcing positive duties to fulfil SERs, as was the case in *Okwanda*, as compared to negative duties of restraint from interference with the enjoyment of SERs, as happened in *PAO*. Many SERs give rise to both negative and positive duties.[42] Negative duties 'protect individuals against intrusion by the State' and are said to be 'determinate, immediately realizable, and resource free'.[43] They are thus relatively easier to enforce. On the other hand, positive duties require 'protection by the State from want or need' and are regarded as being 'indeterminate, programmatic, and resource intensive'.[44] Due to their indeterminate nature and resource implications, positive duties are more difficult to enforce and this is therefore why they are said to require progressive realisation.[45]

The *PAO* case mainly implicated negative duties of restraint, as the main issue in contention was the provisions of the Anti-Counterfeit Act, which acted as an obstacle to accessing generic medication, mostly of benefit to the poor. The process of addressing the issue was less cumbersome. The Court had to analyse the facts of the case and evidence provided to determine whether the issues raised warranted the striking out of the impugned provisions as interfering with the applicants' enjoyment of their constitutional right to health. However, in *Okwanda*, the matters in dispute were more complicated. The applicant wanted the State to provide him free medication and treatment. Multiple complex issues had to be considered.

[40] ibid [51] and [52].
[41] Gauri and Brinks (n 4) 344.
[42] S Fredman, *Human Rights Transformed: Positive Rights and Positive Duties* (Oxford, Oxford University Press, 2008) 68.
[43] ibid 66 and 70.
[44] ibid.
[45] ibid 70.

These included: the applicant's entitlement to the highest standard of health; the applicant's right to healthcare vis-à-vis that of similarly situated individuals not before the court; resource availability to meet the applicant's request; the constitutional mandate for SERs to be progressively realised; and the legitimacy of the Court to adjudicate on polycentric issues, which duty has been argued to mainly lie with the executive and legislature. The critique of the different approaches taken in the two cases therefore remains alive to the more complex challenges in adjudicating positive duties.

iii. Balancing Individual Remedies and Systemic Change

Despite the importance of a contextual approach in mitigating the potential of individual SERs claims to reinforce both beneficiary and policy-area inequality, it should be applied with caution. This is because of its potential to lock out benefits for individual claimants who may end up without immediate relief, despite being genuinely in desperate need. As some commentators have noted, an inquiry into the impact of a SERs claim not only on individual litigants, but also on parties not before the court, should not unjustly lead to litigants in urgent need ending up without a remedy.[46] Talib Kweli aptly captures this point when he states: 'If we say our house is on fire and you say "all houses matter", well that may be true, but all houses aren't on fire now, my house is.'[47]

An example of this is what happened in *Government of the Republic of South Africa v Grootboom*.[48] In the case, the South African Constitutional Court only gave a declaratory order that the State should devise and implement, within its available resources, a comprehensive housing programme that included reasonable measures to ensure that the rights of the poor, and especially those in desperate need, are guaranteed.[49] The judgment has been lauded as being the first time that a court enforced the constitutionality of a socio-economic right. However, the declaratory order that the State should take appropriate steps to cater for the rights of *all* those without adequate access to housing left Mrs Grootboom, and those in the same urgent situation as her, without immediate relief, and she died homeless eight years later. It is for this reason that Davis argues that 'A failure by successful litigants to benefit from constitutional litigation of this kind can only contribute

[46] See D Davis, 'Socio-Economic Rights in South Africa: The Record after Ten Years' (2004) 2 *New Zealand Journal of Public and International Law* 47, 51–56; S Liebenberg and B Goldblatt, 'The Interrelationship between Equality and Socio-Economic Rights under South Africa's Transformative Constitution' (2007) 23 *South African Journal of Human Rights* 335, 354; N Orago, 'Poverty, Inequality and Socio-economic Rights: A Theoretical Framework for the Realisation of Socio-economic Rights in the 2010 Kenyan Constitution' (LLD thesis, University of the Western Cape, 2013) 195–96.

[47] twitter.com/mtvnews/status/751618144918048768.

[48] *Government of the Republic of South Africa v Grootboom* 2000 (11) BCLR 1169 (CC) [99] (*Grootboom*). See also *Soobramoney* (n 22) [31], where the individual claim for renal dialysis was said to be overtaken by the need for the State to manage its limited resources.

[49] *Grootboom* (n 48).

to the long-term illegitimacy of the very constitutional enterprise'. This is because the lack of a tangible benefit for successful litigants in desperate need renders such rights illusionary.[50] A contextual approach should therefore not be applied to defeat a valid and urgently needed individual SERs claim, especially since – using the example of *Grootboom* – despite 'winning' the case, Mrs Grootboom and thousands of other South Africans died without a home.

Thus, an equality-sensitive approach also needs to be applied in the remedial stage of a case. Section III discusses this issue in greater detail and recommends a solution, in the form of an equality-sensitive mixed standard of review, that seeks to balance individual socio-economic needs and systemic change.[51] The individual needs versus systemic change dilemma discussed here, and the role of context in mitigating individualisation, reveals another key challenge to the justiciability of SERs that is also an access-to-justice issue: the limits of adjudication. It is to this that I now turn.

B. Limits of Adjudication

Having argued that a contextual approach is needed for SERs claims to be adjudicated in an equality-sensitive manner, the need to marshal the appropriate evidence for litigation can put a heavy burden on litigants. This raises the question of whether this is an inherent limitation of litigation or whether it reflects the current structure of Kenyan litigation, based on adversarialism. Kenyan courts in recent SERs cases have dismissed a significant number of claims because of the lack of adequate evidence and sufficient particularity but, as this section will argue, it is possible to envisage a different, more inquisitorial role for courts in ensuring justice is delivered to the most disadvantaged. The first sub-section considers the fact-finding and particularisation of claims challenges that have led to the dismissal of a good number of current SERs cases. The second sub-section then considers the extent to which a broadening of the courts' inquisitorial role could provide a solution for this.

i. Fact-finding and Particularisation of Claims

In *PAO*, Ngugi J managed to mitigate the risks associated with the individualised nature of SERs adjudication by conducting a factual and statistical inquiry on the prevalence and effects of HIV/AIDS in Kenya.[52] By applying a fact-finding

[50] Davis (n 46) 56.

[51] Text to nn 169–71.

[52] *PAO* (n 25) [44]–[56]. We are not told whether either of the parties presented these statistics in any of their pleadings, and hence it is assumed that the Court did its own factual and statistical inquiry. Nevertheless, even if either of the parties presented such statistics, the Court did a novel job in skilfully integrating them in its assessment of the claim under the heading 'social context'.

approach, she managed to sketch out the general socio-economic context of disadvantage faced by persons living with HIV/AIDS in the country, and not just the individual claimants in the case. This shows the importance of adducing sufficient evidence and relevant information on social context before the courts in SERs cases.

However, in two other right-to-health cases that had the capacity to set groundbreaking jurisprudence on various aspects of the delivery of SERs, the Kenyan High Court was forced to dismiss the claims because of a lack of particularity and inadequate evidence. The first case was that of *Okwanda*, as discussed earlier.[53] The second case was that of *Kenya Society for the Mentally Handicapped (KSMH) v Attorney General & 7 Others*, which was similarly dismissed because of a lack of particularisation and inadequate evidence.[54]

The *KSMH* case concerned a public interest claim brought on behalf of persons with mental disabilities, whom the petitioner argued were discriminated against due to inadequate policies aimed at the realisation of their SERs. The petitioner averred that there are around 3.6 to 8.5 million Kenyans with different forms of mental, intellectual and psychological disabilities, who remain 'unidentified and unaddressed because of the discriminatory and inadequate State policies'.[55] The petitioning organisation thus sought a declaration that the State had discriminated against persons with mental disabilities in the provision of support and services, in contravention of the Constitution. This was specifically in relation to the general equality and non-discrimination provisions in Article 27, the specific equality and reasonable accommodation guarantees for persons with disabilities in Article 54, and the SERs guarantees in Article 43.[56] They also sought a mandatory order directing the respondents to establish a sound legal framework addressing the needs of persons with mental disabilities in, for example, education, health and financial support.[57]

Despite acknowledging the challenges facing persons with mental disabilities, the case was nevertheless dismissed, with the Court stating that the petition lacked sufficient evidence and particularity. Majanja J observed that

> it is unfortunate that the petition and the supporting deposition are inadequate for this court to conduct an inquiry necessary to reach any conclusions to determine whether rights are violated as alleged. A case such as that presented is not about legal arguments but facts and evidence presented to support legal arguments.[58]

This case, similar to that of *Okwanda*, highlights the importance of presenting sufficient evidence and information. In turn, this will assist the court in taking the

[53] Text to nn 16–22.
[54] *Kenya Society for the Mentally Handicapped (KSMH) v Attorney General & 7 Others* [2012] eKLR (HC) (*KSMH*).
[55] ibid [1].
[56] ibid [5].
[57] ibid [5].
[58] ibid [9].

necessary steps to transform such promise into reality, by holding government to account where an ideal case is brought before it. Such challenges have led to courts signalling to claimants to do more. For example, in one such case, Ngugi J noted that 'parties in the position of the petitioner, should they determine to take on cases which have a bearing on the public interest, must take them on with all due seriousness'.[59] This trend in recent SERs cases exposes the limits of adjudication in terms of the way cases are presented and evidence adduced. It illustrates that, even if courts decide to be stricter and more proactive in adjudicating SERs claims, there is not so much they can do without proper initial prompting by claimants.

Emphasising the observations made by Ngugi J, the East African Centre for Human Rights has stated that the current limits to SERs adjudication in Kenya are mainly a result of 'lack of sufficient preparation and lack of seriousness in the litigation of serious cases of public interest'.[60] The Centre particularly notes that, in the *KSMH* case, the petitioning organisation was in such a hurry to file the case that it did not wait for the completion of a comprehensive study, by the Kenya Human Rights and Equality Commission, capturing the contextual situation of persons with disabilities in Kenya.[61] The study would have helped in particularising the claim and gathering adequate evidence in support of the petition.

Therefore, to some extent, this challenge goes beyond the courts and mainly requires action by claimants to adequately present their cases, with additional help from possible interveners and amici curiae. Such interveners may include civil society organisations that focus on implementation of SERs. Other important interveners include quasi-governmental bodies such as the Kenya Human Rights Commission and the National Gender and Equality Commission, tasked with monitoring the implementation of SERs and the right to equality.[62]

In addition, a lot of thought and background research should go into the planning of collective and public interest litigation on SERs. Consultations with public interest organisations in other jurisdictions that have successfully argued similar SERs claims can also be a helpful approach. However, this may require additional resources and thus could exacerbate the access-to-justice problem.

Suggestions have nevertheless been given on how to navigate such challenges through broadening the courts' inquisitorial role. This is discussed below.

ii. Broadening the Courts' Inquisitorial Role

The dismissal of *Okwanda* and *KSMH* for lack of particularity and inadequate evidence raise the age-old question of whether it is reasonable and practical to

[59] *Consumer Federation of Kenya (COFEK) v Attorney General & 4 Others* [2012] eKLR (HC) [44] (*COFEK*).

[60] East African Centre for Human Rights (EACHRights), *A Compendium on Economic and Social Rights Cases under the Constitution of Kenya, 2010* (2014) 24.

[61] ibid.

[62] www.khrc.or.ke; www.ngeckenya.org.

expect courts to salvage such important cases by broadening their inquisitorial role and seeking additional information from parties or other sources. An equality-sensitive approach would include the courts contemplating how to achieve structural change through changes in their own procedures. The *PAO* case hints that this is possible. In the case, the Court was able to conduct its own factual and statistical inquiry on the prevalence of HIV/AIDS in Kenya and its effects. A converse but equally valid argument, frequently made, is that the court's function – particularly in the common law adversarial judicial system that Kenya subscribes to – rightly has to be prompted by the litigants themselves and is not initiated by the court itself.[63] However, it is argued that the transformative vision of the 2010 Constitution, through entrenchment of justiciable SERs, blurs this line and expects courts to be more proactive in the road towards social transformation. Judicial sensitivity to alleviation of the dire socio-economic conditions of the vulnerable requires a slight departure from the common law adversarial tradition. Courts may be required to take a more hands-on approach, including the broadening of their inquisitorial role, especially when the lives of vulnerable and marginalised groups are at stake.

In India, for example, which is also a common law jurisdiction, the Supreme Court has cited with approval the need for courts to depart from a strict application of the adversarial procedure when it comes to cases that impact on the most disadvantaged. It has particularly stated:

> Therefore, when the poor come before the court, particularly for enforcement of their fundamental rights, it is necessary to depart from the adversarial procedure and to evolve a new procedure which will make it possible for the poor and the weak to bring the necessary material before the court for the purpose of securing enforcement of their fundamental rights. If the adversarial procedure is truly followed in their case, they would never be able to enforce their fundamental rights and the result would be nothing but a mockery of the Constitution. Therefore the Courts should abandon the laissez faire approach in the judicial process particularly where it involves a question of enforcement of fundamental rights and forge new tools, devise new methods and adopt new strategies for the purpose of making fundamental rights meaningful for the large masses of people.[64]

The same reasoning can be applied as to why Kenyan courts need to broaden their inquisitorial role when adjudicating SERs claims. This is because it is mostly cases that affect the poor and disadvantaged that are at the frontline of current SERs claims. In achieving the transformative goal of the Constitution, Chapter 2 argued for a paradigm shift from the previous formalistic legal culture, where courts cared too much about structure, rules and technical limitations, to the adoption of a more proactive approach.[65] To cure the lack of particularity and sufficient evidence

[63] Fuller and Winston (n 3) 385.
[64] *Bandhua Mukti Morcha v Union of India* 1984 (3) SC 161 [9].
[65] Ch 2, text to nn 12–15 and 43–54.

challenges in current SERs jurisprudence would require the court, as the guardian of the Constitution, to ensure that it has the right evidence before it at the onset of an important SERs case. Such information can be obtained either through the application of an inquisitorial procedure or by the court advising the claimants, at the initial stages of the judicial process, to amend their claim to include essential evidence to assist the court in its assessment.

Also, in relation to the need for Kenyan courts to take a more proactive role in the adjudication of SERs cases, the East African Centre for Human Rights has criticised the Court's handling of the lack of particularity and sufficient evidence in the *Okwanda* and *KSMH* cases. It avers that the Court 'was too quick to pull the trigger' in dismissing the cases and could have done more to salvage the claims and to ensure that justice was achieved.[66] In terms of the Court broadening its inquisitorial role, the Centre suggests, for example, that the Court in *Okwanda* and *KSMH* could have saved the cases by ordering the government to adduce information via sworn affidavit on 'the measures it had put in place to ensure the progressive realisation of the rights in question'.[67] I agree with this suggestion because of the difficulty, in many instances, of accessing government information on all plans and intended programmes. Therefore, a shift in the burden of proof to the government to show what it has done and is doing to guarantee constitutionally entrenched SERs can help cure the evidential challenges faced by claimants in SERs litigation. The right to information has indeed been argued to be a powerful tool in making claims for the realisation of SERs and there can also be litigation solely on this basis as further set out in Kenya's Access to Information Act.[68] Furthermore, the requirement for the government to state what it is doing to progressively realise a socio-economic right is merely taking the State to task on the fulfilment of its constitutional obligations to provide and fulfil.

Nevertheless, the lack of sufficient particularisation and evidence for the court to apply in its assessment of such technical cases is a valid concern. It is unfair to expect courts to walk blindly into unfamiliar territory, which may lead to claims of overreaching. This is where amici curiae and interlocutors may come in handy in providing information on various aspects of the case and, in particular, the possible social implications of a court's decision.

The *KSMH* and *Okwanda* cases reveal that courts are just one actor in the process of realising the SERs of vulnerable groups. Civil society and public interest lawyers are also important actors and need to sufficiently particularise their claims and adduce sufficient evidence to aid the courts in coming up with groundbreaking jurisprudence on the realisation of SERs. Additionally, public interest lawyers and bodies monitoring the implementation of SERs need to follow up on individual claims in arguing for the extension of rights guaranteed to an individual

[66] EACHRights (n 60) 25.
[67] ibid.
[68] See Gauri and Brinks (n 4) 7; Access to Information Act No. 31 of 2016, Laws of Kenya.

claimant to others who are similarly situated. As noted earlier, individual SERs claims are still important in overcoming political blockages to the realisation of SERs and may eventually lead to systemic change.[69]

II. Prioritisation of Socio-economic Needs of Vulnerable Groups

Having discussed how an equality-sensitive approach can help to avoid reinforcing inequality and promote equality, this section looks at the extent to which it can actually mitigate inequality by prioritising the needs of vulnerable groups in the adjudication of SERs claims. The grounding for this proposition, as stated in Chapter 7, are the provisions in the 2010 Constitution explicitly recognising the need to prioritise the SERs of vulnerable groups in Kenya.[70] Bolstering these constitutional guarantees is the reason given in the Constitution's drafting history for the inclusion of SERs in general, which are largely meant to ameliorate the dire socio-economic conditions of disadvantaged groups.[71] For example, the Constitution of Kenya Review Commission highlighted poor sanitation and lack of adequate housing concerns raised by slum dwellers (69 per cent of the population in Kenya's capital, Nairobi, at the time) as part of the reason why the rights to adequate housing and reasonable standards of sanitation were constitutionally entrenched.[72] This shows the importance of prioritising the SERs of vulnerable groups. As Bilchitz aptly puts it:

> The urgent interests of beings provide the reasons for many of our duties to others. Talk of duties alone fails to indicate that it is our connection to others who have interests that is of critical importance and which imposes obligations upon us.[73]

Based on the above background, this section analyses recent cases on the right to housing in evaluating the extent to which Kenyan courts have and can actually apply the constitutional mandate to prioritise the SERs of vulnerable groups to mitigate inequality. Such an approach is equality sensitive as the socio-economic disadvantage of vulnerable groups in Kenya, such as the poor, is usually a cause or consequence of status-based discrimination.[74] Thus, by focusing on the most disadvantaged, the requirement seeks to redress the socio-economic redistributive inequalities that are largely caused by status-based recognition harms and

[69] See Gauri and Brinks (n 4) 6.

[70] Ch 7, text to nn 10–27; The Constitution of Kenya 2010, Arts 20(5)(b), 21(3) and 53–57.

[71] Constitution of Kenya Review Commission, *The Final Report of the Constitution of Kenya Review Commission. Approved for issue at the 95th Plenary Meeting held on 10 February 2005* (2005) 112–19.

[72] ibid 118–19.

[73] D Bilchitz, *Poverty and Fundamental Rights: The Justification and Enforcement of Socio-Economic Rights* (Oxford, Oxford University Press, 2007) 73.

[74] See Ch 7, text to nn 3–4 and nn 41–60.

inequalities of participation. It also leads to overall structural change by seeking to move those who are most socially and economically disadvantaged to the same level as benchmark populations.

The section also argues that, in many instances, the duty to prioritise the needs of vulnerable groups will require the immediate amelioration of the dire conditions of the most disadvantaged for them to be free from threats to their survival. As Chapter 7 argued, the constitutional requirement to prioritise the needs of vulnerable groups coincides with the understanding of the minimum core obligation as requiring 'reasonable priority setting in the provision of basic essential levels of each socio-economic right to the most vulnerable and in desperate need'.[75] Therefore, similar to what the minimum core obligation envisages, a failure to prioritise the granting of minimum essential levels of a socio-economic right to a disadvantaged group in desperate need may leave the right devoid of any meaningful content.[76]

The most novel approach taken by courts on the prioritisation of SERs of vulnerable groups so far is in the *PAO* case.[77] Although the Court did not explicitly recognise the constitutional mandate to prioritise the needs of vulnerable groups, the case is a positive development in terms of actual application of the rule. In the case, the urgent need of poor and vulnerable persons living with HIV/AIDS for cheap generic medication trumped rich pharmaceutical companies' need to have expensive branded medication in the market. By making the dire socio-economic situation of persons infected with and affected by HIV/AIDS the cornerstone of its assessment in the case, the Court successfully mitigated inequality.

In some of the recent cases on the right to housing and forced evictions, Kenyan courts have likewise recognised the need to provide urgent relief for some of the most vulnerable groups in the country.[78] Using these cases, this section discusses three themes in interrogating the extent to which Kenyan courts have so far sought to mitigate inequality by prioritising the SERs of vulnerable groups. First, it looks at how courts have sought to prioritise the needs of vulnerable groups in case assessment. Second, the section interrogates how courts can balance the need to respect the executive and legislature's role in coming up with policies and plans for implementing SERs and the granting of effective relief to vulnerable litigants in desperate need of the delivery of a socio-economic right. Third, faced with the reality of resource scarcity, the section looks at whether a resource scarcity defence by the State can trump the prioritisation of urgent socio-economic needs of vulnerable groups.

[75] Ch 7, text to n 18–19.

[76] CESCR, *General Comment No. 3: The nature of States parties' obligations (art. 2, para. 1, of the Covenant)*, 14 December 1990, E/1991/23, [9].

[77] See text to nn 25–41.

[78] See *Mitu-Bell Welfare Society v Attorney General & 2 Others* [2013] eKLR (HC) (*Mitu-Bell High Court* decision); *Satrose Ayuma & Others (on behalf of Muthurwa residents) v Kenya Railways Staff Benefit Scheme & Others* [2013] eKLR; *Susan Waithera Kariuki & 4 Others v Town Clerk, Nairobi City Council & 2 Others* [2011] eKLR (*Susan Waithera*); and *Ibrahim Songor Osman v Attorney General & 3 Others*, High Court Constitutional Petition No. 2 of 2011 (*Ibrahim Songor*).

A. Prioritisation of the Needs of Vulnerable Groups in Case Assessment

In some of the recent cases on the right to housing and forced evictions, Kenyan courts have recognised the need to prioritise the rights of the poor, homeless, slum dwellers and informal settlers, who constitute some of the most vulnerable groups in the country.[79] A good number of High Court decisions on the right to housing have paid particular attention to how forced evictions without relocation or compensation can negatively affect the equal enjoyment of this right by vulnerable groups.[80] Such a position was taken by the High Court in *Mitu-Bell Welfare Society v Attorney General & 2 Others*.[81] Regrettably, some positive aspects of the High Court's decision were overturned and others not taken into account by the Court of Appeal in its recent decision upon appeal by the defendants, as will be discussed here.[82] It is, however, hoped that the Supreme Court will soon have an opportunity to set the record straight and side with the High Court's current series of positive and consistent jurisprudence on the matter.

The *Mitu-Bell* High Court case concerned the forced eviction and demolition of the homes of thousands of families from an informal settlement on public land called Mitumba village, near Wilson Airport in Nairobi, where they had lived for more than 19 years. The evictions took place after a seven-day notice to vacate with no reasons given for the evictions.[83] The community moved to court seeking a declaration that the forced eviction was in contempt of previous court orders not to evict and was also illegal because it took place without due notice, compensation or relocation. They also contended that the forced eviction violated their constitutional rights to housing (Article 43(1)(b)), respect for human dignity (Article 28) and their right to equality and non-discrimination (Article 27).

In its defence, the second respondent (the Kenya Airports Authority) argued that the evictions were necessary to ensure air safety due to the informal settlement's proximity to Wilson Airport's flight path and to curb the security threats the war in Somalia posed.[84] The security threat argument is largely tied to the fact that the area where Mitumba village is located (around South C Estates in Nairobi) is home to a large population of urban Somali refugees.[85] However, the petitioners contended that the evictions were selective and discriminatory as there were other multi-storeyed structures, including residential apartments, surrounding the informal settlement, which were also situated near Wilson Airport but were not demolished.[86]

[79] ibid.
[80] ibid.
[81] *Mitu-Bell High Court* decision (n 78).
[82] See text to nn 102–23.
[83] *Mitu-Bell High Court* decision (n 78) [10].
[84] ibid [13] and [60].
[85] See K Varming, 'Urban Subjects: Somali Claims to Recognition and Urban Belonging in Eastleigh, Nairobi' (2020) 79(1) *African Studies* 1, 10.
[86] *Mitu-Bell High Court* decision (n 78) [13] and [66].

Since no legislation or guidelines have been developed so far on the carrying out of evictions in Kenya, Ngugi J turned to international law applicable to Kenya by virtue of Article 2(5) and (6) of the Kenyan Constitution.[87] In particular, the judge invoked paragraphs 15 and 16 of the guidelines on evictions in CESCR General Comment No. 7 on forced evictions.[88] Paragraph 15 effectively provides for meaningful engagement between the State and those to be evicted, the giving of adequate notice and the following of proper procedures for evictions. Paragraph 16 then provides that '*Evictions should not result in individuals being rendered homeless or vulnerable to the violation of other human rights*' (emphasis added).[89]

After going over the facts and evidence presented in the case, Ngugi J held that the forced eviction and demolition of the petitioners' homes after a seven-day notice, without a relocation option and without following the proper procedures, violated their constitutional rights.[90] She also stated that the selective demolition of the informal settlements alone, and not the multi-storeyed buildings surrounding it, violated the right to non-discrimination and equal protection of the law. It was based on a false assumption that 'terror only resides in the downtrodden informal settlements' in Kenya and, in this case, was only posed by 'the indigent, marginalised, denizens of Mitumba village'.[91] This was said to disregard the State's constitutional obligation to protect the marginalised and ensure social justice and non-discrimination.[92]

Moreover, Ngugi J noted that the State was under a specific constitutional obligation to '*observe, respect, protect, promote and fulfil*' the enjoyment of SERs by the most marginalised and disadvantaged groups in the country that '*suffer disproportionately from the practice of forced eviction*' (emphasis added).[93] This obligation, she argued, meant that the State was not only under a positive duty under Article 43 to progressively take steps to fulfil the right to housing of the petitioners, but was also under a 'negative obligation not to do anything that impairs the enjoyment of these rights', that is, not to take retrogressive measures.[94] The State thus went against its negative obligation by conducting selective and discriminatory demolitions. It also failed to meet its positive obligation to provide and fulfil the right to housing, by evicting the petitioners without providing them with alternative accommodation, rendering them homeless.

Ngugi J then proceeded to conclude that the evictions were not only in violation of socio-economic rights (Article 43), fair administrative action (Article 47) and human dignity (Article 28), but also equality (Article 27) and protection of the

[87] ibid [40].
[88] ibid.
[89] CESCR, *General Comment No. 7: The right to adequate housing (Art.11.1): forced evictions*, 20 May 1997, E/1998/22.
[90] *Mitu-Bell High Court* decision (n 78) [44].
[91] ibid [67] and [68].
[92] ibid.
[93] ibid [69].
[94] ibid [56] and [57].

most vulnerable groups in society (Articles 53 and 56 on children's right to shelter and rights of marginalised groups, respectively).[95] She ordered that the respondents should, within 60 days, provide shelter and access to housing for the former residents of Mitumba village.[96]

This decision touched on two important issues. First, it emphasised that non-discrimination is an immediate duty where a State grants a socio-economic right to some, and not others, in the same or an analogous situation.[97] In the negative connotation of the immediate duty not to discriminate, a State act is similarly discriminatory when, as in the case at hand, and as Ngugi J acknowledged, evictions in the area surrounding Nairobi within Wilson Airport's flight path only affected the informal settlements of the poor and not the luxurious apartments located in the same area.

Second, recognising the urgency of prioritising the right to housing of the poor and vulnerable informal settlers, Ngugi J stated that evictions should not leave those evicted homeless and exposed to harsh conditions threatening their health and life in general.[98] She specifically considered the need to safeguard the SERs of informal settlers, 'who, more often than not, are limited in their capacity to provide for themselves'.[99] This holding shows the explicit awareness by the Court of the need to prioritise housing needs of the most vulnerable. It highlights the critical role an equality-sensitive approach can play in emphasising the immediate nature of the State's obligation to provide SERs, when it involves vulnerable groups in desperate need. It also accords with the requirement of progressive realisation not to take retrogressive measures, such as allowing evictions to be carried out without compensation or relocation, which would leave the petitioners homeless.[100] Such an approach has been taken in a majority of the right-to-housing and forced-eviction cases before the High Court leading up to the *Mitu-Bell* decision.[101]

Despite the largely sanguine tone of current right-to-housing and forced-eviction jurisprudence in the High Court, the recent *Mitu-Bell* Court of Appeal decision marks a fundamental departure from the positive SERs jurisprudence built upon by the High Court over the years.[102]

In its decision on 1 July 2016, the Court of Appeal observed that the High Court had made an error in one of its reliefs. This related to the making of a composite order issuing directives applicable and enforceable not only to the State, which had been found at fault, but also to the Commissioner of Lands, who had

[95] ibid [75].
[96] ibid.
[97] See Ch 7, text to n 16.
[98] *Mitu-Bell High Court* decision (n 78) [49], [52] and [69].
[99] ibid [69].
[100] CESCR, *General Comment No. 7* (n 89) [9].
[101] Text to nn 79–80.
[102] *Kenya Airports Authority v Mitu-Bell Welfare Society & 2 Others* [2016] eKLR (CA) (*Mitu-Bell Court of Appeal* decision).

been duly absolved of any culpability.[103] Regrettably, however, the Court of Appeal focused most of its energies on evaluating this error and other not-so-damaging issues. It then short-sightedly proceeded to dismiss the whole set of reliefs given by the High Court, without substituting them with its own.[104] This unjustly left the initial claimants without a remedy, notwithstanding the three-judge bench's agreement with the High Court's holding that 'the State was responsible for the eviction of residents of Mitumba village and that the State is responsible for the demolition of the residential homes and structures at Mitumba village'.[105] The Court of Appeal also noted the fact that the evictions took place in total disregard of a court order restraining the applicants from demolishing the informal settlement, pending an inter parties hearing and determination of an application for conservatory orders.[106] Yet, despite all these acknowledgements, the Court of Appeal still failed to consider the rights of the evicted informal settlers in its final determination, and left them without any relief.

This brings us to the next issue of deference to the State versus the granting of effective relief to claimants in ensuring that the constitutional mandate to prioritise the needs of vulnerable groups is enforced and not just wishful thinking.

B. Deference versus Effective Relief in Prioritising Socio-economic Rights of Vulnerable Groups

The Court of Appeal in *Mitu-Bell* laid great emphasis on deference to the State, citing Article 20(5)(c) of the Constitution. This relates to the need for courts not to 'interfere with a decision by a State organ concerning the allocation of available resources, solely on the basis that it would have reached a different conclusion'.[107] Nevertheless, it did not say how this specifically applied to the core findings by the High Court on the wrongfulness of the State's forced eviction of informal settlers in Mitumba village without due notice, relocation or compensation. It left open the much-needed inquiry into the difference between a court overstepping its mandate, by delving into issues of policy setting, and a court as the guardian of the Constitution, holding the State accountable for failure to meet its constitutional obligations.

This is in contrast to the way in which the High Court attempted to navigate the distinction between illegitimate intrusion into the work of a State organ and holding the State accountable. It did this primarily through its choice of a remedy, namely by granting a structural interdict which did not prescribe to the State what it needed to do, but required it to draw up a plan which the Court would then be

[103] ibid [141](a).
[104] ibid [142].
[105] ibid [140].
[106] ibid [31].
[107] ibid [34] and [100].

responsible for in ensuring it accords with the constitutional requirements and is implemented.[108] Accordingly, the High Court required a report to be filed in the form of an affidavit in relation to current State policies and guidelines on how shelter and housing is to be provided to marginalised groups within 60 days.[109] The Court also made an order for meaningful engagement between the parties and relevant stakeholders towards an agreed resolution of the applicant's grievance within 90 days, thus also considering the third issue of participation when taking an equality-sensitive approach.[110] This is a better way of holding the State accountable without intruding, as the structural interdict deferred to the government the policy and resource-allocation duties. It gave the State flexibility in deciding how it would meet the claimants' housing needs, while also enabling the High Court to keep a watchful eye over the protection of the informal settlers' right to housing. This was meant to ensure that former residents of Mitumba village did not end up with a nominal remedy without actual enforcement. Therefore, such an approach both respects the separation of powers and 'shields the court from accusations that it has usurped functions reserved for the other organs of state'.[111]

Unfortunately, the Court of Appeal did not develop this approach in a coherent manner. To the contrary, the Court of Appeal rejected the application of structural interdicts and retention of supervisory jurisdiction and held that, once a case is closed, no further orders can be given (*functus offficio* doctrine). However, even in this holding, the Court seemed to have contradicted itself. This contradiction can be seen in three key rulings and observations made in the judgment. First, the Court of Appeal made contradictory statements as to the meaning and applicability of structural interdicts. A reading of the Court of Appeal's reasoning reveals that, in one breath, the Court rejects the application of structural interdicts in Kenya as well as the retention of supervisory jurisdiction by a court over its orders. In this regard, the Court held that 'In the instant case, the trial court erred in delivering a judgment and then reserving outstanding matters to be dealt with by the court. Save as authorized by law, upon delivery of judgment, a court becomes *functus officio*'.[112] It then proceeded to hold that the application of supervisory orders is 'unknown to Kenyan law'.[113] Finally, the Court, in contradiction with the position it had taken earlier and the eventual determination, held that 'a supervisory order can be made pursuant to the provisions of *Article 23 (3)* of the 2010 Kenya Constitution'.[114] This provision gives courts wide discretion to grant

[108] The High Court applied a 'report back to court' structural interdict model whereby 'the defendant is required to report back to the court with a plan on how he or she intends to remedy the violation' and a fixed date is given to that effect. See C Mbazira, *Litigating Socio-Economic Rights in South Africa: A Choice Between Corrective and Distributive Justice* (Cape Town, Pretoria University Law Press, 2009) 189.

[109] *Mitu-Bell High Court* decision (n 78) 79.

[110] ibid.

[111] Mbazira (n 108) 189.

[112] *Mitu-Bell Court of Appeal* decision (n 102) [72] and [142].

[113] ibid [71].

[114] ibid [112]. See also the eventual holding in [141] (c) and (d).

appropriate relief. The resulting judgment failed to recognise that the uniqueness of supervisory orders, like structural interdicts, is the capacity of the court to retain jurisdiction in order to compel the State or a State organ to fulfil its obligations to a successful litigant. Such orders particularly compel the State 'to engage with the plaintiffs in meaningful dialogue because of the knowledge that the doors of the court are open to the plaintiffs'.[115]

The Court of Appeal thus fundamentally misunderstands what a structural interdict, and supervisory orders in general, do – they are not meant to vary the court's judgment but to supervise the implementation of the court's orders. Several Kenyan scholars have noted that such set-backs or confusion when trying to balance numerous competing constitutional interests could be the effect of 'teething problems' because of the radical departure from a previous legal framework that did not include SERs.[116]

Also, the eventual holding rejecting the applicability of supervisory orders flies in the face of demand by the transformative nature of the 2010 Constitution for a new legal culture to implement the unique provisions therein. New constitutional guarantees, such as the inclusion of SERs, inject new life to judicial adjudication and require that new approaches be taken by courts to ensure their implementation. Structural interdicts/supervisory orders have been argued to be unique approaches important in the judicial implementation of SERs, specifically in cases involving 'poor litigants who may not have the resources to institute another suit in case of non-compliance by the defendant'.[117] The Court of Appeal in *Mitu-Bell* missed this point, leaving the claimants who had 'won' on grounds of unlawful eviction without an effective remedy.

Roach and Budlender emphasise the importance of an effective and meaningful remedy for poor successful litigants, which, they rightly note, has 'greater weight than the principle of respecting institutional roles'.[118] They also note that structural interdicts are particularly effective in tackling governmental non-compliance in situations where it exudes 'incompetence, inattentiveness and intransigence'.[119] In the *Mitu-Bell* case, the State had already shown its intransigence by defying an earlier court order restraining the applicants from evicting residents of Mitumba village.[120] Moreover, the government only indicated the applicable Guidelines on Settlement and Evictions in an affidavit to the Court when seeking to comply with Ngugi J's orders in the *Mitu-Bell* High Court decision requiring it to do so

[115] Mbazira (n 108) 182.

[116] I Ndegwa, 'A roof over Wanjiku's head: Enforcement of the Right to Housing under the Constitution of Kenya' in J Biegon and G Musila (eds), *Judicial Enforcement of Socio-Economic Rights under the New Constitution: Challenges and Opportunities for Kenya* (Nairobi, Kenya Section of the International Commission of Jurists, 2012) 173.

[117] Mbazira (n 108) 182–83.

[118] K Roach and G Budlender. 'Mandatory Relief and Supervisory Jurisdiction: When Is It Appropriate, Just and Equitable?' (2005) 122 *South African Law Journal* 325, 343.

[119] ibid 345.

[120] See *Mitu-Bell High Court* decision (n 78) [5]; *Mitu-Bell Court of Appeal* decision (n 102) [6].

within 60 days from the day of the judgment.[121] This shows the positive impact the structural interdict applied by the High Court had in bringing to the government's attention the urgent need for such guidelines.

Second, the Court of Appeal's rejection of the applicability of structural interdicts is contradictory because it ignores their use by the Supreme Court. As the Court of Appeal noted, the Kenyan Supreme Court has applied structural interdicts, for example in *Communications Commission of Kenya & 5 Others v Royal Media Services Limited & 5 Others*.[122] In the case, the Supreme Court ordered the first appellant to consider the respondents' application for licences and to notify the Court's registry within 90 days on the fulfilment of the Court's orders.[123] The rejection of courts' retention of supervisory jurisdiction by the Court of Appeal thus seems to overrule the practice of the Supreme Court, whose judgments hold the overall precedential value. Hence, the Court arguably overstepped its mandate. Such confusion in the handling of SERs cases that have an impact on vulnerable groups has the effect of reinforcing inequality and marginalisation.

Third and last, the Court of Appeal only relied on one aspect of Article 20(5), deference to the State's decision on the allocation of available resources to fulfil SERs (Article 20(5)(c)). But the thrust of Article 20(5) is much broader. In particular, the Court failed to require the State to follow Article 20(5)(b), which states that, even if resources are scarce, the State should nevertheless take steps to prioritise the SERs of vulnerable groups. As has been argued in this section, the application of a structural interdict helps maintain a balance between granting the State flexibility on the best way to realise SERs and giving claimants an effective remedy.

However, as much as it is essential to prioritise the needs of vulnerable groups in the country, there is also the reality of resource scarcity. A practical application of the constitutional mandate to prioritise the SERs of vulnerable groups therefore needs to be accompanied by an appreciation of the resource impediments that this requirement faces. This point is discussed below.

C. The Duty to Prioritise Socio-economic Rights of Vulnerable Groups and the Reality of Resource Scarcity

A key challenge to fulfilling SERs of vulnerable groups in a developing nation like Kenya is the reality of resource scarcity. Indeed, as was stated in Chapter 7, Article 20(5) of the Constitution allows the State to make a claim that it does not have enough resources to implement a socio-economic right provided for under Article 43. However, the provision gives guidelines on how such a defence should

[121] See *Mitu-Bell Court of Appeal* decision (n 102) [12] and [13].

[122] *Communications Commission of Kenya & 5 Others v Royal Media Services Limited & 5 Others*, Supreme Court Petition No. 14 of 2014.

[123] ibid [415].

be made. It places the onus of proof on the State to show that resources are not available and directs that, in allocating resources to realise SERs, the State should prioritise the needs of vulnerable groups and individuals in the country.[124] The court in evaluating the State's defence is required not to interfere with a State organ's decision on 'allocation of available resources, solely on the basis that it would have reached a different conclusion'.[125] This last provision acknowledges that, in most instances, there will be competing socio-economic needs and the State will have to make its own value judgement on the best way to meet each of these needs. All things considered, the major take-home point in Article 20(5) is that, even though there is the reality of resource scarcity, these requirements place an obligation on the State to try and ensure that the rights of vulnerable groups are guaranteed as a matter of priority. This is in appreciation of the essential need to ameliorate the dire conditions of vulnerable groups.

Moreover, as Chapter 7 discussed, even though SERs in Article 43 are subject to progressive realisation because of the reality of resource constraints, these rights also have aspects that require immediate realisation. According to the CESCR, these include the obligation to take steps towards realising SERs, the duty not to discriminate, and the minimum core obligation, which coincides with the need to prioritise the SERs of vulnerable groups.[126]

In prioritising the SERs of vulnerable groups, the presence of many disadvantaged groups in Kenya with competing socio-economic needs, and the fact that almost half the population is considered poor, means that a more pragmatic approach to meeting these needs, acknowledging genuine resource constraints, will have to be developed. Such an approach will also depend on the right in question.

For instance, when it comes to the right to housing, meeting the needs of vulnerable groups could be further divided into two categories, in terms of priority. The first category could consist of the most vulnerable groups that require a roof over their heads as a matter of imminent urgency, because the lack of it would threaten their very survival. This category would then include those rendered homeless because of either conflict, natural disasters or unlawful forced evictions. The housing rights of these groups should be immediately realised either in the form of basic housing structures, or the allocation of alternative land or money, as has been done in the past to resettle evicted slum dwellers and internally displaced persons.[127] Not meeting this essential level of the right to housing would deprive the right of its raison d'être – its most essential content.[128] Applying the

[124] Art 20(5)(a) and (b); Ch 7, text to nn 13–19.

[125] Art 20(5)(c).

[126] Ch 7, text to nn 16–17; CESCR, *General Comment No. 7* (n 89) [10].

[127] For example, the provision of alternative land and/or money by the government in resettling persons who were left internally displaced after the 2007/2008 post-election violence in Kenya. Also, in *Ibrahim Songor* (n 78), informal settlers who had been forcefully evicted without relocation or compensation were granted Ksh 200,000 (US$2,000) each as reparation.

[128] CESCR (n 89) [10].

requirements in Article 20(5)(b) on the need to prioritise the vulnerability of various individuals and groups when implementing SERs, it is argued that a resource scarcity defence cannot trump the meeting of such imminent urgent needs.

The second category could consist of vulnerable groups such as slum dwellers who live in poorly built, but relatively habitable, shanties or those living in mud huts, whose vulnerability can be flexibly ameliorated by an application of mid-term and long-term housing programmes. This second category will thus still be subject to progressive realisation considering the reality of resource scarcity. What is envisioned here is something like the holding of the South African Constitutional Court in *Grootboom*, that for a housing programme to be reasonable it 'must be balanced and flexible and make appropriate provision for attention to housing crises and to short, medium and long-term needs'.[129]

An even greater concern is the prevalence of corruption in Kenya, narrowly defined as 'abuse of public power (or public office) for private gain'.[130] This works to further skew the allocation of the already scarce resources for implementing SERs in favour of the well off, at the expense of the indigent. According to a 2019 Afrobarometer survey report on corruption, 45 per cent of public service users in Kenya reported having to pay a bribe to get a public service, 18 per cent to access medical treatment, 14 per cent to obtain school placements for their children, 48 per cent to get help from or avoid problems with the police, 35 per cent to obtain household services and 38 per cent to obtain official documents like identity cards.[131] Therefore, a major consequence of corruption is that it creates an additional financial burden to accessing basic services for all citizens, but especially for the poor, who are often unable to afford bribes.[132]

This illuminates the harms of corruption in skewing the distribution of social goods that largely affect vulnerable groups, like the poor and persons with disabilities, who end up getting the short end of the stick in the provision of their SERs. To remedy this, in adjudicating SERs claims, courts need to bear in mind the necessity of tackling corruption where it is said to have occurred, especially because of its capacity to exacerbate status-based inequality.

These kinds of issues were recognised in *Glenister v President of the Republic of South Africa & Others* before the South African Constitutional Court, which provides a model on how Kenyan courts could intervene in such cases.[133] The case concerned the obligation of the South African government to establish and maintain an independent anti-corruption body. Ngcobo CJ, giving the main judgment of the Court, observed that corruption poses a threat to both the fight

[129] *Grootboom* (n 48) [44].

[130] Y Jong-Sung and S Khagram, 'A Comparative Study of Inequality and Corruption' (2005) 70 *American Sociological Review* 136, 137.

[131] C Pring and J Vrushi, *Global Corruption Barometer Africa 2019: Citizens' Views and Experiences of Corruption* (Transparency International and Afrobarometer, 2019) 38.

[132] E Uslaner, 'Corruption and Inequality' (2011) *CESifo DICE Report* 20, 21.

[133] *Glenister v President of the Republic of South Africa & Others* [2011] ZACC 6 (CC) (*Glenister*).

against poverty and the delivery of SERs.[134] In explaining the need and rationale behind combating corruption, Moseneke DCJ and Cameron J in their joint judgment stated that 'There can be no gainsaying that corruption threatens to fell at the knees virtually everything we hold dear and precious in our hard-won constitutional order'.[135] They went on to highlight that corruption undermines human dignity, equality and various SERs.[136] The Court then proceeded to hold that the South African State was constitutionally obliged to establish and maintain an independent anti-corruption entity.[137]

The Court in *Glenister* not only recognised the capacity of corruption to undermine the guarantee of equality and skew the allocation of SERs to the detriment of the poor, but, in applying this context, also proceeded to grant an effective remedy. Similarly, in applying an equality-sensitive approach not only in case assessment, but also at the remedial stage, Kenyan judges need to go further than just giving 'toothless' acknowledgements or declarations against corruption. This happened in *Kepha Omondi Onjuro & Others v Attorney General & 5 Others*, where, despite the High Court taking note of the corruption complaints by the petitioners, it merely emphasised that the housing project in issue should only benefit 'those who genuinely deserve to reap the benefits of the project', and 'care must be taken to ensure that those who deserve to benefit from the project are the ones who actually benefit therefrom'.[138] Kenyan courts are vested with broad powers under Article 23 of the Constitution to grant appropriate relief. Hence, courts have no excuse for not giving an effective relief in SERs claims citing corruption as an impediment to ensuring SERs programmes reach those they are intended to benefit.

The analysis in this section has shown that an equality-sensitive approach is essential in pinpointing the status-based and redistributive inequality-specific reasons why it is important to prioritise the SERs of vulnerable groups. This then helps mitigate such inequality.

III. Desirability of an Equality-sensitive Approach in Setting Standards of Review for Assessing Socio-economic Rights Claims

This section considers best practices derived from cases analysed in various parts of the chapter and makes recommendations on the role an equality-sensitive approach can play in setting standards of review by courts for assessing SERs claims going forward. Coming up with the appropriate standard for assessing SERs

[134] ibid [57].
[135] ibid [166].
[136] ibid [167], [172] and [200].
[137] ibid [189] and [192].
[138] *Kepha Omondi Onjuro & Others v Attorney General & 5 Others* [2015] eKLR (HC) [149].

cases is crucial because 'The standards and tests courts rely on and courts delineate in the course of socio-economic rights litigation, may affect and influence the degree to which courts can translate abstract rights into tangible reality'.[139]

This section specifically considers the effect that various standards of review may have on realising the socio-economic needs of vulnerable groups. It argues that courts, as guardians of the Constitution,[140] should adopt a standard of review that applies equality as an interpretative tool in the judicial enforcement of SERs that have a bearing on status-based equality, to avoid reinforcing structural injustices. To this extent, it recommends a mixed standard of review that incorporates a reasonableness approach and the value of equality in safeguarding the rights of vulnerable groups.

A. The Reasonableness Standard of Review

As was highlighted in Chapter 7, the full version of Article 20(5) of the Kenyan Constitution provides:

> (5) In applying any right under Article 43, if the State claims that it does not have the resources to implement the right, a court, tribunal or other authority shall be guided by the following principles—
>
> (a) it is the responsibility of the State to show that the resources are not available;
>
> (b) in allocating resources, the State shall give priority to ensuring the widest possible enjoyment of the right or fundamental freedom having regard to prevailing circumstances, including the vulnerability of particular groups or individuals; and
>
> (c) the court, tribunal or other authority may not interfere with a decision by a State organ concerning the allocation of available resources, solely on the basis that it would have reached a different conclusion.

This provision expressly incorporates salient elements of a reasonableness standard of review. However, it avoids setting a generic reasonableness test by giving more specific guidelines which make it clear that the government must justify a lack of resources to implement a socio-economic right. The guidelines in Article 20(5) contain some of the valuable principles on the reasonableness standard of review developed in South Africa. This derives from the text of the South African Constitution, which requires the State, when implementing SERs, to take *reasonable* measures, within its available resources, to progressively realise these rights.[141]

[139] See J Chowdhury, 'Judicial Adherence to a Minimum Core Approach to Socio-Economic Rights – A Comparative Perspective' (2009) 27 *Cornell Law School Inter-University Graduate Student Conference Papers* 1, 1.

[140] The Constitution of Kenya 2010, Art 23 on the authority of courts to uphold and enforce the Bill of Rights and Art 165 on the determination of questions as to whether provisions of the Constitution have been contravened.

[141] The 1996 South African Constitution, ss 26(2) and 27(2).

The South African Constitutional Court in the *Grootboom* case established the two main issues to be considered in a reasonableness approach.[142] First, Yacoob J stated that a margin of discretion should be given to the legislature and executive for them to decide on the content of the socio-economic measure or programme to be adopted.[143] This accords with Article 20(5)(c) of the Kenyan Constitution, which states that a court should not interfere with the decision of a State organ on the allocation of resources for realising SERs 'solely on the basis that it would have reached a different conclusion'. This position has been affirmed by the Kenyan High Court in *Consumer Federation of Kenya (COFEK) & 3 Others v Attorney General & 4 Others* on the right to food.[144] In the case, Ngugi J stated that, as long as the State's measures are sound, it is not up to the Court to enquire as to whether other more desirable or favourable measures could be adopted, or if public money could be better spent.[145] As Ngugi J explained, this is because there is usually a wide range of possible measures open for the State to adopt that could meet the requirement of reasonableness. Once adopted measures are shown to do so, the requirement is met.[146]

The second key aspect of the reasonableness approach, as was noted in *Grootboom*, is the obligation of the State to prioritise the immediate needs of those in desperate need in order for a programme implementing a socio-economic right to be considered reasonable.[147] As Davis observes, 'the Court insisted that the concept of reasonableness meant more than an assessment of simple statistical progress, and that evidence had to be provided to show that there was sufficient attention given to the needy and most vulnerable'.[148] In accordance with this mode of review, the Court in *Grootboom* held that the State's housing programme was unreasonable as it lacked any component providing for those in desperate need.[149] Article 20(5)(b) of the Kenyan Constitution makes explicit the requirement to prioritise vulnerable groups in the delivery of SERs and does not leave it to a generic reasonableness test.

Several commentators have praised the South African Constitutional Court's application of reasonableness in *Grootboom*.[150] Notably, the decision has been lauded as being democracy promoting. By requiring sensible priority setting by the State to provide low-cost housing for those in desperate need, the Court avoided giving itself the role of overseeing the public purse and immersing itself in

142 *Grootboom* (n 48).
143 ibid [41].
144 *COFEK* (n 59).
145 ibid [39] and [40].
146 ibid [40].
147 *Grootboom* (n 48) [68].
148 Davis (n 46) 51–52.
149 *Grootboom* (n 48) [66]–[69].
150 See C Sunstein, 'Social and Economic Rights – Lessons from South Africa' (1999) 11 *Constitutional Forum* 123; C Steinberg, 'Can Reasonableness Protect the Poor? A Review of South Africa's Socio-Economic Rights Jurisprudence' (2006) 123 *South African Law Journal* 264.

'setting allocative priorities'.[151] Such an approach is indeed helpful in enabling the court to hold the State accountable for its constitutional obligations without delving into polycentric issues of policy making and resource allocation that lie within the proper mandate of the executive and legislature.

However, various criticisms have been levelled against the reasonableness standard of review, as applied by the South African Constitutional Court in *Grootboom*.[152] The main criticism of the approach is the failure of the Court to adopt the minimum core obligation approach in providing the right to housing for those in desperate need.[153] In this regard, the Court's application of a reasonableness approach without taking into account a minimum core content meant that 'a government programme will pass constitutional muster if it plans to cater for the poor in the fullness of time, even if it fails to prioritize their interests over other less urgent interests'.[154] This also runs the risk of rendering illusionary the SERs of vulnerable groups in urgent need.

Nevertheless, the Court in *Grootboom*, by recognising the failure of the State to prioritise the needs of those in desperate need, applied some element of the minimum core obligation. Bilchitz specifically observes that the only way the Court could have reached the conclusion that the government's housing programme was unreasonable, for not including the short-term needs of those in desperate need, would only have been possible through a recognition of the minimum core obligation.[155] However, as noted earlier, it is unfortunate that this minimal recognition was not enough for the Court to acknowledge an individualised right to housing to be immediately provided for the individual litigants in the case.

Importantly, Davis notes that the South African Constitutional Court has been reluctant to impose any excessive burden on the State by interpreting the rights to health and housing as incorporating a guarantee of the minimum essential levels of these rights. This has in effect ensured that 'no direct claim can be made by a litigant against the State for the delivery of a minimum core of rights'.[156] In consequence, the lack of a tangible benefit to poor successful litigants in urgent need, as in the *Grootboom* case where Mrs Grootboom died eight years later, penniless and without a house, renders such rights illusionary.[157] The South African Constitutional Court has, however, granted immediate remedies to informal settlers in some of the right-to-housing cases that followed *Grootboom*.[158]

[151] See Sunstein (n 150) 123, 127 and 130; Davis (n 46) 60.
[152] See Steinberg (n 151) 267–68; Davis (n 46) 54–55.
[153] Liebenberg and Goldblatt (n 46) 354.
[154] Steinberg (n 151) 268.
[155] D Bilchitz, 'Giving Socio-Economic Rights Teeth: The Minimum Core and Its Importance' (2002) 119 *South African Law Journal* 484, 486. See also Steinberg (n 150) 280.
[156] Davis (n 46) 54.
[157] See ibid 56; text to nn 49–50.
[158] See *City of Johannesburg Metropolitan Municipality v Blue Moonlight Properties 39 (Pty) Ltd & Another* [2011] ZACC 33 (CC); *Occupiers of 51 Olivia Road v City of Johannesburg* [2008] ZACC 1 (CC).

Some of the Kenyan case law improves on the South African position by giving individual remedies and prioritising the needs of vulnerable groups, as reflected in the text of Article 20(5)(b), although this is not consistently the case. In a majority of right-to-housing and forced-eviction cases, the Kenyan High Court has granted individual remedies to poor informal settlers in recognising that forced eviction without adequate notice, relocation or compensation will render nugatory their right to housing.[159] For example, similar to the observation of Ngugi J in the *Mitu-Bell* High Court case, Musinga J observed in *Susan Waithera* that it was unconstitutional to forcefully evict the applicants in the case from the houses they had occupied for over 40 years with the consequence that they are rendered homeless. The Court held that the government had an obligation to provide alternative housing, resettlement or access to productive land, if eviction was to be undertaken humanely.[160] The Court of Appeal in *Mitu-Bell* unfortunately failed to consider the need to prioritise the urgent needs of poor litigants.[161] However, it is hoped that the Supreme Court will side with the High Court, if the case or one similar to it, is appealed.

Also noteworthy is the fact that some of the recent right-to-housing cases in Kenya can be distinguished from the facts in *Mitu-Bell*, and hence the Court of Appeal's holding may not affect the positive jurisprudence set in these cases. For instance, in *Ibrahim Songor*, informal settlers who had been forcefully evicted without adequate notice, relocation or compensation were granted Ksh 200,000 (US$2,000) each as reparation.[162] This is different from the judgment in the *Mitu-Bell* High Court case, which required the parties to meaningfully engage and come up with an appropriate resolution to the grievances of the evicted slum dwellers within 90 days.[163]

Additionally, in *Satrose Ayuma*, the petitioners did not object to their eviction but only 'desired a more humane programme for eviction'.[164] The main contention in the case was the cruel, inhuman and degrading manner in which the eviction was carried out. This particularly related to the fact that, even before the expiry of the 90-day period given to the residents to vacate the suit premises, the respondents were said to have disconnected the water supply and demolished toilets and bathrooms to force the petitioners out of the suit premises.[165] The case can thus be distinguished from *Mitu-Bell*, where the key contention was forced eviction without adequate notice, compensation or relocation. However, similar to the *Mitu-Bell* High Court decision, Lenaola J also granted a structural interdict in *Satrose Ayuma*, requiring the parties to agree on a humane programme of eviction and file it in court within 60 days following the judgment.[166]

[159] See n 78.
[160] *Susan Waithera* (n 78) [16].
[161] *Mitu-Bell Court of Appeal* decision (n 102).
[162] *Ibrahim Songor* (n 78).
[163] Text to n 110.
[164] *Satrose Ayuma* (n 78) [111(ii)].
[165] ibid [4].
[166] ibid [111(ii)(e)(v)].

All in all, on the one hand, it is apparent that implementation of SERs can be justifiably limited because of the resource constraints that necessitate progressive realisation of these rights. Hence the need for reasonable priority setting by the State and the reason why Kenyan courts should give a level of deference to the State in coming up with policies and programmes for this purpose. However, on the other hand, courts as guardians of the Constitution have the obligation to hold the State accountable for unreasonably failing to fulfil these obligations, in particular the constitutional mandate to prioritise the SERs of vulnerable groups. To this extent, an application of Article 24 of the Kenyan Constitution also comes in handy in requiring that limitations to fundamental rights should be '*reasonable and justifiable in an open and democratic society based on … equality*' (emphasis added) and should not derogate from the core essential content of a right.[167] These provisions, coupled with the constitutional duty to prioritise the needs of vulnerable groups in the delivery of SERs, show the essential nature of some consideration of the value of equality within the standard of reasonableness.

Due to the valid criticisms of the reasonableness approach set out in this section, suggestions have been made for a mixed standard of review that includes the value of equality alongside the reasonableness standard of review.[168] Such a mixed approach is the best way to counter the demerits of a reasonableness approach, and is particularly important in developing an equality-sensitive standard of scrutiny in the adjudication of SERs claims.

B. Proposal for a Mixed Standard of Review

This section analyses the potential for the adoption of an equality-sensitive mixed standard of review that integrates reasonableness and the value of equality in the assessment of SERs cases that have a bearing on equality.

What is argued for here is that, the standard of review adopted by Kenyan courts should capitalise more on the specific provisions in the Constitution. Article 20(5) of the Constitution, arguably, provides a two-pronged mixed standard of review, incorporating both reasonableness and the value of equality, which is articulated by the need to prioritise the needs of vulnerable groups. Article 20(5)(b) sets out the goal to be achieved ('ends test') – to prioritise the needs of the most disadvantaged when realising SERs. The 'means test', on how to progressively realise SERs as required under Article 21(2) of the Constitution, is concerned with whether the plan the State has put before it is a reasonable means of achieving the pre-determined end goal. Article 20(5)(c) provides a space for deference by specifying that the court cannot substitute the decision of a State organ with its own. Nevertheless, the court can demand for the State to show what it is doing to meet

[167] Art 24(1) and 24(2)(c).
[168] Liebenberg and Goldblatt (n 46) 355; Orago (n 46).

the goal of prioritising the needs of the most disadvantaged when realising SERs; and that such measures are a reasonable means of achieving this goal. Moreover, where the State relies on shortage of resources to justify falling short of achieving the ends, it must adduce evidence to support its claims (Article 20(5)(a)).

To determine the socio-economic needs of vulnerable groups that should be prioritised, including the needs of the particular claimant(s) before them, Kenyan courts need to look at the overall context of disadvantage relating to the socio-economic right at issue. The context of disadvantage to be considered should range from not just status-based harms but also material disadvantage, disadvantaged groups that have to conform to dominant norms to get their rights, and inequalities of participation.[169] These considerations encompass the four issues – recognition harms, redistributive harms, participatory harms and the ways in which SERs can lead to overall structural change – that should be considered for SERs adjudication to be equality sensitive. Consequently, such an inquiry would demand 'stringent justifications from the state in situations where the denial of access to socio-economic rights creates or reinforces patterns of inequality and marginalisation'.[170]

Importantly, when applying the 'means test', courts should not be too deferent to the State and the Kenyan Constitution provides guidelines on what courts should and should not be deferent. As stated earlier, Article 20(5)(c) requires courts not to interfere with a State organ's decision for the allocation of resources to realise a socio-economic right, on the basis that a different conclusion could have been reached. However, per a joint reading of paragraphs (b) and (c) of Article 20(5), in the 'ends' and 'means' tests set out at the beginning of this section, courts should interrogate the reasonableness of the State's priority setting as regards measures to determine whether it achieves the set end goal of prioritising the socio-economic needs of vulnerable groups. The court cannot vary the State's decision, but it can say it is unreasonable. Hence, when viewed in this way, leaving vulnerable groups in urgent need of housing without a remedy, as discussed in the chapter, is unreasonable. The same can be said of corruption in programmes to assist the most disadvantaged to have access to the right to housing, as lining people's pockets is never reasonable because resources are used for the wrong ends. In such cases involving poor litigants, the application of a mixed standard of review followed by an equality-sensitive remedy, such as a structural interdict, would be the best approach to avoid reinforcing status-based inequality.

The proposed mixed standard of review is therefore inherent within the relationship between paragraphs (b) and (c) of Article 20(5) of the Constitution. Such an approach consolidates the arguments made throughout the chapter on how Kenyan courts can apply an equality-sensitive approach to avoid reinforcing inequality, promote equality and mitigate inequality when adjudicating

[169] Liebenberg and Goldblatt (n 46) 357–59.
[170] ibid 359.

SERs claims. Nonetheless, its application may need adjustment on a case-by-case basis in addressing further questions, such as who the disadvantaged and most disadvantaged are, especially when it comes to the interaction between status and material disadvantage.

IV. Conclusion

As this chapter has shown, a closer look at cases such as *PAO* and the *Mitu-Bell* High Court decision reveal that, on the one hand, there is a positive set of cases where Kenyan courts have taken an equality-sensitive approach when adjudicating SERs. This is by recognising the vulnerability of various disadvantaged groups and how a socio-economic right, if implemented in a way that fails to consider the lived experiences of poverty and discrimination such groups face because of their status, may reinforce their disadvantage. However, even in these cases, such an approach is taken without expressly discussing the various constitutional provisions obliging the State to prioritise the needs of vulnerable groups when implementing SERs.

On the other hand, decisions like that of the Court of Appeal in *Mitu-Bell* show that too little attention is paid to the importance of applying an equality-sensitive approach when adjudicating SERs cases. This undermines the delivery of these rights to the vulnerable and most disadvantaged. Shedding light on these issues, the chapter has then argued that the application of an equality-sensitive approach in the adjudication of SERs claims needs to be more robust. This is in order to hold the State accountable for the fulfilment of its obligations and granting appropriate relief to the poor and those in desperate need. As the chapter has recommended, an equality-sensitive approach can be adopted through the application of a mixed standard of review that combines a reasonableness approach and the value of equality. This will enable courts to better respond to the marginalisation and vulnerability of disadvantaged groups, as the Constitution envisions, and afford them equal concern and respect.

Conclusion: Finding Harmony

This book has shown that the development of indigenous jurisprudence on the conceptualisation, interpretation and application of equality concepts in the Kenyan Constitution encounters various hurdles. The major one has been the lack of guidance and agreement on how to approach the interpretation of the multiple and interrelated conceptions of equality in the Constitution, and the absence of an equality test or a principled approach on how to embark on an equality analysis. As has been argued, development of a coherent approach in this area is imperative as the lack of clarity offers limited guidance to legal practitioners, and other pertinent players, on what is required of them by law in addressing inequalities.

From this background, the book has critically analysed whether a coherent conception of the competing and interrelated notions of equality in the Constitution can be discerned or developed. Based on the discussions in the various chapters, two analytical frameworks, particularly as advanced in Chapters 3 and 7, have been developed and applied as principled approaches that can be taken in the harmonious interpretation of competing and interrelated equality concepts in the 2010 Kenyan Constitution, to create internal coherence. These are: (1) the *equal concern and respect approach*, which begins with an interrogation of what treatment as an equal means to various individuals whose rights are in issue in a court case; and (2) the *four-dimensional approach* to conceptualising, interpreting and applying equality.

Finally, as all the chapters have shown, a contextual and purposive approach to the interpretation of equality provisions in the Constitution is desirable. There is a need to refer to history and context when interpreting equality provisions. This is in recognition of the fact that the law does not operate in a vacuum but is indeed a product of its social context. This also refers to the importance of appreciating the transformative nature of the Constitution, which would mean that judges ought to be alive to past injustices, even as they seek to consider what various principles of equality mean in terms of societal developments going forward.

BIBLIOGRAPHY

Books

Abiad N, *Sharia, Muslim States and International Human Rights Treaty Obligations: A Comparative Study* (London, British Institute of International and Comparative Law, 2008)
Barak A, *Purposive Interpretation in Law* (Princeton, NJ, Princeton University Press, 2007)
Bilchitz D, *Poverty and Fundamental Rights: The Justification and Enforcement of Socio-Economic Rights* (Oxford, Oxford University Press, 2007)
Bork RH, *The Tempting of America: The Political Seduction of the Law* (London, Sinclair-Stevenson, 1990)
Dawson C and Russello GJ, *Religion and Culture* (Washington, DC, Catholic University of America Press, 2013)
Dworkin R, *A Matter of Principle* (Oxford, Oxford University Press, 1985)
—— *Is Democracy Possible Here? Principles of a New Political Debate* (Princeton, NJ, Princeton University Press, 2008)
—— *Law's Empire* (Cambridge, MA, Harvard University Press, 1986)
—— *Taking Rights Seriously* (Cambridge, MA, Harvard University Press, 1977)
Ely JH, *Democracy and Distrust: A Theory of Judicial Review* (Cambridge, MA, Harvard University Press, 1980)
Faden R and Beauchamp T, *A History and Theory of Informed Consent* (New York, NY, Oxford University Press, 1986)
Federation of Women Lawyers (FIDA-Kenya), *Protection Against Female Genital Mutilation: A Review of the Implementation of the Children's Act* (Nairobi, FIDA-Kenya, 2009)
—— *The Prohibition of Female Genital Mutilation Act 2010, Abridged Version* (Nairobi, FIDA-Kenya, 2014)
Fraser N and Honneth A, *Redistribution or Recognition? A Political-Philosophical Exchange* (London, Verso, 2003)
Fredman S, *Human Rights Transformed: Positive Rights and Positive Duties* (Oxford, Oxford University Press, 2008)
—— *Discrimination Law* (2nd edn, Oxford, Oxford University Press, 2011)
Frye M, *Politics of Reality: Essays in Feminist Theory* (Trumansburg, NY, The Crossing Press, 1983)
Gauri V and Brinks D, *Courting Social Justice: Judicial Enforcement of Social and Economic Rights in the Developing World* (New York, NY, Cambridge University Press, 2008)
Ghai YP and Cottrell J, *Kenya's Constitution: An Instrument for Change* (Nairobi, Katiba Institute, 2011)
—— and Ghai JC (eds), *Ethnicity, Nationhood and Pluralism: Kenyan Perspectives* (Nairobi, Katiba Institute, 2013)
—— and McAuslan P, *Public Law and Political Change in Kenya: A Study of the Legal Framework of Government from Colonial times to the Present* (Nairobi, Oxford University Press, 1970)
Ghanea N, *Women and Religious Freedom: Synergies and Opportunities* (Washington DC, United States Commission on International Religious Freedom, 2017)
Hancock A, *Solidarity Politics for Millennials: A Guide to Ending the Oppression Olympics* (New York, NY, Palgrave-Macmillan, 2011)
Hepple B, *Equality: The New Legal Framework* (Oxford, Hart Publishing, 2011)
Hirsch SF, *Pronouncing and Persevering: Gender and the Discourses of Disputing in an African Islamic Court* (Chicago, IL, University of Chicago Press, 1998)

Jjuuko FW (ed), *The Independence of the Judiciary and the Rule of Law: Strengthening Constitutional Activism in East Africa*, vol 2 (Kampala, Kituo cha Katiba, 2005)
Kakwani N and Silber J (eds), *The Many Dimensions of Poverty* (New York, NY, Palgrave Macmillan, 2007)
Kenya National Bureau of Statistics, *2019 Kenya Population and Housing Census Volume IV: Distribution of Population by Socio-economic Characteristics* (Nairobi, Kenya National Bureau of Statistics, 2019)
Kenyatta J, *Facing Mount Kenya* (New York, NY, Vintage Books, 1965)
Khaitan T, *A Theory of Discrimination Law* (Oxford, Oxford University Press, 2015)
Kiragu E, Wachira M and Kangatta-Lan E, *Status of Women and Girls in Kenya: Urgent Need to Uphold Human Rights* (Nairobi, Centre for Rights Education and Awareness, 2007)
Liebenberg S, *Socio-Economic Rights: Adjudication Under a Transformative Constitution* (Cape Town, JUTA, 2010)
Lister R, *Poverty* (Cambridge, Blackwell/Polity Press, 2004)
Mbazira C, *Litigating Socio-Economic Rights in South Africa: A Choice Between Corrective and Distributive Justice* (Cape Town, Pretoria University Law Press, 2009)
Musila G (ed), *Handbook on Election Disputes in Kenya: Context, Legal Framework, Institutions and Jurisprudence* (Nairobi, Law Society of Kenya, GIZ and the Kenyan Judiciary, 2013)
—— and Biegon J, *Judicial Enforcement of Socio-Economic Rights under the New Constitution: Challenges and Opportunities for Kenya* (Nairobi, Kenya Section of the International Commission of Jurists, 2012)
Mazrui A, *The Politics of Gender and the Culture of Sexuality: Western, Islamic, and African Perspectives* (E Anwar ed, Lanham, MD, Rowman & Littlefield, 2014)
Mwangi P, *The Black Bar: Corruption and Political Intrigue within Kenya's Legal Fraternity* (Nairobi, Oakland Media Services, 2001)
Ng'ang'a W, *Kenya's Ethnic Communities: Foundation of the Nation* (Nairobi, Gatundu Publishers Limited, 2006)
Njonjo KS, *Exploring Kenya's Inequality: Pulling Apart or Pooling Together?* (Nairobi, Society for International Development, 2013)
—— *Youth Fact Book: Infinite Possibility of Definite Disaster?* (Nairobi, Institute of Economic Affairs, 2010)
Nussbaum M, *Women and Human Development: The Capabilities Approach* (Cambridge, Cambridge University Press, 2000)
—— *Women and Human Development: The Capabilities Approach* (Vol 3, Cambridge, Cambridge University Press, 2001)
Ogot BA, *History of the Southern Luo* (Vol 1, Nairobi, East African Publishing House, 1967)
Okin SM, *Justice, Gender, and the Family* (New York, NY, Basic Books, 1989)
Ousseina A, *Muslim Women in Postcolonial Kenya: Leadership, Representation, and Social Change* (Madison, WI, University of Wisconsin Press, 2013)
Pojman LP and Westmoreland R (eds), *Equality: Selected Readings* (Oxford, Oxford University Press, 1997)
Rae D, *Equalities* (Cambridge, MA, Harvard University Press, 1981)
Rawls J, *A Theory of Justice* (Cambridge, MA, The Belknap Press of Harvard University Press, 1971)
Raz J, *Morality of Freedom* (Oxford, Clarendon Press, 1986)
Sen A, *Development as Freedom* (Oxford, Oxford University Press, 1999)
—— *Inequality Reexamined* (Oxford, Oxford University Press, 1992)
—— *Social Exclusion: Concept, Application and Scrutiny* (Manila, Asian Development Bank, 2000)
Smith A, *An Enquiry into the Nature and Causes of the Wealth of Nations* (E Cannan ed, vol 1, London, Methuen, 1776)
Society for International Development (SID), *Pulling Apart: Facts and Figures on Inequality in Kenya* (Nairobi, SID, 2004)
Tayob A (ed), *Constitutional Review in Kenya and Kadhis Courts: Selected Papers Presented at the Workshop* (Cape Town, St. Paul's University's Department of Religious Studies and Centre for Contemporary Islam of the University of Cape Town, 2010)
The Equal Rights Trust and Kenya Human Rights Commission, *In the Spirit of Harambee: Addressing Discrimination and Inequality in Kenya* (London, Prontaprint Bayswater, 2012)

United Nations Development Programme (UNDP), *Human Development Report 2010: The Real Wealth of Nations – Pathways to Human Development* (New York, NY, Palgrave Macmillan, 2010)
Wangila MN, *Female Circumcision: The Interplay of Religion, Culture, and Gender in Kenya* (Maryknoll, NY, Orbis Books, 2007)
Wintemute R, *Sexual Orientation and Human Rights: The United States Constitution, the European Convention, and the Canadian Charter* (Oxford, Clarendon, 1995)
Young IM, *Justice and the Politics of Difference* (Princeton, NJ, Princeton University Press, 1990)

Contributions to Edited Books

Baer S, 'Equality' in Rosenfeld M and Sajó A (eds), *The Oxford Handbook of Comparative Constitutional Law* (Oxford, Oxford University Press, 2012)
Baxi U, 'Preliminary Notes on Transformative Constitutionalism' in Vilhena O, Baxi U and Viljoen F (eds), *Transformative Constitutionalism: Comparing the Apex Courts of Brazil, India and South Africa* (Johannesburg, Pretoria University Law Press, 2013)
Biegon J, 'The Inclusion of Socio-Economic Rights in the 2010 Constitution: Conceptual and Practical Issues' in Biegon J and Musila G (eds), *Judicial Enforcement of Socio-Economic Rights under the New Constitution: Challenges and Opportunities for Kenya* (Nairobi, Kenya Section of the International Commission of Jurists, 2012)
Boso L, 'Equality and Non-discrimination' in Martin R, Areff S and Miyandazi V (eds), *Global Perspectives on Human Rights: Oxford Human Rights Hub Blog* (3rd edn, Oxford, Oxford Human Rights Hub, 2016)
Chesworth J, 'Kadhi's Courts in Kenya: Reactions and Responses' in Tayob A (ed), *Constitutional Review in Kenya and Kadhis Courts: Selected Papers Presented at the Workshop* (Cape Town, St. Paul's University's Department of Religious Studies and Centre for Contemporary Islam of the University of Cape Town, 2010)
Clifford J, 'Equality' in Shelton D (ed), *The Oxford Handbook on International Human Rights Law* (Oxford, Oxford University Press, 2013)
Fredman S, 'Living Trees or Deadwood: The Interpretive Challenge of the European Convention on Human Rights' in Barber N, Ekins R and Yowell P (eds), *Lord Sumption and the Limits of the Law* (Oxford, Hart Publishing, 2016)
Ghai YP, 'Ethnicity, Nationhood and Pluralism: The 2010 Kenya Constitution' in Ghai YP and Ghai J (eds), *Ethnicity, Nationhood and Pluralism: Kenyan Perspectives* (Nairobi, Katiba Institute, 2013)
Kimeu S, 'Historical and Legal Foundations of the Kadhi's Courts in Kenya' in Tayob A (ed), *Constitutional Review in Kenya and Kadhis Courts: Selected Papers Presented at the Workshop* (Cape Town, St. Paul's University's Department of Religious Studies and Centre for Contemporary Islam of the University of Cape Town, 2010)
Kymlicka W, 'Two Models of Pluralism and Tolerance' in Heyd D (ed), *Toleration: An Elusive Virtue* (Princeton, NJ, Princeton University Press, 1998)
Mraja M, 'Current Debates on the Harmonized Draft Constitution of Kenya' in Tayob A (ed), *Constitutional Review in Kenya and Kadhis Courts: Selected Papers Presented at the Workshop* (Cape Town, St. Paul's University's Department of Religious Studies and Centre for Contemporary Islam of the University of Cape Town, 2010)
Musila G, 'The Transformative Promise of the 2010 Constitution and New Electoral Laws' in Musila G (ed), *Handbook on Election Disputes in Kenya: Context, Legal Framework, Institutions and Jurisprudence* (Nairobi, Law Society of Kenya, GIZ and the Kenyan Judiciary, 2013)
Ndegwa I, 'A Roof Over Wanjiku's Head: Enforcement of the Right to Housing under the Constitution of Kenya' in Biegon J and Musila G (eds), *Judicial Enforcement of Socio-Economic Rights under the New Constitution: Challenges and Opportunities for Kenya* (Nairobi, Kenya Section of the International Commission of Jurists, 2012)

Okoth-Ogendo HWO, 'Constitutions without Constitutionalism: Reflections on an African Political Paradox' in Greenberg D, Katz S and Wheatley S (eds), *Constitutionalism and Democracy: Transitions in the Contemporary World* (Oxford, Oxford University Press, 1993)

Sabbagh D, 'Affirmative Action' in Rosenfeld M and Sajó A (eds), *The Oxford Handbook of Comparative Constitutional Law* (Oxford, Oxford University Press, 2012)

Tayob A, 'Muslim Responses to Kadhis Courts as Part of Kenya's Constitutional Review' in Tayob A (ed), *Constitutional Review in Kenya and Kadhis Courts: Selected Papers Presented at the Workshop* (Cape Town, St. Paul's University's Department of Religious Studies and Centre for Contemporary Islam of the University of Cape Town, 2010)

Journal Articles and Working Papers

Ackerman B, 'Beyond Carolene Products' (1985) 98(4) *Harvard Law Review* 713

Albertyn C, 'Substantive Equality and Transformation in South Africa' (2007) 23 *South African Journal of Human Rights* 253

—— and Kentridge J, 'Introducing the Right to Equality in the Interim Constitution' (1994) 10 *South African Journal of Human Rights* 149

Alkire S, 'Capability Approach and Well-Being Measurement for Public Policy' (2015) 94 *OPHI Working Paper* 1

Allison JWF, 'Fuller's Analysis of Polycentric Disputes and the Limits of Adjudication' (1994) 53 *Cambridge Law Journal* 367

Balkin JM, 'Framework Originalism and the Living Constitution' (2009) 103 *Northwestern University Law Review* 549

Befort S and Donesky T, 'Reassignment under Americans with Disabilities Act: Reasonable Accommodation, Affirmative Action, or Both' (2000) 57 *Washington and Lee Law Review* 1045

Bennett TW, 'Re-Introducing African Customary Law to the South African Legal System' (2009) 57(1) *American Journal of Comparative Law* 1

Bilchitz D, 'Giving Socio-Economic Rights Teeth: The Minimum Core and Its Importance' (2002) 119 *South African Law Journal* 484

Brest P, 'The Misconceived Quest for the Original Understanding' (1980) 60 *Boston University Law Review* 204

Brinks D and Gauri V, 'The Law's Majestic Equality? The Distributive Impact of Judicializing Social and Economic Rights' (2014) 12 *Perspectives on Politics* 375

Brodsky G and Day S, 'Denial of the Means of Subsistence as an Equality Violation' (2005) *Acta Juridica* 149

Carcien M, 'Rawls and Reparations' (2010) 15 *Michigan Journal of Race and Law* 267

Choudhry S, 'Globalization in Search of Justification: Toward a Theory of Comparative Constitutional Interpretation' (1999) 74 *Indiana Law Journal* 819

Chowdhury J, 'Judicial Adherence to a Minimum Core Approach to Socio-Economic Rights – A Comparative Perspective' (2009) 27 *Cornell Law School Inter-University Graduate Student Conference Papers* 1

Cliteur P, 'State and Religion against the Backdrop of Religious Radicalism' (2012) 10(1) *International Journal of Constitutional Law* 127

Collins H, 'Discrimination, Equality and Social Inclusion' (2003) 66(1) *Modern Law Review* 16

Crenshaw K, 'Demarginalizing the Intersection of Race and Sex: A Black Feminist Critique of Antidiscrimination Doctrine, Feminist Theory and Antiracist Politics' (1989) *University of Chicago Legal Forum* 139

Cusack S and Pusey L, 'CEDAW and the Rights to Non-Discrimination and Equality' (2013) 14(1) *Melbourne Journal of International Law* 1

Davis D, 'Socio-Economic Rights in South African: The Record after Ten Years' (2004) 2 *New Zealand Journal of Public and International Law* 47

Davis DM, 'Constitutional Borrowing: The Influence of Legal Culture and Local History in the Reconstitution of Comparative Influence: The South African Experience' (2003) 1 *International Journal of Constitutional Law* 181

de Beer RJ and Vettori S, 'The Enforcement of Socio-Economic Rights' (2007) 10(3) *Potchefstroom Electronic Law Journal* 1

Du Plessis L, 'Religious Freedom and Equality as Celebration of Difference: A Significant Development in Recent South African Constitutional Case-Law' (2009) 12(4) *Potchefstroom Electronic Law Journal* 10

Farber D and Frickey P, 'Is Carolene Products Dead – Reflections on Affirmative Action and the Dynamics of Civil Rights Legislation' (1991) 79 *California Law Review* 685

Ferraz O, 'The Right to Health in the Courts of Brazil: Worsening Health Inequities?' (2009) 11 *Health and Human Rights* 33

Finerty C, 'Being Gay in Kenya: The Implications of Kenya's New Constitution for its Anti-Sodomy Laws' (2012) 45 *Cornell International Law Journal* 431

Fitzgerald J, 'The Road to Equality? The Right to Equality in Kenya's New Constitution' (2010) 5 *The Equal Rights Review* 55

Flood C and Gross A, 'Litigating the Right to Health: What Can We Learn from a Comparative Law and Health Care Systems Approach?' (2014) 16 *Health and Human Rights* 62

Fredman S, 'Foreign Fads or Fashions: The Role of Comparativism in Human Rights Law' (2015) 64(3) *International and Comparative Law Quarterly* 631

—— 'From Dialogue to Deliberation: Human Rights Adjudication and Prisoners' Rights to Vote' (2013) *Public Law* 292

—— 'Redistribution and Recognition: Reconciling Inequalities' (2007) 23 *South African Journal of Human Rights* 214

—— 'Substantive Equality Revisited' (2016) 14(3) *International Journal of Constitutional Law* 712

Freedman B, 'A Moral Theory of Informed Consent' (1975) 5(4) *The Hastings Center Report* 32

Fukuda-Parr S, 'The Human Development Paradigm: Operationalizing Sen's Ideas on Capabilities' (2003) 9(2–3) *Feminist Economics* 301

Fuller L and Winston K, 'The Forms and Limits of Adjudication' (1978) 92 *Harvard Law Review* 353

Gardner J, 'On the Ground of Her Sex(uality)' (1998) 18 *Oxford Journal of Legal Studies* 167

Goldblatt B and Albertyn C, 'Facing the Challenge of Transformation: Difficulties in the Development of an Indigenous Jurisprudence of Equality' (1998) 14 *South African Journal of Human Rights* 248

Griffiths J, 'What Is Legal Pluralism?' (1986) 18(24) *Journal of Legal Pluralism and Unofficial Law* 1

Hickman T, 'Constitutional Dialogue, Constitutional Theories and the Human Rights Act 1998' (2005) *Public Law* 306

Hirschl R, 'The Rise of Comparative Constitutional Law: Thoughts on Substance and Method' (2008) 2 *Indiana Journal of Constitutional Law* 11

Holmes E, 'Anti-Discrimination Rights Without Equality' (2005) 68 *Modern Law Review* 175

International Labour Office (ILO), *Employment, Growth and Basic Needs: A One-World Problem* (Geneva, ILO, 1976)

Jackson VC, 'Constitutions as "Living Trees"? Comparative Constitutional Law and Interpretive Metaphors' (2006) 75 *Fordham Law Review* 921

Joireman S, 'Inherited Legal Systems and Effective Rule of Law: Africa and the Colonial Legacy' (2001) 39(4) *Journal of Modern African Studies* 571

Jong-Sung Y and Khagram S, 'A Comparative Study of Inequality and Corruption' (2005) 70 *American Sociological Review* 136

Kamau W, 'Law, Pluralism and the Family in Kenya: Beyond Bifurcation of Formal Law and Custom' (2009) 23(2) *International Journal of Law, Policy and the Family* 133

Karlan P and Rutherglen G, 'Disabilities, Discrimination, and Reasonable Accommodation' (1996) 46(1) *Duke Law Journal* 1

Klare KE, 'Legal Culture and Transformative Constitutionalism' (1998) 14 *South African Journal of Human Rights* 146

Kuria GK and Vazquez AM, 'Judges and Human Rights: The Kenyan Experience' (1991) 35 *Journal of African Law* 142

Langa P, 'Transformative Constitutionalism' (2006) 17 *Stellenbosch Law Review* 351

Liebenberg S and Goldblatt B, 'The Interrelationship between Equality and Socio-Economic Rights under South Africa's Transformative Constitution' (2007) 23 *South African Journal of Human Rights* 335

Loenen T, 'The Equality Clause in the South African Constitution: Some Remarks from a Comparative Perspective' (1997) 13 *South African Journal of Human Rights* 401

McClain L, 'Red Versus Blue (And Purple) States and the Same-Sex Marriage Debate: From Values Polarization to Common Ground?' (2008) 77 *UMKC Law Review* 415

McCrudden C, 'Common Law of Human Rights? Transnational Judicial Conversations on Constitutional Rights' (2000) 20 *OJLS* 499

—— 'Legal Research and the Social Sciences' (2006) *Law Quarterly Review* 632

—— 'Rethinking Positive Action' (1986) 15 *Industrial Law Journal* 219

McLachlin B, 'The Evolution of Equality' (1996) 54 *Advocate* 559

Merry SE, 'Gender Justice and CEDAW: The Convention on the Elimination of All Forms of Discrimination Against Women' (2011) 9(1) *Journal of Women in the Middle East and the Islamic World* 49

Modirzadeh NK, 'Taking Islamic Law Seriously: INGOs and the Battle for Muslim Hearts and Minds' (2006) 19 *Harvard Human Rights Journal* 191

Muhula R, 'Horizontal Inequalities and Ethno-regional politics in Kenya' (2009) 1 *Kenya Studies Review* 85

Muigai G, 'Political Jurisprudence or Neutral Principles: Another Look at the Problem of Constitutional Interpretation' (2004) *East African Law Journal* 1

Munoru GGS, 'The Development of the Kenyan Legal System, Legal Education and Legal Profession' (1973) 9 *East African Law Journal* 1

Mureinik E, 'A Bridge to Where? Introducing the Interim Bill of Rights' (1994) 10 *South African Journal of Human Rights* 31

Murray C, 'Kenya's 2010 Constitution' (2013) 61 *Neue Folge Band Jahrbuch des öffentlichen Rechts* 747

Murray R and Wheatley S, 'Groups and the African Charter on Human and Peoples' Rights' (2003) 25(1) *Human Rights Quarterly* 213

Musila G, 'A Preliminary Assessment of the Kenyan Truth, Justice and Reconciliation Commission Bill, 2008' (2008) 5 *African Renaissance* 40

Mutua M, 'Justice Under Siege: The Rule of Law and Judicial Subservience in Kenya' (2001) 23 *Human Rights Quarterly* 96

—— 'The African Human Rights System: A Critical Evaluation' (2000) *Human Development Occasional Papers* (1992–2007) 1

Nickel J, 'Strong Affirmative Action' (1990) 17(1) *Journal of Ethnic and Migration Studies* 49

Ongoya EZ, 'The Law, the Procedures and the Trends in Jurisprudence on Constitutional and Fundamental Rights Litigation in Kenya' (2010) II *Kenya Law Review* 1

Orago NW, 'Limitation of Socio-Economic Rights in the 2010 Kenyan Constitution: A Proposal for the Adoption of a Proportionality Approach in the Judicial Adjudication of Socio-Economic Rights Disputes' (2014) 16 *Potchefstroom Electronic Law Journal* 169

Phillips A, 'Defending Equality of Outcome' (2004) 12(1) *Journal of Political Philosophy* 1

Porter B, 'Expectations of Equality' (2006) 33 *Supreme Court Law Review* 23

Pothier D, 'Connecting Grounds of Discrimination to Real People's Real Experiences' (2001) 13 *Canadian Journal of Women and the Law* 37

Pound R, 'Mechanical Jurisprudence' (1908) 8(8) *Columbia Law Review* 605

Raday F, 'Culture, Religion, and Gender' (2003) 1(4) *International Journal of Constitutional Law* 663

—— 'Gender and Democratic Citizenship: The Impact of CEDAW' (2012) 10(2) *International Journal of Constitutional Law* 512

Raz J, 'Free Expression and Personal Identification' (1991) 11 *Oxford Journal of Legal Studies* 303

Roach K and Budlender G, 'Mandatory Relief and Supervisory Jurisdiction: When Is It Appropriate, Just and Equitable?' (2005) 122 *South African Law Journal* 325

Salvadori C, 'Twelve Mosques: The History of Islam in Kenya' (2009) 38(1) *Kenya Past and Present* 33

Scalia A, 'Originalism: The Lesser Evil' (1988) 57 *University of Cincinnati Law Review* 849
—— Keynote Address: Foreign Legal Authority in the Federal Courts (2004) 98 *Proceedings of the ASIL Annual Meeting* 305
Sealy-Harrington J, 'Assessing Analogous Grounds: The Doctrinal and Normative Superiority of a Multi-Variable Approach' (2013) 10 *Journal of Law & Equality* 37
Selznick P, '"Law in Context" Revisited' (2003) 30(2) *Journal of Law and Society* 177
Sen A, 'Development as Capabilities Expansion' (1989) 19 *Journal of Development Planning* 41
—— 'Human Rights and Capabilities' (2005) 6(2) *Journal of Human Development* 151
Shadle BL, 'Changing Traditions to Meet Current Altering Conditions: Customary Law, African Courts and the Rejection of Codification in Kenya, 1930–60' (1999) 40(3) *Journal of African History* 411
Sihanya B, 'Constitutional Implementation in Kenya, 2010–2015: Challenges and Prospects' (2011) *FES Kenya Occasional Paper* 5
Smith J, Theano C, Torbett L, and Toussaint J, 'Women's Land and Property Rights in Kenya – Moving Forward into a New Era of Equality: A Human Rights Report and Proposed Legislation' (2009) 40 *Georgetown Journal of International Law* 1
Steinberg C, 'Can Reasonableness Protect the Poor? A Review of South Africa's Socio-Economic Rights Jurisprudence' (2006) 123 *South African Law Journal* 264
Stroud S, 'The Aim of Affirmative Action' (1999) 25(3) *Social Theory and Practice* 385
Sullivan DJ, 'Gender Equality and Religious Freedom: Toward a Framework for Conflict Resolution' (1992) 24 *New York University Journal of International Law and Politics* 795
Sunstein C, 'Social and Economic Rights – Lessons from South Africa' (1999) 11 *Constitutional Forum* 123
Taylor R, 'Rawlsian Affirmative Action' (2009) 119(3) *Ethics* 476
Thomas K, 'Selected Theories of Constitutional Interpretation' (2011) *Congressional Research Service* 1
Tushnet M, 'Dialogic Judicial Review' (2009) 61 *Arkansas Law Review* 205
Uslaner E, 'Corruption and Inequality' (2011) *CESifo DICE Report* 20
Varming K, 'Urban Subjects: Somali Claims to Recognition and Urban Belonging in Eastleigh, Nairobi' (2020) 79(1) *African Studies* 1
Wesson M, 'Equality and social rights: An exploration in light of the South African Constitution' (2007) *Public Law* 748
Wilson S and Dugard J, 'Taking Poverty Seriously: The South African Constitutional Court and Socio-Economic Rights' (2001) 22 *Stellenbosch Law Review* 664
Young IM, 'Equality of Whom? Social Groups and Judgments of Injustice' (2001) 9 *Journal of Political Philosophy* 1

Reports

Advance Africa, *Kenya Universities and Colleges Central Placement Service (KUCCPS)* (2015)
African Commission on Human and Peoples' Rights and International Work Group for Indigenous Affairs, *Report of the African Commission Working Group of Experts on Indigenous Populations/ Communities* (2005)
Centre for Rights Education and Awareness, *Respect the Rule of Law – On the Implementation of the Constitutional Principle on the 'Not More Than Two Thirds Gender' Principle* (2015)
Cilliers J, Hughes B and Turner S, *Reducing Poverty in Africa: Realistic Targets for the Post-2015 MDGs and Agenda 2063* (African Futures Paper 10, 2014)
Committee of Experts on Constitutional Review, *Final Report of the Committee of Experts on Constitutional Review* (2011)
Constitution of Kenya Review Commission, *Report of the Constitution of Kenya Review Commission, Volume four Constituency Constitutional Forum Reports: Constituency No. 6, Westlands; Constituency No. 24, Lamu East; Constituency No. 136, Nakuru Town; Constituency No. 40, Mandera East; Constituency No. 185, Kisumu Town West; Constituency No. 11, Likoni; and Constituency No. 138, Molo. Approved for issue at the 66th Meeting of the Commission held on 20 March 2003* (2003)

—— *The Final Report of the Constitution of Kenya Review Commission. Approved for issue at the 95th Plenary Meeting held on 10 February 2005* (2005)
East African Centre for Human Rights, *A Compendium on Economic and Social Rights Cases under the Constitution of Kenya, 2010* (2014)
East African Collaboration for Economic, Social & Cultural Rights, *Kenya Civil Society Shadow Report on Economic, Social and Cultural Rights* (2014)
Ellis A, Cutura J, Dione N, Gillson I, Manuel C and Thongori J, *Gender and Economic Growth in Kenya: Unleashing the Power of Women* (Washington, DC, The World Bank, 2007)
Equal Rights Trust, *Declaration of Principles on Equality* (London, Equal Rights Trust, 2008)
—— *Economic and Social Rights in the Courtroom: A Litigator's Guide to Using Equality and Non-Discrimination to Advance Economic and Social Rights* (London, Equal Rights Trust, 2014)
Fredman S, *A Comparative Study of the Anti-Discrimination and Equality Laws of the USA, Canada, India and South Africa* (European Communities, 2012)
Hickey S and du Toit A, *Adverse Incorporation, Social Exclusion and Chronic Poverty* (Working Paper No. 81, Chronic Poverty Research Centre, University of Manchester, June 2007)
International Labour Office, *Employment Incomes and Equality: A Strategy for Increasing Productive Employment in Kenya* (1972)
Judges and Magistrates Vetting Board, *Restoring Confidence in the Judiciary* (Interim Report, 2013)
Kenya Land Alliance, *A Case for Women's Land Rights in the Proposed New Constitution* (2006)
—— and FIDA-Kenya, *Women, Land and Property Rights and the Land Reforms in Kenya* (Policy Brief 2006)
Kenya National Assembly, *Report of the Parliamentary Select Committee on the Review of the Constitution on the Reviewed Harmonized Draft Constitution* (2010)
Kenya National Bureau of Statistics, *2003 Kenya Demographic Health Survey* (2003)
—— *2014 Kenya Demographic and Health Survey* (2014)
—— *Basic Report on Well-Being in Kenya: Based on the 2015/2016 Kenya Integrated Household Budget Survey (KIHBS)* (2018)
—— *Kenya Facts and Figures 2014* (2014)
—— *Kenya National Survey for Persons with Disabilities – Main Report* (2008)
Khan S, Combaz E and Fraser E, *Social Exclusion: Topic Guide* (revised edn, Birmingham, University of Birmingham, 2015)
Murray C, *Beginner's Guide to the Proposed Constitution: Chapter by Chapter* (2009) constitutionnet.org/sites/default/files/beginners_guide_to_proposed_const_chap_by_chap.pdf
Musila G, *Framework Briefing Paper on How the New Constitution Addresses Social Exclusion and Marginalization of Women, Ethnic Minorities/Indigenous Groups and the Poor* (Nairobi, Report for Oxfam GB, November 2011)
Mutunga W, *Progress Report on the Transformation of the Judiciary: The First Hundred and Twenty Days, 19 October 2011* (2011)
National Cohesion and Integration Commission (NCIC), *Ethnic Audit of Parastatals in Kenya* (Nairobi, NCIC, 2016)
Nyagudi PA, 'Overview of the Current Policies, Legislation and Programmes for Persons with Disabilities in Kenya' in *Launch of PWD Web Portal and e-Accessibility Workshop for Persons with Disabilities* (Laico Regency, Nairobi: National Council for Persons with Disabilities, 2012)
Owino K, Owiro D, Marchant M and Jairo S, *Implementing the Constitutional Two-Thirds Gender Principle: The Cost of Representation* (2015)
Pring C and Vrushi J, *Global Corruption Barometer Africa 2019: Citizens' Views and Experiences of Corruption* (Transparency International and Afrobarometer, 2019)
Public Service Commission, *Diversity Policy for the Public Service* (Nairobi, The Government Printer, 2016)
Raffaelli R, *Dissenting Opinions in the Supreme Courts of the Member States, European Parliament Study, Directorate General for Internal Policies Policy Department C: Citizens' Rights and Constitutional Affairs* (2012)

Randa J and Gubbins P, *Kenya Economic Update: Time to Shift Gears – Accelerating Growth and Poverty Reduction in the New Kenya* (Washington, DC, World Bank Group, 2013)
Republic of Kenya, *Report of the Committee on the Administration of Justice: Summary of Recommendations 24* (1998)
—— *Final Report of the Task Force on Judicial Reforms* (Nairobi, Government Printer, 2010)
Robeyns I and van der Veen RJ, *Sustainable Quality of Life: Conceptual Analysis for a Policy-relevant Empirical Specification* (AH Bilthoven, Netherlands Environmental Assessment Agency, 2007)
Truth Justice and Reconciliation Commission (TJRC), *Report of the Truth, Justice and Reconciliation Commission* Volume IIB (Kenya TJRC 2013)
United Nations Children's Fund (UNICEF), *Poverty Reduction Begins with Children* (New York, NY, UNICEF, 2000)
United Nations Development Programme, *Kenya Human Development Report 2015, Work for Human Development: Briefing Notes for Countries on the 2015 Human Development Report* (2015)
United Nations Human Rights Council, *Oral statement on 'Minorities and Effective Participation in Economic Life' by the Centre for Minority Rights Development (CEMIRIDE), UN Human Rights Council Forum on Minority Issues, Third Session, Geneva December 14–15, 2010* (2010)
United Nations Human Settlements Programme, *Nairobi Urban Sector Profile* (Nairobi, UN-HABITAT, 2006)
Walsh J, *Double Standards: Women's Property Rights Violations in Kenya* (Human Rights Watch Vol. 15(5)(A), March 2003)
World Bank, *World Development Report 2000/01: Attacking Poverty* (Washington, DC, Oxford University Press for the World Bank, 2000)
World Health Organization, *The Global Burden of Disease: 2004 Update* (2004)

Newspaper Articles

Abdi D, 'Real Gains for Muslim Women', *Kenyan Woman* (Nairobi, Issue Number 01, January 2010)
Ayaga W and Ng'etich J, 'Why Kenyan MPs shot down gender bill', *Standard Digital* (Nairobi, 6 May 2016)
Jillo R, 'Court Orders Vetting of Judges to Start Thursday', *Capital News* (Nairobi, 21 February 2012)
Jipeshughuli, 'Why Aren't Kenya's Affirmative Action Funds Working?' *Jipeshughuli* (Nairobi, 6 March 2017)
Lucheli I, 'Vetting Board Finds Five High Court Judges Unfit to Serve', *The Standard* (Nairobi, 22 December 2012)
Mukaindo P, 'A Case of Mistaken Identity? Demystifying the "Constitutional Court" in Kenya', *Kenya Law* (Nairobi, 2 May 2013)
Nyagah R, 'KEWOPA wants gender balance provision implemented now', *Kenyan Woman* (Nairobi, 1 June 2015)
Oluoch F, 'As Kenya election approaches, two-thirds gender rule hands over parliament', *The EastAfrican* (Nairobi, 28 April 2017)
—— 'More women elected in Kenya, but the numbers still fall short', *The EastAfrican* (Nairobi, 12 August 2017)
Orengo P, 'Kenya's Gay Movement Seeks Stamp of Approval', *The Standard* (Nairobi, 9 July 2013)
Owino K, 'The "two-thirds" gender rule can be implemented – affordably', *The Daily Nation* (Nairobi, 14 May 2015)
Sunday Nation Team, 'Ask your Question: Wilfred Lichuma', *The Daily Nation* (Nairobi, 4 May 2017)
'The Review of the Constitution of Kenya under Constitution of Kenya (Amendment) Act, 2008 and the Constitution of Kenya Review Act, 2008' *The Daily Nation* (Nairobi, 16 June 2009)
Wainaina E, '22 women for Parliament as regions elect first female MPs', *The Daily Nation* (Nairobi, 11 August 2017)

Theses and Unpublished Papers

Atieno R, 'Explaining Female Labour Force Participation: The Case of Kenya's Informal Sector and the Effect of the Economic Crisis' (Annual IAFFE Conference, Buenos Aires, 22–24 July 2010)

Baraza N, 'Family Law Reforms in Kenya: An Overview' (Heinrich Böll Foundation's Gender Forum, Nairobi, 30 April 2009)

McConnachie C, 'What Is Unfair Discrimination? A Study of the South African Constitutional Court's Unfair Discrimination Jurisprudence' (DPhil Thesis, University of Oxford, 2014)

Mutunga W, 'The 2010 Constitution of Kenya and its Interpretation: Reflections from the Supreme Court Decisions' (University of Fort Hare Inaugural Distinguished Lecture Series, 16 October 2014)

Orago N, 'Poverty, Inequality and Socio-economic Rights: A Theoretical Framework for the Realisation of Socio-economic Rights in the 2010 Kenyan Constitution' (LLD thesis, University of the Western Cape 2013)

INDEX

www.ingramcontent.com/pod-product-compliance
Lightning Source LLC
Chambersburg PA
CBHW071351220926
51613CB00008B/80
9781509941193